FOREIGN POLICY MAKING IN WESTERN EUROPE

Foreign Policy Making in Western Europe

A comparative approach

edited by
WILLIAM WALLACE
Royal Institute of International Affairs
W. E. PATERSON
University of Warwick

PRAEGER PUBLISHERS
Praeger Special Studies

New York • London • Sydney • Toronto

BL British Library Cataloguing in Publication Data

327.4
F 714

Foreign policy making in Western Europe.
1. Europe, Western—Foreign relations
I. Wallace, William, b. 1941
II. Paterson, William Edgar
327.4   D1058

PRAEGER PUBLISHERS, PRAEGER SPECIAL STUDIES
383 Madison Avenue, New York, N.Y. 10017, U.S.A.

Published in the United States of America in 1978
by Praeger Publishers
A Division of Holt, Rinehart and Winston, CBS, Inc.

© 1978 by William Wallace and W. E. Paterson

Library of Congress Catalog Card Number: 78–58844

Printed in Great Britain

79-8555

Contents

Figures

Table

Contributors

David Allen	Senior Lecturer in European Studies – Loughborough University.
Jan Deboutte	Research Assistant – Department of Political Studies, University of Leuven, Belgium.
Ib Faurby	Lecturer in International Politics, Aarhus University, Denmark.
Christopher Hill	Lecturer in International Relations, London School of Economics.
William E. Paterson	Senior Lecturer, Department of Politics, Warwick University.
Donald Sassoon	is completing his Doctorate on the PCI.
Alfred von Staden	Senior Lecturer in International Relations, Leyden University, The Netherlands.
William Wallace	Director of Studies, The Royal Institute of International Affairs, London

Abbreviations

CAP	:	Common Agricultural Policy
CIEC	:	Committee on International Economic Co-operation
COREPER	:	Committee of Permanent Representatives (EC)
COREU	:	EC telex system
CP	:	Communist Party
CSCE	:	Conference on Security and Co-operation in Europe
DC	:	Italian Christian Democratic Party
EC	:	European Community
EDC	:	European Defence Community
EEC	:	European Economic Community
EFTA	:	European Free Trade Association
EPC	:	European Political Community
FEOGA	:	European Agricultural Guidance and Guarantee Fund
GATT	:	General Agreement on Tariffs and Trade
IEA	:	International Energy Authority
IMF	:	International Monetary Fund
LO	:	Swedish TUC
MBFR	:	Mutual Balanced Force Reduction
NATO	:	North Atlantic Treaty Organisation
OECD	:	Organisation for Economic Co-operation and Development
OPEC	:	Organisation of Petroleum Exporting Countries
PCI	:	Italian Communist Party
PSI	:	Italian Socialist Party
TUC	:	Trades Union Congress
UN	:	United Nations
UNCTAD	:	United Nations Commodity Trade and Development

Foreword by *William E. Paterson*

The present volume owes its inception to a continuing dissatisfaction on the part of the editors with the available literature in the field. This literature falls more or less neatly into two categories. The first category is theoretical in intent, i.e. the intention is to produce generalised propositions of an 'if . . . then' character, and is best represented by the work of James Rosenau.[1] The second group is concerned to present a survey of a whole range of national policies rather than to explain foreign policy at the level of theory.[2]

Both approaches seem to us to suffer from serious limitations. The first approach, undertaken almost exclusively by American scholars, often involves a number of built-in assumptions and values derived ultimately from American experience, which may or may not be relevant elsewhere. It is also often characterised by a certain hauteur in which the testing of the hypotheses and the provision of empirical evidence is left to other researchers. The second group normally suffers from being too descriptive and making very little real effort to incorporate the insights of the first approach. It is also rare indeed for a survey volume to look at the foreign policy of any West European country other than Britain, France or West Germany.

The choice of Western Europe for this volume is almost self-evident. It is the area in which we have the greatest experience, an area moreover still of importance in international politics. There is to date no satisfactory treatment of the making of foreign policy in any single West European state, with the exception of Britain which has been relatively well covered.[3] A focus on Western Europe with its high level of economic development and mutual interaction has also enabled the contributors to analyse the implications for foreign policy of concepts like 'interdependence' and 'transnationalism'.[4]

This volume, then, concentrates on the formulation of foreign policy rather than the content. This of course raises the definitional problem, of the extent to which it is still possible to talk in any meaningful sense, given 'interdependence' and the internationalisation of domestic politics, of foreign policy. After a lengthy analysis of the implications of interdependence, William Wallace concludes that 'Interdependence has not decreased the role of nation states in international life, on the contrary, it has increased it.' In effect the actors (i.e. no longer confined to Foreign Offices) and the issues may have changed but it is still possible to talk of foreign policy.

Bureaucratic politics?

In recent years, especially in the United States, increasing attention has been focused

1

on the explanation of foreign policy decisions and actions in terms of competing bureaucratic perspectives and interests. The 'bureaucratic politics' approach is evaluated critically by a number of the contributors. While finding the concept useful, Christopher Hill exposes some of its conceptual ambiguities.[5] William Wallace concludes a detailed consideration of bureaucratic politics in Bonn, London and Paris thus:

> But in no case can the observer safely ascribe the outcome to bureaucratic politics alone. Foreign policy in Paris, Bonn and London, as (one suspects) in most other capitals, emerges out of the continuous interaction between political direction and administrative habit, against the background provided by cultural tradition and constitutional authority.[6]

This view is shared by Ib Faurby:

> It one accepts the basic line of argument of this chapter, bureaucratic battles, however energetically fought, are not the main determinants of policy. International and societal forces, as well as other factors at the governmental level, narrowly limit the area within which purely bureaucratic factors can shape foreign policy.[7]

Despite the slightly sceptical conclusions all the contributors devote a great deal of time to analysing the bureaucracies and in particular, how they have responded to the challenges of a changing international environment. William Wallace looks in detail at the internal organisation and attempts at reform in the relevant ministries in Bonn, London and Paris.[8] Jan Deboutte and Alfred van Staden expose extremely interesting differences in the patterns of organisational response in Belgium and the Netherlands.[9] The attempts by the bureaucracy of the Commission of the EC to deal with foreign policy are analysed by David Allen.[10]

One of the most interesting findings to emerge from the contributions is the 'conservative' nature of the foreign office bureaucracies. Christopher Hill lists some general reasons for this phenomenon.[11] These factors include bureaucratic procedures, in particular the 'Standard Operating Procedures'. Also where countries like the typical West European state have been used to playing an important role in international politics, stable bureaucracies are likely to represent a force for caution, since radical change is likely to be associated with diminution of status for their own country and diplomatic service.

It does also seem to be the case that in all the countries studied foreign service recruitment is normally from the more privileged strata of society, that these were often the strata with which the foreign service had the most intimate contact and they were normally perceived as being 'Conservative'.[12] This does seem to be one sense in which, despite the increasingly elastic boundary between domestic and international politics, the foreign services remain to some extent distinct from the rest of the national civil services, a point which was made in the report on the organisation of Britain's external relations by the Central Policy Review Staff which appeared in early 1977.[13]

The impact of non-governmental groups on the formulation of foreign policy

James Rosenau, in distinguishing between foreign and domestic policy 'issue–areas', argued that foreign policy was typically carried out in a restricted, centralised, decision-making structure, in contrast to domestic policy where power and responsibility were typically dispersed amongst a number of centres.[14] This picture of foreign policy as largely a governmental activity is broadly confirmed by the contributions. Public opinion, however defined, tends to be only sporadically involved in foreign policy. This lack of interest is reflected by the legislatures, where only the Dutch Parliament makes a sustained effort to take a critical interest in foreign policy matters. In normal times foreign policy questions have a low visibility and it is rare for them to lead to major changes in the political and party system. The major exceptions to this general picture in recent years were the EC issue in Norway and Britain and *Ostpolitik* in the Federal Republic. Both these issues involved 'core–values' in the countries concerned and public and party interest was high. Only in Italy does there seem to be a very marked partisan identification in the foreign office bureaucracy (though everywhere socialists seem to be under-represented) and that appears to have more to do with patronage than any marked cleavage of policies.[15] Even in Scandinavia where the level of interest group activity and organisation is unprecedentedly high, interest group influence on foreign policy formulation is considerably less than in domestic policy. An interesting exception to the general lack of influence of cause groups is Holland where they have been successful in recent years in influencing policy towards South Africa.[16]

Large/small states

The contributions to this volume tend to support the view that there is no qualitative difference between the making of foreign policy in large and small West European states. All the states that have been studied here, belonging as they do to the better off and better educated nations in the world, are able to support fairly complex foreign policy making apparatuses and to be represented in a high proportion of the other countries in the international system. This, together with their participation in a large number of multilateral international organisations ensures that, unlike many small and weak nations elsewhere, they are normally quick to perceive events and developments in the international system. They are of course often constrained by various factors, in particular lack of military capability, from affecting these events, though the alliance relationship with the United States, participation in the European Community and relative financial strength does afford the typical small West European state more opportunity to influence the international system than many small and weak nations elsewhere in the world.

The general impression of foreign policy making in Western European states that emerges from the contributions to this volume is one that differs in various ways

3

from conventionally held conceptions of foreign policy making in the United States. In contrast to the role of the United States Congress, or more especially the Senate, the role of the legislatures is minimal. The impression given by the contributions is that foreign policy making is a routine activity, largely concerned with regulating intra-European and Atlantic relations. It is noticeable that the contributions implicitly at least, by devoting relatively little attention to it, play down the importance of the political leadership and emphasise the role of the bureaucracy in this process. This is a valuable contrast to many American accounts which, because of their interest in 'crises' rather than routine policy emphasise the role of political leadership, especially the President. Within the bureaucracy, foreign offices in West European states still seem to play a more dominant and assured role than does the State Department in the United States.

This volume is largely concerned with describing present practice in relation to foreign policy making in the various West European states. It does however contain some indications of possible change. It seems clear that the role and nature of the various foreign offices is coming under increasing scrutiny. The changing content of foreign policy issues has led almost everywhere to questions about the fitness of foreign offices to deal with the 'new issues'. There have, too, been more complaints than in the past about the social exclusiveness of the foreign services. Despite the increased involvement of the Commission of the European Community in the field of foreign policy making, it seems unlikely at the moment that there will be any radical developments in this area in the near future. However the participation of Communist parties in the governments of both Italy and France, if it occurred, would probably lead to a change of the political consensus inside the Community. This might change the nature of foreign policy making in West European states since it would make intra-European relations contentious. This would be likely to make foreign policy the subject of partisan identification and increase the present low level of public involvement. At the time of writing a victory of the Left in France begins to look more unlikely and the chances of change correspondingly reduced.

William E. Paterson
September 1977

Notes

[1] See especially James N. Rosenau, *The Scientific Study of Foreign Policy*, The Free Press, New York, 1971.

[2] F. S. Northedge (ed.), *The Foreign Policies of the Powers*, Faber, London, 1968, and R. C. Macridis (ed.), *Foreign Policy in World Politics*, Prentice Hall, New Jersey, 1976.

[3] W. Wallace, *The Foreign Policy Process in Britain*, RIIA, London, 1975, and R. Jones, *The Changing Structure of British Foreign Policy*, Longmans, London, 1974.

[4] On interdependence see R. Cooper, 'Economic Interdependence and Foreign Policy in the Seventies', *World Politics*, 24 February 1972. On transnationalism see

R. Keohane and J. Nye (eds), 'Transnational Relations and World Politics', Harvard, Cambridge, 1972.

[5]   See ch. 1 pp. 17–20.

[6]   p. 48.

[7]   p. 124.

[8]   pp. 41–48.

[9]   pp. 58–69.

[10] ch. 6.

[11] pp. 17–18.

[12] Viz inter alia pp. 18, 62, 63, 84.

[13] This report referred to 'the middle classness' of the Foreign Office.

[14] J. Rosenau, 'Foreign Policy as an Issue-Area' in *Domestic Sources of Foreign Policy*, Free Press, New Jersey, 1971.

[15] Donald Sassoon claims that this is also true of the Defence Ministry see p. 95.

[16] pp. 75–76.

1 A theoretical introduction

CHRISTOPHER HILL

Commentators have always been interested in the foreign policies of Western European states because of their perennial historical importance. It is only relatively recently, however, that attention has turned seriously towards the processes by which foreign policies are made – if one excludes the interest in such institutional questions as secrecy and administrative efficiency that has existed since the First World War. This widening of focus has been general. For what it is worth social scientists may certainly claim to have introduced the terms 'decision-making' and 'policy-makers' into common usage.[1] In itself this is an excellent thing. A new dimension of analysis has been opened up, the simple personification of states has been made more difficult, and greater understanding may lead to greater accountability. But on the other side of the coin is the danger that we have witnessed only the flowering of yet another academic fashion, with all its accompanying jargon and ephemerality. Writers may pay lip-service to the importance of studying policy-making, without fully understanding how they are to proceed with the task or why it is important in the first place. It is therefore essential for any book that seeks to provide data on decision-making in foreign policy to begin by assessing the state of theory in the subject. This will enable the various empirical studies to cohere and provide a sense of purpose. Consequently this essay begins with a brief discussion of the progress of the subject area known as 'foreign policy analysis', including an evaluation of attempts to reach an overreaching theory of foreign policy. It continues by breaking down the area into its main strands of interest, and ends by suggesting which approach is likely to prove most fruitful for the future course of research. Although in no sense a blueprint for the country studies which follow, this should at least familiarise the reader with the basic preoccupations of those who aim to explain why foreign policies take the forms that they do.

General theory

Interest in decision-making has arisen more or less parallel to the general growth of activity in the social sciences. Hopes that the same systematic method which seemed to characterise advance in the natural sciences could be fruitfully applied to the study of society, produced in the middle decades of this century a wave of theoretical writing in political science as much as in economics, psychology and sociology. If the branch known as international relations was a little slow to follow the early trend, ground was soon made up in many of the universities of the United

7

States. Much theoretical energy was naturally directed towards explaining change in the whole 'system' of international relations, but a growing body of work became concerned with the 'micro' question of how to account for the behaviour of individual states in the system.[2] The search for 'a theory of foreign policy' was enthusiastically under way.

Theory-building has been an erratic business, pursued in almost as many ways as there are disciples of the approach. Broadly speaking, however, there have been three main streams of work discernible. The most widely known of these, because it has been found most navigable by traditionalists, has been the 'conceptual models' perspective employed by Graham Allison and his colleagues at Harvard. Using the concept of 'paradigm' developed by Robert Merton, Allison demonstrates how different theories, each of some real explanatory power, can be plausibly constructed from the same body of data.[3] To some extent these theories will be complementary, to some extent mutually exclusive, but their ultimate truthfulness will depend not only on how well they fit the facts but also on what questions they leave unasked through making (inevitably) restrictive initial assumptions. Thus Allison argues that much previous study of international relations has assumed that states are unitary bodies seeking to maximise certain universal goals (such as power, security, and 'the national interest'), with the consequence that many important domestic influences on decision have simply been ignored. A circular logic operates whereby some factors are not highlighted because they were not in the first instance deemed important enough to analyse. Allison (and later Halperin) shows that models other than the traditional 'rational actor' approach can explain a great deal of state behaviour that would otherwise appear anomalous. In particular the dimensions of 'bureaucratic politics' and 'organisational process' are added to the analysis of foreign policy, while later work by John Steinbruner has identified 'cybernetic' and 'cognitive' models of policy-making and applied them in detail to the case of the multilateral force issue in 1964.[4]

In principle there is no reason why the human imagination should not continue to formulate new paradigms illuminating a range of aspects of foreign policy. The advantage of such an approach to theory is that it concedes from the beginning, and builds upon the likely truth that human affairs are complex and multi-layered and can only be fully understood when observed from a number of standpoints. If social science cannot be value-free, then it is as well to admit the relativity of a particular interpretation and to seek to multiply the angles until the subject is viewable in the round. The disadvantages, however, are equally clear. On the one hand, there are diminishing marginal returns from a policy of looking for 'new' dimensions of analysis; refinement and reinterpretation can easily degenerate into scholasticism. On the other, the cataloguing of paradigms evades the issue of how to distinguish between the more and the less fruitful approaches. How are we to aggregate the various models presented as partial explanations? What logical next steps can be taken to determine which patterns of behaviour tend to be dominant in which circumstances (to the extent that such rules of thumb are feasible)? What you see may well depend on where you sit, but which seats give the best view in the house?

The second school of thought among contemporary foreign policy theorists would probably argue that the problem of relativism can be overcome by taking a truly scientific approach, in which hypotheses are strictly tested against replicable data using a standard methodology, so that theory can be gradually constructed from the accumulating stock of validated or falsified propositions. Patrick McGowan has written: 'The single unifying feature of systematic studies of foreign policy is their attempt to derive, validate, and evaluate general explanatory sentences about foreign policy'.[5] By 'general explanatory sentences' McGowan means 'if . . . then' statements that link together two variables in such a way that they can have predictive as well as retrospective capacities of explanation. An example he gives is: 'If a democracy lacks political unity, then its foreign policies will not be aggressive'.[6] Here a principle has been abstracted from specific historical contexts in the hope that it can be applied to future as well as past events, and across the whole range of democratic states. A wide range of techniques for establishing such generalisations is regarded as acceptable by proponents of this school, for despite a definite quantifying bias, one of their principal inspirations has been James Rosenau, whose prolific writings have largely been couched in the 'literary' form, and have had the wider impact for being so. Rosenau is wedded to the importance of theory and scientific method, but he regards particular methods, from content analysis through to simulation, as being essentially secondary to this overall aim, and therefore takes a liberal view of the 'measurement' problem.[7]

Nevertheless the McGowan and Shapiro approach is distinctive, for it reverts back to the macro level of analysis, instead of delving into decision-making like an Allison or Snyder.[8] The aim is to tackle generalisation head-on, not to hope that it will emerge as a spin-off from detailed case studies decked out with conceptual trappings. As a result the main focus is behaviourist, in the sense that attempts are made to correlate outputs (types of foreign policy behaviour) with inputs (types of influences on that behaviour) in a comparative framework, i.e. conclusions should refer to at least two states, and preferably to whole classes of states.[9] The search is essentially that for *patterns* in foreign policy,[10] and in making this the major immediate target the McGowan school is both more ambitious and less individualistic than most other foreign policy analysts, who are largely satisfied with elaborating on the workings of single factors in policy-making, still flushed as they are with feelings of liberation from the conventions of diplomatic history.

The third stream of theoretical activity is less clearly articulated as a separate approach than the others, but it exists as a clear 'middle way' nevertheless. Many of those who study foreign policy have a great deal of sympathy with the spirit of scientific enquiry if not with all its methods or shows of optimism. They may not be sanguine about the prospect of general theory, and they may be sceptical about the attempt to test objectively endless lists of uninteresting propositions, but they are still interested in probing behind the surface of international relations, so as to gauge the extent to which decision-making contributes to events (and simply how it happens). These middle men are currently concerned with *taxonomies* and with creating an agreed *framework* for research (or, if you will, an agreed paradigm).

The figure most prominently associated with what may be termed a cautious commitment to science, is Michael Brecher, whose own phrase expresses his outlook more pithily – 'structured empiricism'. Brecher has been the inspiration behind a continuing comparative project of investigation into crisis decision-making, but he is best known for his two-volume survey of the foreign policy process in Israel.[11] In these books he builds on the ideas thrown up previously by Richard Snyder, Joseph Frankel and others, and outlines in full a scheme for the study of foreign policy that most people will accept.[12] It is in essence a taxonomy, but does not deserve the patronising response the term often evokes, since it is both exhaustive in its coverage, and sensitive to its limitations.

Brecher's achievement is to have shown how a general dictum of foreign policy analysis – that the domestic sources of foreign policy are of considerable significance to international relations – can be applied in detail to a country and to specific cases, without losing sight of the comparative perspective. We are shown how conventional narratives of foreign policy can be improved by breaking down vague generalisations about 'parliament' or 'the mood of the country' into the actual mechanisms through which influences can be exerted over governments, and by attempting to weight the importance of one factor against another, both domestic and external. This is far more productive than taking a whole predictive model, in all its detail, and applying it to cases in the hope of finding a single explanatory theory. It is also more realistic than hoping to build theory from the results of endless specific hypotheses tested against the whole mass of available data. At the same time, it suggests a uniform approach for analysing foreign policy, so that case studies may be easily compared, and it is explicitly concerned with concepts, generalisations, and causes.

The health of theory about foreign policy, therefore, is good if not a life insurer's dream. The search for comprehensive explanations able to predict events in detail remains an over-ambitious, even absurd, target. But the negative accomplishment of treating diplomacy and decision in a more sophisticated way, relating them to 'normal' politics on the home front and accepting that they do not simply happen, like moves in chess, is both definite and widely recognised. *Per contra*, what concerns this author is not that the subject will die but that respectability may lead to ossification. Apparently discrete sub-areas can soon become self-justifying and incestuous.

There are two obvious and sensible ways of guarding against a loss of momentum. One of these is to recognise that foreign policy analysis is in many respects parasitical upon developments elsewhere in the social sciences. What the subject has brought to international relations largely consists of insights from psychology, the sociology of organisations, mainstream political science and even geography.[13] The originality of the Snyders and Rosenaus has lain principally in their ability to see the importance of developments outside their own field, and to bring them together in a way that throws light upon the special problems of foreign policy. An acceptance that continued borrowing will be necessary (although not enough in itself, of course), should ensure that (a) conventional wisdoms are regularly tested against new ideas; (b) there is no pretence of treating foreign policy as entirely distinct from generalised discussions of power, bureaucracy, democracy and the like (this would be ironic in view of the subject's basic purpose); (c) the study of decision-making as an integrated subject can progress without its process being confused with the different *contexts* in which decisions are made; (d) the increasing intermeshing of foreign and domestic policies, especially in the economic sphere, is not distorted.

The other present need is to work within the existing capacity of the subject. As we shall see, considerable progress has been made in explaining how particular factors in policy-making operate, even if we are far from integrating them into a general theory. Energies should therefore be devoted towards continuing this trend, involving the study of such particular matters as the problems posed by crisis decisions, small-group behaviour, or the machinations of bureaucracy. Through concentration on separate dimensions we can achieve the worthwhile gain of knowing broadly in what kind of circumstances various factors come into play, how profound is their impact, and how much is to be attributed to particular context.[14] This kind of approach begs a number of theoretical questions (e.g. how we are to know which are the important 'dimensions' to isolate) but then so does any model or framework in the social sciences. What it does do, however, is to throw up researchable questions, and ones that relate directly to the actual experiences of politics as perceived by participants at all levels. The kinds of variables listed by Brecher are not always institutional, but they do include interest groups, administrative departments, economic élites, and so on. Whatever the virtues of strict behaviourism, it cannot be denied that it often makes political science inaccessible to any but the specialist, partly by a tendency to regard institutions as of only superficial importance – politics being about 'underlying' patterns of behaviour. On the premise that the purist approach has shown little signs of producing sufficient major insights to compensate for its aloofness, this chapter will therefore proceed to discuss the main areas of research in terms of political argument as well as science.

The main areas of research

(1)   *Crisis*

The great majority of academic analyses of politics since 1945 have come from the United States, and this has led to a predictable fear of 'culture-bound' theories being foisted on the non-American world. The term 'cultural imperialism' is not unknown, denoting the concern of some that the use of misleading models necessarily leads to inappropriate remedies for practical problems, because too well-tailored to specifically American attitudes on democracy and development.[15]

Crises are a case in point. Much of the literature on foreign policy analysis focuses on the major dramas of international politics, which the Great Powers naturally monopolise. Events like Korea, Suez, Cuba and Vietnam have been the cases most used as source material for theory. This is understandable, but it presents problems for those interested in routine decisions or countries less involved in nuclear diplomacy. Even the countries of Western Europe, for all their dual representation on the Security Council, seem more concerned with economic negotiations than high politics. Suez and Algeria are embarrassing memories, and repetitions of *mea culpa* do not seem very helpful to politicians preoccupied with the new style of Lomé and Rambouillet.

It would be a mistake, however, to believe that the study of crisis is of only limited interest. For one thing, this is an area where general and non-banal conclusions have been drawn. Defining crisis as the condition in which participants feel their core values to be under threat, their future to be at the crossroads, and the need for a major decision to be pressing,[16] then we can say with reasonable confidence on the basis of studies made so far that crisis tends to distort normal decision-making, with important consequences for the substantive decisions produced. For example, it would probably be agreed that the tension intrinsic to crisis has in itself the result of steadily narrowing the options that decision-makers perceive open to them (but not their adversaries) at the time.[17] Even in the Cuban missile crisis, where John Kennedy tried consciously to avoid the narrowness of vision that he saw in the months leading up to the outbreak of World War I, the emergency Excom decisional group narrowed the choice down to either a blockade or a military strike within twenty-four hours of the twelve-day deliberations beginning. Policies of continuing secret diplomacy, of 'do nothing' or of working mainly through the UN, were not seriously considered.[18] This tendency is also evident in British policy during late March 1939, in American reactions to the invasion of South Korea in 1950, and in Soviet attitudes towards Czechoslovakia in 1968.[19]

The cases mentioned are those which have received most detailed investigation, and they also provide evidence for other propositions of importance to all students of foreign policy. The supporting data cannot be given here, but there are good reasons for believing that a crisis atmosphere leads to decision-making being centred on small *ad hoc* groups which may reflect the sympathies of top leadership more than those of the whole governing cabinet or party. Naturally this makes it even more difficult than usual to exercise any influence on policy from outside official circles, and public participation in any form becomes unlikely at the very times when foreign policy is of maximum relevance to the lives of the majority. The obvious dangers of such changes in procedure are compounded by the scope for misperception and over-simplification created by crises. In circumstances of stress and uncertainty communications with adversaries becomes difficult, time is perceived as being of the essence (perhaps more than need be), and stereotypes are resurrected or reinforced. The classic example of Anthony Eden's view of Colonel Nasser is simply an extreme case of the norm. Hitler slipped into accepting the image of Neville Chamberlain as the appeaser, and was consequently surprised when Britain did decide to fight over Poland.[20] Similarly, in the weeks prior to the

Six-Day War in 1967 Israeli leaders displayed the 'holocaust syndrome' in which strategic calculations were infected by an exaggerated emotional fear for the very existence of the state of Israel.[21] In other words, decision-makers can, to a degree, exaggerate crises, unnecessarily polarise conflict, and make ill-considered decisions.

But, it may still be said, even if generalisations can be drawn from Great Power confrontations, they will only be relevant to the Great Powers and to their politico-military crises; the contemporary states of Western Europe now have very different preoccupations. To this reasonable point there are several cogent replies. First, it is a mistake to underestimate the continuing political component in the foreign policies of contemporary Western European states. Although within the European Communities and the international system in general, inter-state relations seem to revolve increasingly around differential rates of inflation, commodity markets and oil exploration, it must be remembered both that particular problems always change and that the disputes which surface in the EC's Council of Ministers, the CIEC, or the Group of Ten, are not simply technical in their implications. They are questions of political economy, involving disputes over values and the distribution of benefits. So that to the extent that foreign policy centres on functional issues, it will still involve important clashes of interest and/or ideology, with the inbuilt potential for polarisation contained in any intransigent behaviour.

This has been well illustrated by the Cod War, which spilled over into the issues of defence and East-West relations. Moreover there is no reason to believe that this affair was anachronistic. One of the most severe setbacks for the Community, after all, was the aftermath of the Yom Kippur war. The oil embargo and the war itself imposed great strains on relations between member states and between the United States and Europe. Traditional international politics continues in the rest of the world, at least, and inevitably rebounds continuously onto Europe. Nor is there any sign that Europe wishes to ignore the wider system. Even leaving aside France's Second Empire reflexes over the Lebanon and Zaire, the growing consensus on the need for a common European foreign policy of some kind testifies to the surviving desire to play an important role in world affairs, if not as individual middle-rank states, then as a collectivity.[22] Enlargement of the Nine, as seems likely to take place in the next few years, may or may not enhance the possibility of a united foreign policy, but it will certainly add to the strategic and political preoccupations of members. Greece and Portugal would bring major problems with them, not least that of EC relations with NATO and the future of the latter's southern flank.

The second reason for including crisis in any analysis of foreign policy making in Western Europe is that crisis is not a circumstance associated only with the imminence of war. Stress, anxiety and uncertainty are regular features of all aspects of life, and everyone from the ordinary individual through Oxfam or Rio Tinto-Zinc to the Ministry of Defence will undergo periodic crises in the sense that they will feel their respective rationales under major and immediate threat. Moreover crises need not always occur on the grand scale; they may be compartmentalised.

13

Belgium may be distracted by an internal crisis over relations between Flemings and Walloons; the common agricultural policy may place the British Cabinet in dire straits over butter prices; France may find her relations with Spain and her own internal security threatened by the activities of Basque insurgents based in the French Pyrenees. None of these instances represent great international conflicts in which the survival of states, or the system itself, is at stake. But they do stand for the way in which important foreign policy decisions, even if on limited issues, do fairly regularly have to be taken under far less than the ideal conditions of calm and maximum scanning of information. While, therefore, any science of 'crisis-management' is likely to founder on the capacity of human beings to outwit theories purporting to explain them, an understanding of the characteristic pressures exerted by a crisis can only be beneficial.[23]

(2) *Psychology*

The recent popularity of 'psycho-history' has perhaps discredited as much as furthered the cause of psychology among political scientists.[24] It can appear as a dubious adjunct to the unfashionable practice of ascribing great weight in history to charismatic individuals. Of what real use, it might be said, is a knowledge of Lenin's devotion to his executed brother when trying to explain the course of the Russian Revolution? But to take this attitude is to misconceive the uses of psychological analysis and to trivialise the issues.

We have already seen that conditions of crisis can affect the way in which decision-makers perceive antagonists and threats. Collective and individual attitudes can be one significant, semi-independent variable in the process of decision. And it is this statement which should be the starting point for the analysis of all policy-making. For to be interested in how decisions are made almost presupposes a distinction between how actors see the world, and how it is (or might otherwise be seen). The assumption that policy formulation can affect the quality of foreign policy, can hardly be divorced from the proposition that the degree of accuracy of decision-makers' images of the outside ('operational') world will affect the success of their actions.[25] Most writers see information as necessarily passing through the 'prism' of decision-makers' attitudes and values before emerging, 'interpreted', to stimulate decisions. In this straightforward sense the importance of perceptions is clear, and most scholars in the field probably cannot remember how they looked at international relations before the insight. Nevertheless, we should take care, when arguing on the basis that different groups see problems in varying ways, not to slip into the philosophical quagmire of assuming that there is a definite reality against which these perceptions can be measured, because mappable by the 'objective' outside analyst.

It is clear that we can also use the notion of perception in more specific ways. As Robert Jervis above all has shown, many examples can be found of decision-makers seeing phenomena in ways which are influenced more by extraneous considerations, such as their understanding of history or their personal background, than by the

14

strict content of the information available at the time.[26] One of the more important of these extra factors has been identified by Irving Janis in a highly suggestive if not always convincing book. He argues that when people come together to take a decision, there is a tendency for 'group-think' to operate unless it is consciously counteracted. By this Janis means that individuals are subject to the powerful pull of the group's consensus, and are likely to submerge their own doubts or disagreements because of social and emotional inhibitions against challenging the conventional view – especially when expressed by those of more senior rank. He cites the decisions of Autumn 1950 to enter North Korea, and of April 1961 to go ahead with the Bay of Pigs invasion, as well as the series of decisions taken by Lyndon Johnson's 'Tuesday lunch' group over Vietnam, as instances of 'fiascoes' brought about partly by the comforting atmosphere of mutual support in which most groups tend to conduct their business. The Marshall Plan and the Cuban missiles crisis, however, are seen as cases where painful mutual criticism and the deliberate appointment of devil's advocates to examine the weaknesses of proposed options reduced the margin for error in the eventual policy produced.[27]

Obvious criticisms can be made of the group-think thesis, both in its details and its central thrust – consensus has perhaps other more important origins than mere conformism, for example, since the outside environment sets prior limits to choice – but it is still a theory of considerable plausibility because it treats foreign policy decision-makers neither as different animals from those making other types of decision, nor as a collection of disparate individuals. Small groups of all kinds share some salient characteristics, and it is not before time that what social psychology has to say about them should be applied to foreign policy.

Of a whole range of general psychological traits that can be identified as also applying to politicians and their advisers, only a small number can be mentioned here. But another syndrome that students of foreign policy should take seriously is cognitive dissonance. This phenomenon occurs when incoming information suggests a different view from that which a person holds by predisposition. Given that there are three alternative reactions – ignoring the information, changing one's opinions, or interpreting it in a way that actually supports one's predispositions – the theory predicts that people will often behave in either the first or the third way, so as to reduce the psychological tension or 'dissonance' caused by having to challenge an existing outlook.[28] It can be argued that cognitive dissonance is a particularly apposite concept for international relations, because statesmen are more easily cocooned from the realities of foreign affairs than are their counterparts making domestic policy. Full information is harder to come by and stereotypes may become correspondingly deep-rooted and resistant to change. Indeed the whole question of information and its sifting merits particular attention from students of foreign policy since decisions will often hang on the quality of knowledge used to reduce uncertainty.

The 'perceptions' approach to foreign policy is frustrating as well as rewarding in the way it leads inexorably into a discussion of rationality, and thereby to mainstream political discussion. The vocabulary of a psychological analysis of politics cannot help but contain words like 'misperception', 'distortion', and 'stereotype', which imply a positivist belief in the improvement that can take place in policy if certain procedures/attitudes are adopted. This belief is a major tenet of the concept of rationality, whether used to describe how people do behave, or how they ought to behave. Other central notions are the necessity of calculating means to suit ends, or vice versa, and the maximising of (unbiased) information. Despite the basic nature of such a perspective to any study of policy-making, however, at least two dilemmas constantly recur to bog down discussion: (1) how to define rationality (2) how to bridge the gap between the desirability of rational policy-making in principle, and the apparent incapability of practitioners to behave rationally on any consistent basis.

Nevertheless the psychological approach to foreign policy itself suggests some ways out of this cul-de-sac. If we relax the assumption that adherence to basic max-ims of rationality will usually point specifically to the most preferable action to take in the circumstances, and instead limit using the word 'rational' to descriptions of the procedures of policy-making, we rule out a fair proportion of disputes over the rationality of a given policy. Even this restriction evades a number of problems, but at least it accepts that policies and attitudes in themselves cannot be irrational; it allows for the variations brought about by different values, cultures, and circum-stances. If 'rational behaviour' is kept for describing how people go about taking a decision and making sense of the outside world, then definitions of rationality become much more manageable. Otherwise confusion rapidly follows.

At the same time we must also direct attention to the actual content of the policies pursued, and a liberal interpretation of 'psychology' makes this possible. In order to understand why one decision is preferred to another, we need to describe the set of attitudes held collectively by those responsible, and at four levels. First of all, the *particular images* of the environment and its various components (e.g. enemies, institutions, problems) need to be delineated, particularly those which are of long standing. Next, it is crucial to uncover the *operating assumptions*, or rules of thumb, on which decisions are made. If Neville Chamberlain's belief in the untrustworthiness of Russian negotiators is a specific, targetted image, then his belief in the importance of negotiation in international relations was an operating assumption. Thirdly, the *values*, or articles of faith, which act as permanent touch-stones for all our deliberations about new problems, must be the next layer revealed by any analysis of attitudes. But these in turn are unlikely to be randomly adhered to or unrelated. Ultimately any investigation of foreign policy will turn to the overall *belief-systems* or ideologies of decision-makers. Only in the context of a general outlook can it be seen why various precepts are held, and why some are more dispensable than others. With a knowledge of ideology (although the methodology of achieving it is difficult to settle on) it should be possible to make broad but definite predictions about, for instance, which policies will be pursued with special resolve, and which will be sacrificed if needs be.[29]

The psychological dimension of foreign policy has been outlined at some length because this author believes that it is of especial importance, and not simply one among many discrete areas of enquiry. On the contrary, it hardly needs hiving off at all. Ideally, a concern for attitudes, perceptions and values should be part of the texture of any analysis of policy, at whatever level of generality. Otherwise it will inevitably be difficult to take into account the fact that decisions emerge, or 'flow', over time. Models of decision-making that concentrate on structure, whether institutional or functional, are intrinsically static and difficult to use to explain change. By the same token any prescription of 'better' policies must consider the different histories and situations of the range of states to whom the theory may be applied, and this can really only be done via the study of political culture. Finally, deep-seated beliefs run as a stratum beneath the divisions between departments or issues and they therefore point towards the shared characteristics of participants in the policy process; bureaucratic politics and other pluralist perspectives tend to highlight contrasts, and it is as well to redress the balance. In sum, the mechanics of policy-making take their momentum from ideas and ideals, and we need to be generally sensitive to the fact.

(3) *Bureaucracy*

The paradox about almost all knowledge is that it is constantly necessary to aggregate, then disaggregate, in turn. The moment a generalisation is made it can be broken down, and whenever detailed insights are achieved, immediate reactions are to think of the wider context. Thus it is no contradiction of the argument made above for a certain holism of approach, to revert back to the particular area of bureaucracy and foreign policy.

Any sensible treatment of bureaucracy will conform to the distinction made by Allison between the 'organisational process' and the 'bureaucratic politics' models, while perhaps seeking to qualify or fill out each of them. The first of these models appears to be the more sophisticated of the two, in its emphasis on the intrinsic problems encountered by any attempt to administer policies affecting large numbers of people and the allocation of massive resources. Bureaucratic politics, in contrast, seems to demand that an adherent swallow a whole (conflictual) view of human nature in order to accept its descriptive value.

The literature on the processes of administration has been steadily accumulating since the nineteenth century, and particularly since the writings of Max Weber and Robert Michels. This tradition can now be judged to have produced a body of work which is of considerable use to those concerned with political decision-making.[30] The major arguments that need to be taken into account by students of foreign policy decision-making begin with the well known characterisation of bureaucracy as a conservative force in society. Conservatism can be seen as attaching to the administrative procedures themselves (filing systems are by definition retrospective, precedents are institutionalised through research departments and the writing of background papers) or equally in the characters of those who operate the system (being temperamentally disposed to order, continuity, and deference to authority). Either way, the very existence of large and well established bureaucracies can plausibly be said to inhibit change, with harmful effects if foreign policy thereby fails to adjust to new circumstances. The incoherent, and possibly tardy British withdrawal from East of Suez, is a case in point.[31]

By the same token, it is interesting to treat bureaucracy as the repository of values for a political system. So far as an impersonal process can be said to have a memory, then it is likely to reside principally in the permanent administrative structure. The continuity of personnel and procedures helps also to preserve the major principles by which policy is evaluated. In particular, career officials are likely to nurture those attitudes which will be acceptable to most of their fly-by-night political masters, even though they will come from different parties. Where countries have been used to playing important parts in international relations, as those of Western Europe have, stable bureaucracies are even more likely to represent a force for centrism and caution, since radical change is likely to be associated with diminution of status for their own country and diplomatic service.[32] Naturally this will vary according to the extent in different countries to which career officials are subordinated to incoming political appointees, but even in the USA where continuity is regularly disrupted, those who work in the State and Defence Departments have nevertheless helped to perpetuate some relatively long standing traditions (such as the US commitment since 1947 to Europe, and the need to 'lead' public opinion). As a result US foreign policy is less susceptible to violent change than is often supposed.[33]

Another interesting aspect of the process of administration is its quality of routine. Classical Western bureaucracy was supposed to contribute an advance by laying down set procedures which would ensure the exercise of functions independent of the whims of individuals, and this is still generally accepted to be desirable. But the principle of automatic operation is double-edged. Although it is important to have a pool of equally competent and interchangeable personnel, the Standard Operating Procedures (SOPs) which they develop so as to ensure regularity, also have the effect of reducing the flexibility of an organisation. SOPs can take many forms, from training schedules that 'cannot' be disrupted (Pearl Harbour), to a foreign office that liaises more with one sister department than another.[34] Whatever the habits are, they are inevitable, and they inevitably make adaptation less a smooth progression than a series of sharp, infrequent jumps. The history of the British Diplomatic Service's adjustment to the increasingly economic character of British external relations, is a case in point.[35]

In combination with the sheer size of the machine, standard procedures also mean that it is difficult to galvanise administration into rapid, major action, as with the prolonged preparations of the Anglo-French expedition to Suez in 1956.[36] It is perhaps an exaggeration to suggest that all bureaucracies are monoliths of extreme rigidity, but they certainly tend towards inflexibility, just as smokers tend to damage their lungs (but not all do so). In this sense the 'organisational process model' is useful because it can incorporate not only the physical, tabulated arrangements by which administration functions, but also some of the purely psychological tendencies that we have noted in the previous section. Steinbruner's demonstration of how human beings rely on 'tracked-thinking' (i.e. ideas that run along well worn lines) closely parallels the preference of administration for clearly specified routines.[37]

It is easy to see from the study of process alone that lack of co-ordination is always one of the major problems for any foreign policy machine. Different departments even within a foreign ministry can easily slip into methods which may be idiosyncratic and hard to shift. The effects of such parochialism are highlighted even further, however, by the 'bureaucratic politics' paradigm. This presents policymaking as being dominated by the self-interest, even rivalries, of the separate departments of state. Their staff are seen as socialised into making the narrow concerns of their own unit the major priority. Policy formulation therefore becomes as much a process of pulling and hauling between rival groups as one of strategic calculation. The tendency is exaggerated by the fact that different departments genuinely have different perspectives on the national interest. Treasuries tend to push for financial stringency, defence ministers for higher arms expenditure, and foreign offices for measures that do not upset existing relations with other states.[38]

If the logic of this view of decision-making is fully accepted, it makes it a matter of some surprise that foreign policy should ever appear to possess any overall coherence. And certainly Allison and Halperin regard 'foreign policy' as being a misnomer for the collection of compromises and partialities which they identify as normal. In fact it is unlikely that the model will ever be accepted as generally applicable to foreign policy. For one thing, the case is clearly overstated. To generalise about interaction between states being dominated by what happens within their respective administrations is to invite the ridicule usually poured on single-factor explanations in social science. A more fundamental objection has been made by Lawrence Freedman in a well judged recent appraisal.[39] Freedman points out that the dichotomy posed by Allison between the rational and the political/bureaucratic is false because it rests on a very narrow definition of politics – namely, that it is the result of separate interests attempting to 'win' the game of policy formulation. If, by contrast, policies are defined as argument about the legitimate distribution of resources, then bureaucratic divisions can be placed in perspective as merely one among many factors helping to determine which values hold sway in government. Elements such as political culture, levels of economic development, or the social bases of power, can then be introduced to the analysis.

Criticism of the bureaucratic politics 'conceptual lens' can be taken further by the argument that in essence it differs little from the 'rational' model which so frequently comes under fire. If the rational paradigm assumes that states aim at maximising their interests, which in turn are concerned principally with power and security, then bureaucratic politics differs only through its attack on the state as unitary actor. For in focusing on departmental competition within the state, it also takes self-interest and power as being the motives for action. Few people will need convincing that this is a questionable, and one-dimensional view of human nature, whether levelled at states, departments, or individuals.

The last major objection to the bureaucratic politics approach is that it is culture-bound. Pluralist politics in Washington, encouraged by the division of powers in the American constitution, do not necessarily provide representative data for generalisations that will extend to the one-party systems of Eastern Europe, or the narrowly based élites of many less developed countries.[40]

Nevertheless, the Allison and Halperin paradigm should not be discarded simply because it can be seen to be over-ambitious. It has provided us with a series of detailed hypotheses about administrative behaviour, in the context of foreign policy, which we did not have before. Even if bureaucratic politics is likely to turn out to be more of a partial than a general theory, it does seem to have identified a set of powerful forces which operate in any well established bureaucracy. Departmental rivalries *do* seem to be ubiquitous, and incremental policy-making is at least as common as grand strategy, even if the extent to which such forces predominate in policy-making will be dependent on other factors, and particularly on the historical traditions which shape systems of government in differing ways. We should therefore make use of the American perspective and see how far it is applicable elsewhere. Western European societies, where central bureaucracies have been established and influential for some three hundred years, are the ideal place to start.

(4) *Domestic society*

Curiosity about decision-making naturally leads first to the government and its professional advisers. But other 'domestic sources' should not be neglected, despite the conventional assumption that foreign policy is the preserve of a small élite. Even if this is the case – and the increasingly wide ramifications of external policy bring it into doubt – it is important to know precisely how such élites operate, and to what extent they are responsive, at least, to the needs of their domestic constituency (as they frequently profess to be).

An institutional approach will make these questions more concrete. For instance, legislatures are usually supposed to exercise some ultimate control over foreign policy, if only through the ultimate power of the purse. Whether they do so, and how, is another matter. Even bearing in mind the variation of circumstances that can occur (the contrast between Mrs Ghandi's emergency and the period after her electoral defeat, or between the United States and Britain, are warnings enough against wild generalities) it should be possible to plot the strengths and weaknesses of representative assemblies charged with ensuring that statesmen are accountable.

In any catalogue of domestic influences on foreign policy the information media will rank high. Newspapers (foreign as well as home) have always been an important part of the day of politicians and diplomats both because of the information they can provide and the effect their commentaries may have in the wider community. *Causes célèbres* are made not born, and the press is a necessary condition for their success; the Zinoviev Letter, Suez, and Watergate all spring readily to mind. On the other hand, prestigious journals often have special relationships of various kinds with government, and these will also repay scrutiny. *The Times, Al Ahram* and *Pravda* fall into this category.[41] Beyond the press, radio and television have played increasingly important roles during this century in presenting international affairs to the public, sometimes informing, sometimes manipulating. Even if the global village is not yet at hand, the effects on both society and politicians of the growing mountains of information about world affairs, must be brought in to any analysis of the interplay between foreign and domestic affairs.[42]

It is not currently popular to conduct enquiries into the exercise of power. Nevertheless power is a term in constant use, and it would be perverse to pretend that many important facets of life are not determined by groups (whether states, governments, classes or combinations) implementing their own preferences despite opposition from other interested parties – if it is in this that power consists. Thus it is worthwhile attempting some estimates, however rough, of the relative power of the groups in question. This is especially true of pressure groups, which are proliferating in industrialised countries and are often the only practicable channels of access to policy-makers. When so much energy is devoted to organisations like Amnesty International and the European Movement it is important to know what pay-offs their activities receive. Equally, major economic groups like trade unions and employers' organisations have rapidly realised that national economic policy is as much determined by the transnational movement of capital and commodities as by Treasury budgeting. Accordingly they are now central contributors to the debates about international political economy which continually take place within states, and as such should figure prominently in any analysis of contemporary foreign policy.[43] By the same token, worthwhile research is waiting to be done on the specialist institutes for the study of international affairs which now exist in most developed countries. Although these organisations do not have the sanctions or rewards to exert actual leverage, they may still, over a period of time, profoundly shape the way in which decision-makers think. Their position as half-way houses between governments and the academic world is one of great potential importance.

Last and probably least of the various domestic 'institutions' which are relevant to the making of foreign policy, comes the mass public. Almost all the research directed towards 'public opinion' has concluded that it is of peripheral importance in the area of external affairs. The general public is seen as having little or no interest in foreign affairs – elections usually being fought on tangible, domestic issues – no expertise, and relatively little opportunity to influence policy, because of the norms of secrecy and *raison d'état* which prevail.[44] Despite the truth in all this, there may be more to the concept of public opinion than meets the eye. Decision-makers in many countries, after all, seem genuinely to believe their own rhetoric that they are in some way constrained by the 'mood' of the public and that their scope for leadership is strictly limited. It may be that this very perception itself acts as an inhibition on politicians, and a form of indirect influence for the rest of us. It would certainly be interesting to know how justified the belief is, and what its implications are for actual policy. As with many aspects of politics, the nature of the issue may decide whose views are heard, or sought.

Apart from checking off the potential members of what is sometimes called 'the foreign policy community', the main concern when looking at the domestic dimension should be to demonstrate that foreign policy is not made in a vacuum, on the basis of the state of the international game, but rather reflects the particular values and priorities of the community from which it comes. This may be evident from the social and educational backgrounds of decision-makers, but their influence is notoriously difficult to assess. More revealing is the way in which a society distributes its resources. Although the demands of the home front will not always be incompatible with defence and diplomacy, there is an implicit tension and different countries rank their goals differently. Conscription may be imposed even though educators and industrialists are strongly committed to higher education training programmes; immigrant workers may be sent home in times of unemployment, thus endangering relations with their parent country; most commonly, the social service and defence departments may be in direct competition for limited financial resources. Moreover, the European Communities create special conflicts for their members, who have treaty obligations that at times can become serious domestic liabilities. How such problems are resolved reveals a good deal about the place of domestic factors in a country's overall calculus of priorities.[45]

Even more fundamentally, a society colours foreign policy via its whole political and cultural complexion. The international orientation of a country is not likely to be simply the product of geographical situation or size. Proximity to the Soviet Union may explain why both Sweden and Iran are quite heavily armed, but it does not tell us why the one is neutral and internationalist and the other assertive and regionally active. The answers clearly lie in the unique ways in which the two societies have evolved. In this sense foreign policy is the way in which a country expresses its individual heritage and character to the outside world. Its internal experiences will inevitably help to determine what kind of foreign policy is pursued, whether co-operative/individualist, cautious/risky, costly/inexpensive, or whatever.

The relationship between internal and external factors is two-way. In some ways a foreign policy will be an outcrop of society, but it also mediates the world at large into domestic life. No country can be truly isolationist, and from this viewpoint foreign policy is a way of formulating a coherent response to the multiple external problems that arise from the attempts to achieve growth or security. This feedback can take the form of constraints upon freedom to make a whole range of policies – aid with strings, IMF finance, and demands for ideological conformity are such constraints – or it can help to set new goals for a society. Mussolini's Italy, for example, was profoundly affected by the Duce's desire to emulate the international status of Hitler and the Nazis. Similarly, Greece's setbacks in 1974 over Cyprus led to the fall of the Colonels' régime and to a reassessment of the state of Greek political life. Here as elsewhere, foreign policy and domestic politics were of vital importance to each other.

(5)   The external environment and cross-national linkages

This kind of evidence demonstrates the impact which the international system can have on policies right across the board, and it demonstrates the poverty of any analysis that seeks to elevate either the domestic or the foreign to the position of primary explanation. The two perspectives are not in competition. Rather, the making of foreign policy must be seen within the context of models of the whole international system, even though the decision-making focus will inevitably concentrate on the inner workings of government. The most elementary understanding of systems theory will make it clear that no unit or sub-system can be understood without reference to the overall system and its environment. In the case of the modern nation–state, while it is technically possible to support some kind of decent, societal life even if totally cut off from the outside, the almost universal goals of economic growth and effective security make this very difficult, as the history of post-war Burma indicates.

There is a particularly live danger of becoming too inward-looking when examining the foreign policy of an individual state, of not looking to the regional and global environments. Even powerful states like the United States and Soviet Union are partially dependent on the functioning of systems outside their unilateral control, at the levels of strategy, resources, finance, and trade. For lesser countries the behaviour of their neighbours, or of international markets, can be little short of vital. Therefore a knowledge of the systemic constraints or opportunities which different states live with (the givens) and of their ability to deal with them is almost a prerequisite of eventually turning towards domestic affairs. This is obviously true for a country like Israel, whose very survival depends on the politics of the Middle East, but it also applies to those in less dramatic circumstances, such as Belgium, Australia, Poland, or Thailand.

This is not to propose a theory of geo-political determinism. The great schemes of Mackinder and Mahan are now more of historical than practical value. Nevertheless the familiar questions posed by determinism – how much freedom of action do single countries have? How far does the possession of certain attributes predispose to particular kinds of international posture? – will always be of continuing relevance. In philosophical terms men will always act as if their fate were in their own hands, but they can save much wasted time and energy by an awareness of the more inevitable restrictions imposed on them by circumstances (and indeed, of their freedoms; if anything, most men of affairs are over-sensitive to the impediments to action). Hegel and Marx might have regarded this as 'working with history' rather than against it; but the Sprouts have provided a rather less metaphorical approach to the problem of inevitability. Their continuum, from voluntarism to determinism, via environmentalism, possibilism, cognitive behaviourism, and probabilism, caters for most conceivable positions, and has been unjustly neglected by empirical studies of foreign policy.[46] These concepts can be used to illuminate particular events, and the events used to refine our understanding of causes. At present Othello's resigned 'It is the cause, it is the cause . . .' still stands to remind us of how little we understand of the impersonal forces which we create but cannot command.

Most contemporary interest in the external environment is, however, centred on the roles of non-governmental actors. Subsequent analysis takes two forms. The first derives from Rosenau's scheme for observing 'linkage politics'. This was designed to make possible study of those elements of international relations which are not catered for by the conventional analysis of state policies. Noticing that many groups in domestic society themselves intervene in foreign affairs, bypassing their governments, and that processes inside a country (like education) can be directly affected by developments abroad, Rosenau proposed a simple tabulation of all the cross-linkages which can occur between domestic and international variables, by the three processes of penetration, reaction, and emulation. The analysis can easily be extended to include the interactions between peoples, independent of officialdom; press activities in one country are quickly taken up in another, for example.[47]

The linkage 'matrix' of 144 frames was disowned by its author almost as soon as it was produced, in a shrewd retreat from the criticisms being heaped on it for, among other things, a lack of any underlying theory to give direction to empirical research. Nonetheless it was clear that the *concept* of linkage met a real need, and it has been used frequently as one way of describing a world in which states are the major but not the only actors. So long as linkages are not seen as being independent variables alone, they are a useful addition to our vocabulary.[48]

The second form taken by a 'beyond the nation–state' analysis of foreign policy is rather more powerful. The notion of 'interdependence' is already as familiar to politicians as to scholars,[49] and there is obviously some truth in the argument that nuclear weapons, trade, technology, and the pressure on resources have made all states dependent on others for the success of both domestic and foreign policies. However this is still a long way from being a reason for neglecting policy analysis in favour of describing patterns of interdependence, or the 'international regimes' seen by Joseph Nye and Robert Keohane as being central to the explanation of modern world politics.[50] While the transnational perspective is valuable in its concentration on the common problems and processes encountered in advanced capitalist states, that of decision-making makes at least three major contributions which are anything but made redundant by interdependence.

First, not all states are sufficiently developed to be enmeshed in the web of economic and administrative transactions that bring about mutual reliance. The majority are poor and non-industrialised. Even among the Western European powers, which are highly interpenetrated, some states are far weaker than others. Britain and Italy depend heavily on the prospects for growth in West Germany, while the Scandinavian countries hope that the more powerful members of NATO will be able to sustain the strength of the alliance, although they have little to offer in return. In other words, even in a homogeneous region, states will have sufficiently diverse preoccupations and capabilities to make them want to pursue policies which are not identical with those of their neighbours, and which may indeed be incompatible with them. Just as centralisation leads to a separatist re-action, so homogeneity breeds a desire for diversity. And this is the second point. Whatever the fate of the nation–state, there are always likely to be sub-units of some kind in the world system, with separate policies towards those whom they see as 'outside' their own communities, as 'foreign'. The tension between macro and micro appears to be universal, and the actors who operate at the micro level will by definition have decision-making processes worth studying, whether they are states, provinces, functional organisations, corporations, or rebels against a monolithic Eurasian régime.

The final asset of the policy-making vantage point, even in a cobweb world of interdependence, is that it cannot help but raise political and moral questions. Given that government will remain a specialised business, run by a few for the many, it is important to have clear points of accountability, where those who are responsible for decisions are accessible to argument and challenge. Already it is difficult to know who to address, let alone who should have control, over such vital issues as the exploitation of North Sea oil, the amount of credit to be injected into states suffering from inflation and unemployment, or the response of Western Europe to a rise in Soviet arms spending. One of the better known characteristics of the multinational corporation is its lack of a single locus of responsibility, and this is becoming true of state activities as well. Confusion has certainly been engendered by the proliferation of institutions in response to problems that cut across state boundaries, but it is also due to the very failure of politicians and commentators to make sense of what is happening, in terms of deciding who should properly have what powers. Myths still abound about the sovereignty of parlia-ments, on the one hand, and about national impotence in the face of inter-dependence on the other, and they will be perpetuated unless questions are asked about how decisions are actually made, and with how much freedom from constraint. If discussion takes place at the level of international society alone, power will remain elusive and incrementalism will inevitably become even more rife. Only by taking cross-sections through decisions can we know how they might realistically be made better or differently, in terms of the appropriate distribution of powers between nations, regional bodies, and universal institutions.

Conclusion

It is quite possible that we shall never have a theory of foreign policy. Even if the epistemological difficulties about generalising in social science are surmounted,[51] foreign policy may still be too particular a phenomenon to generate theories of its own.[52] What this introduction has tried to show however, is simply that caution along these lines need not lead us straight back into individualistic case studies, or what a leading historian has called 'the sterile triviality of so much historical research'. As Lawrence Stone went on to argue, for all their faults social scientists 'can direct attention to problems of general relevance . . . they can ask new questions and suggest new ways of looking at old ones; they can supply new categories, and as a result may suggest new ideas'.[53] More than this, social scientists can still generalise, even without being able fully to explain what they observe. In the context of foreign policy this means breaking down international behaviour into its different contexts and sets of causes, and attempting to make statements which are more than merely commonplace about how these factors influence decisions. Moreover this must be done in a way which has meaning for those concerned with actual political dilemmas, whether as policy-maker or critic. The present volume takes a limited class of states (but one whose actions can have major impact outside their own area) and attempts to uncover the forces which shape their foreign policies. It focuses on institutions as well as processes. The strategy is a good one not only because of the 'OECD bias' of foreign policy analysis, but also because the aim is limited enough to have a real chance of adding to knowledge.

Notes

*I am indebted to Professor Geoffrey Goodwin of the London School of Economics for his comments on an earlier draft of this chapter.
[1]   These terms have been in increasingly wide use since the early 1950s, after the gradual emergence during the previous two decades both of formal decision analysis (through game theory) and of a political science literature questioning the degree to which institutions of government behaved as they were supposed to do. See the entries under 'Decision-Making' in the *International Encyclopaedia of Social Science*, Macmillan and Free Press 1968, and the *Oxford English Dictionary Supplement*, OUP 1972.
[2]   The distinction between macro and micro constitutes what has become known as 'The Level of Analysis Problem in International Relations', thanks to J. David Singer's article of that title in 1961 (now available in *International Politics and Foreign Policy*, revised edition, Free Press 1969, edited by James N. Rosenau). One of the first works to take explicitly and analytically an 'actor' perspective was George Modelski's *A Theory of Foreign Policy*, Praeger 1962.
[3]   G. Allison, 'Conceptual Models and the Cuban Missile Crisis', *American Political Science Review*, September 1969, and *Essence of Decision*, Little, Brown 1971, especially p. 32.
[4]   J. Steinbruner, *The Cybernetic Theory of Decision*, Princeton University Press 1974.
[5]   Patrick J. McGowan (ed.), *Sage International Yearbook of Foreign Policy Studies*, volume 1, Sage 1973, p. 14.
[6]   Op. cit., p. 13.
[7]   See for example *Comparing Foreign Policies*, Sage 1974, pp. 17-18, and *In Search of Global Patterns*, Free Press 1976, pp. 1-6.
[8]   Richard Snyder was of course the pioneer of decision-making models of

foreign policy; see R. C. Snyder, H. W. Bruck, and Burton Sapin (eds), *Foreign Policy Decision-Making*, Free Press 1962, the heart of which was first published in 1954 as *Decision-Making as an Approach to the Study of International Politics*, Princeton University Press. His work is not given separate prominence here because (a) it was too detailed to breed many empirical applications and (b) its important elements have been subsumed into the work of later writers.

[9] Strictly speaking much work even of this kind is not truly behaviourist, because it often relies on concepts that are not easy to operationalise, such as 'cooperative behaviour', or 'escalation' (P. McGowan and H. Shapiro, (eds), *The Comparative Study of Foreign Policy*, Sage 1973, pp. 98-9).

[10] Or what M. Sullivan has termed 'national attributes'. See the useful Part 4 of his *International Relations: Theories and Evidence*, Prentice Hall 1976. Certainly all taxonomies and models imply that some patterns will be found, but the 'national attribute' school differs in both its commitment to the feasibility of wide generalisation, and its attempt to begin analysis by demonstrating input–output correlations on at least a regional and preferably a global basis.

[11] M. Brecher, *The Foreign Policy System of Israel*, OUP 1972, and *Decisions in Israel's Foreign Policy*, OUP 1974. Brecher's work on crisis is represented by his article 'India's devaluation of 1966: linkage politics and crisis decision-making', *British Journal of International Studies*, vol. 3, no. 1, April 1977, and by an article outlining the framework of the current project, to appear shortly in *International Studies Quarterly*.

[12] Joseph Frankel, through his books *The Making of Foreign Policy*, 2nd edition, OUP 1967, *National Interest*, Pall Mall 1970, and *British Foreign Policy 1945-73*, OUP/RIIA 1975, has made the most distinctive of European contributions to foreign policy analysis.

[13] For example Allison's *Essence of Decision*, op. cit., owes a substantial debt to the work of such figures as Herbert Simon, Richard Neustadt, Richard Cyert and James March (pp. 162 and 301).

[14] This will inevitably leave open for debate the question of how exactly recurrent factors will operate in particular circumstances. In my view we have to accept defeat on the issue of detailed scientific prediction in social science, except where the variables are strictly quantifiable, as with votes and money.

[15] See for instance Johan Galtung's discussion of the related idea of 'scientific colonialism' in L. L. Horowitz (ed.), *The Rise and Fall of Project Camelot*, MIT Press 1974, revised edition, pp. 281-312.

[16] Readers may notice the difference between this and Charles Hermann's widely used definition, which isolates surprise, short time and a high threat to values as the characteristics of a crisis. C. Hermann, *Crises in Foreign Policy*, Bobbs-Merrill 1969, p. 29; also *International Crises: Insights from Behavioural Research*, Free Press 1972, edited by Hermann.

[17] This view is supported by O. R. Holsti, in his *Crisis, Escalation, War*, McGill/Queen's University Press 1972, pp. 143-69, and by Brecher in vol. II (op. cit.) pp. 564-5 and 574. On the other hand J. Kalicki shows that over a long period

'a crisis system' may become more stable through the actors involved learning more about each other and about crisis-management. However this is rather a different matter from the question of the pressures experienced by decision-makers once a period of acute crisis begins (J. Kalicki, *The Pattern of Sino-American Crises*, CUP 1975).

[18] See R. Kennedy, *The Thirteen Days*, Macmillan, London 1969, pp. 28–38, and R. Hilsman, *To Move a Nation*, Delta 1964, pp. 194–204.

[19] The evidence for these assertions is too lengthy to cite here, but see S. Aster, *1939: The Making of the Second World War*, A. Deutsch 1973, chs. 3 and 4; G. Paige, *The Korean Decision*, Free Press 1968, pp. 293–5; Part I of P. Windsor and A. Roberts, *Czechoslovakia 1968*, Chatto & Windus 1969 especially pp. 78–9.

[20] N. Rich, *Hitler's War Aims*, vol. I, A. Deutsch 1973, pp. 124–30.

[21] M. Brecher, vol. II op. cit., pp. 335–6 and 559.

[22] This consensus is perhaps only tentative at present, but it is evident among both member governments and 'attentive opinion'. See Geoffrey Goodwin, 'The External Relations of the European Community – Shadow and Substance' in *British Journal of International Studies*, April 1977, and William Wallace and David Allen, 'Political Co-operation: Procedure as substitute for policy' in Helen Wallace, William Wallace and Carole Webb (eds), *Policy-Making in the European Communities*, John Wiley and Sons 1977.

[23] This is also, broadly, the view of Phil Williams's useful *Crisis Management*, Martin Robertson 1976, and of Coral Bell's *The Conventions of Crisis*, OUP 1971.

[24] An early example is A. L. and J. L. George, *Woodrow Wilson and Colonel House*, The John Day Co., 1956; more recent is R. G. L. Waite, *The Psychopathic God: Adolf Hitler*, Basic Books 1977.

[25] The distinction between 'operational' and 'psychological' was originally drawn by H. and M. Sprout, 'Environmental Factors in the study of International Politics, *Journal of Conflict Resolution*, December 1957. It had also been fundamental in Snyder's earlier work, but less explicitly.

[26] R. Jervis, 'Hypotheses on Misperception', *World Politics*, April 1968; *The Logic of Images in International Relations*, Princeton UP 1970; *Perception and Misperception in International Politics*, Princeton UP 1976.

[27] I. Janis, *Victims of Group-think*, Houghton Mifflin 1972.

[28] L. Festinger, *A Theory of Cognitive Dissonance*, Row Peterson 1957. Festinger is the originator of the concept, of which a succinct explanation is given in N. F. Dixon, *On the Psychology of Military Incompetence*, Jonathan Cape 1976, pp. 164–6.

[29] This point will be lent extra force by a reading of E. May, *'Lessons' from the Past: The Use and Misuse of History in American Foreign Policy*, OUP 1973. J. C. Farrell and A. P. Smith (eds), *Image and Reality in World Politics*, Columbia UP 1968, also contains useful material on the centrality of general images of international relations. R. Axelrod (ed.), *The Structure of Decision*, Princeton UP 1976, terms these belief-systems 'cognitive maps' and presents a method for describing them formally.

[30] Helpful summaries can be found in M. Albrow, *Bureaucracy*, Macmillan 1970; M. J. Hill, *The Sociology of Public Administration*, Weidenfeld and Nicolson 1972; and D. S. Pugh, D. J. Hickson and C. R. Hinings, *Writers on Organizations*, Penguin, 2nd edition, 1971.

[31] See P. Darby, *British Defence Policy East of Suez, 1947-68*, OUP 1973, for evidence of lack of inter-departmental co-ordination and long term planning.

[32] Even in France, where administrators have been self-conscious about the need for expertise and planning, in practice the exclusive nature of the bureaucratic élite has made difficult re-examination of the old dicta about the centrality of France and French culture in world affairs. H. W. Ehrmann, *Politics in France*, Little, Brown 1968, pp. 140-1.

[33] B. C. Cohen, *The Public's Impact on Foreign Policy*, Little, Brown 1973, especially pp. 62-3, is revealing on the continuity of State Department attitudes relative to public opinion.

[34] For instance, while the State Department has not always been on warm terms with the Pentagon, it has been relatively close to the Department of Labor. J. F. Campbell, *The Foreign Affairs Fudge Factory*, Basic Books 1971, pp. 195-203, 212-5.

[35] The traditionally low status of economic expertise in the Foreign Office, coupled with an antagonism between the department and the Treasury, meant that a scramble to catch up on economic skills took place in the Office in the 1960s, boosted by some of the recommendations of Plowden and Duncan. See W. Wallace, *The Foreign Policy Process in Britain*, RIIA 1975, chapter 6, and P. Byrd, 'Trade and Commerce in External Relations' in R. Boardman and A. J. R. Groom (eds), *The Management of Britain's External Relations*, Macmillan 1973.

[36] H. Thomas, *The Suez Affair*, Penguin, revised edition, 1970, pp. 50-2.

[37] Steinbruner, op. cit., pp. 126-8.

[38] See Allison, op. cit., M. Halperin, *Bureaucratic Politics and Foreign Policy*, Brookings 1974, and the two authors' joint 'Bureaucratic Politics: A Paradigm and some Policy Implications' in R. Tanter and R. H. Ullman (eds), *Theory and Policy in International Relations*.

[39] L. Freedman, 'Logic, Politics, and Foreign Policy Processes', *International Affairs*, July 1976.

[40] A point stressed by F. B. Weinstein in 'The Uses of Foreign Policy in Indonesia: An approach to the Analysis of Foreign Policy in the Less Developed Countries', *World Politics*, April 1972.

[41] C. Seymour-Ure, *The Political Impact of Mass Media*, Constable 1974.

[42] For instance J. Hale, *Radio Power*, Elek 1975, highlights the way that radio broadcasting cannot help but influence both domestic and international politics.

[43] R. J. Lieber has shown the way in his *British Politics and European Unity: Parties, Elites, and Pressure-Groups*, University of California Press 1970.

[44] K. J. Holsti, *International Politics*, 2nd edition, Prentice Hall 1974, pp. 381-6.

[45] H. and M. Sprout, 'The Dilemma of Rising Demands and Insufficient

Resources', *World Politics*, XX, 1968; G. Kennedy, *The Economics of Defence*, Faber 1975.

[46] H. M. Sprout, *The Ecological Perspective on Human Affairs*, Princeton UP 1965.

[47] J. N. Rosenau (ed.), *Linkage Politics*, Free Press 1969.

[48] For both the reappraisal and the citations of the frequent use of the concept of linkage, see J. N. Rosenau 'Theorizing across systems: Linkage politics revisited' in J. Wilkenfeld (ed.), *Conflict Behaviour and Linkage Politics*. The term is also used in the rather different sense of the linkages made by governments between separate issues, so as to gain extra bargaining leverage. See the articles on Atlantic Relations in *International Affairs*, April 1976, by William Wallace, Ann-Margaret Walton, and David Rudnick.

[49] See, for example, James Callaghan's 'Challenges and Opportunities for British Foreign Policy', Fabian Tract 439, 1975, in which 'the new world of interdependence' is a central theme.

[50] As expressed in 'The Study of Transnational Relations Reconsidered', a paper given to the 1976 annual conference of the British International Studies Association by Robert Keohane. This was a preview of the forthcoming work by Nye and Keohane, *Power and Interdependence*, Little, Brown.

[51] Such difficulties are discussed in A. MacIntyre 'Is a science of Comparative Politics Possible?' in P. Laslett, W. G. Runciman, and Q. Skinner (eds), *Philosophy, Politics and Society*, 4th Series, Basil Blackwell 1972.

[52] A problem raised by H. MacDonald, 'The Case against Special Subjects in International Studies', *Millennium: Journal of International Studies*, Autumn 1975, in criticism of C. J. Hill, 'The Credentials of Foreign Policy Analysis', *Millennium*, Autumn 1974.

[53] Lawrence Stone, *The Causes of the English Revolution 1529-1642*, Routledge and Kegan Paul 1972, p. 22.

2 Old states and new circumstances: the international predicament of Britain, France and Germany

WILLIAM WALLACE

If, as American theorists of foreign policy have so often claimed, the analytical insights derived from studies of the relatively open processes of Washington policy-making are 'also relevant to other countries', they should above all be relevant to the major states of Western Europe.[1] Britain, France and Western Germany each have distinctive systems of government, it is true, different economic strengths and weaknesses, and distinctive perceptions of their national interests and of the international environment within which their governments operate. But this said, they have more in common with the United States than any other group of states in the international system. They too are open societies, governed by constitutional means with a democratic political tradition stemming from similar historical roots to that of the United States. They share the problems of advanced industrial societies; face the same intractable dilemmas: inflation versus unemployment, protection of domestic industries versus the benefits of international competition, expenditure on defence and investment versus expenditure on welfare or higher domestic consumption. Behind the differing rhetoric of 'social democracy' or 'advanced liberalism', all three governments share with the United States the real problems of managing mixed economies, in which state intervention in industry is unavoidable and international co-operation inescapable. Their government machinery is similarly extensive and complex, bringing in its train problems of co-ordination and coherence, of bureaucratic inertia and political control. If comparative study of foreign policy is possible beyond the most general theoretical abstractions, then comparison must be possible here.

In looking at the making of foreign policy, rather than at the foreign policy field as a whole, and in looking in detail at particular countries, the relevance of the more abstract and 'pure' foreign policy theory is necessarily limited. We are concerned here, in James Rosenau's terms, with the comparative study of particular foreign policies rather than with the study of comparative foreign policy *per se*.[2] How far, we may ask, do America's major European partners share her predicament of international interdependence, and share too her perception of the implications of that predicament? How far are their governments similarly riven by internal dissension and bureaucratic politics? How far has the penetration of their domestic politics by foreign actors, and the involvement of domestic actors in international activities, undermined the old certainties of foreign policy and foreign policy-making, leaving governments faced with problems of policy management which are at once domestic and intergovernmental?

The rhetoric of interdependence has for long been an established part of trans-atlantic diplomacy: proclaimed by Mr Macmillan and President Kennedy at the beginning of the 1960s, recognised and resisted by President de Gaulle, reasserted (and reinterpreted) by Dr Kissinger in his 'Year of Europe' initiative of 1973. Academic studies of interdependence have flourished in the United States in recent years, examining in some detail the mutual dependencies between the United States and its international partners in different areas of policy.[3] Studies of interdependence in Western Europe have so far been more limited in scope. The rhetoric of integration, a process which was understood as leading gradually but irreversibly towards the establishment of a supranational European government, clouded academic, and political appreciation of the implications of interdependence within Western Europe.[4]

The reality of interdependence – the degree to which national economies, societies and governments are vulnerable to developments in other countries, and in their turn affect developments in other countries, whether intentionally or unintentionally, by their own actions – is however qualitatively different in Western Europe from the position in which the United States find itself. Economically, the major states of Western Europe are much more sensitive than the USA to international trends, much more dependent on foreign markets for their production and on foreign suppliers for their raw materials. Exports amounted to some 7·2 per cent of America's gross domestic product in 1975, compared to 19·2 per cent for Britain, 16 per cent for France, and 21·3 per cent for Germany. For each of these three major European states, their most important trading partners were their West European neighbours, with whom they exchanged manufactures, components, agricultural produce and services within a partly-integrated international economy. The creation of such an integrated West European economy had of course been one of the aims of post-war American foreign policy, promoted both by the conditions attached to Marshall Plan assistance to their war-damaged economies and by continuing diplomatic pressure throughout the fifties and early sixties. The United States' commitment to a high degree of West European interdependence was deepened by the success of American companies in taking advantage of the opportunities presented by expanding and relatively open European markets. A multinational framework of industrial activity has thus been created, which yet further restricts the ability of any one European government to manage its economy or alter its domestic priorities independently.

Dependence on external suppliers for vital raw materials is also markedly higher for these countries than for the United States. In 1974 France depended on imports of oil for 71·3 per cent of its total energy requirements. Britain (since North Sea oil had not yet begun to flow) supplied 53·2 per cent of its energy needs from imported oil, West Germany 51·8 per cent; while the United States, with a far higher consumption of energy per head, drew only 16·9 per cent of its requirements from overseas sources. Europe's oil suppliers lay outside the mutually dependent and close-knit network of the advanced industrial countries. Overwhelmingly, European imports of energy came from the Arab states of North Africa and the Middle East. West European countries were therefore far more vulnerable to political influences and economic pressures from the Arab oil producers than their American ally – as the events of October–December 1973 clearly demonstrated. Their higher degree of dependence on external sources of raw materials also demanded a more active European response to the developing countries' demands for a 'new international economic order' after the 1973 Middle East War, though the British Prime Minister's 'Kingston initiative' of 1975 petered out in the recriminations of UNCTAD IV, and the French President's later proposal for a 'North-South dialogue' in the form of a restricted–membership conference did not foreshadow particular European generosity in the detailed discussions of the Conference on International Economic Co-operation.

If American students of international politics have become convinced of the realities of interdependence in economic issues, those whose attention centres on security and defence issues have been more struck by the continuing autonomy of the nation-state.[5] Yet even for these larger European powers, the exercise of sovereignty in matters of defence has become conditional upon the co-operation of allies. Most importantly, all three depend in the last resort upon the protection of the United States, extended both through the American conventional contribution to Western European defence and through the 'nuclear guarantee' of the US strategic deterrent. In spite of the efforts of the British and French governments to maintain independent arms industries, the steadily increasing costs of research, development and production have gradually forced them towards the policy of intergovernmental collaboration in military procurement which the German government had adopted by choice. Formal sovereignty remained, in terms of national control over the deployment of forces and their potential use (though constrained for West Germany by its commitments under Western European Union). But unilateral use of force by any of these powers was inconceivable by the end of the 1960s, except in such limited skirmishes as the repeated fisheries disputes between Britain and Iceland.

The partly undirected drift towards a high degree of economic interdependence within Western Europe has been accompanied by a parallel drift towards an interpenetration of societies. In spite of the barriers of language and of national cultures, a partly-integrated West European society may be said to be emerging, founded upon faster and cheaper travel by road, rail and air, upon shared television programmes, football competitions and popular music, upon student exchanges, holidays in the same Mediterranean resorts, and intermarriage.[6] Transnational links and formal groupings have grown up among business and banking leaders, among farmers, and (more slowly) among trade unions, which serve to bring pressure to bear upon different governments in support of common interests and to bypass the traditional diplomatic channels of intergovernmental communication in transmitting confidential information on common concerns.[7] Links between political parties, though not as close as post-war enthusiasts for European integration had hoped they would become, provide another direct channel of communication between political systems; and may even form the basis for common 'foreign policy' actions, as the activities of Europe's social democratic parties in assisting their partner in Portugal during 1976–77 were held by some to indicate.[8]

The political focus for the activities of these transnational groups is provided by the multilateral framework of international organisations within which governments attempt to manage European and Atlantic interdependence. The most important of these is clearly the European Community; but the intricate patterns of intergovernmental consultation and co-operation spread far beyond Brussels and far beyond the competences of the Treaty of Rome. On international and domestic economic issues, British, French and German officials and central bankers meet each other and their colleagues from other western industrial countries at the Bank of International Settlements in Basle and at the many committees and working parties of the Organisation for Economic Co-operation and Development in Paris. Within the security field, Britain and Germany are leading members of NATO and of the Eurogroup; France remains half in half out of NATO, and (while refusing to join the Eurogroup) co-operated in 1975–76 in the establishment of a new European Programme Group to further co-operation in military procurement. The Council of Europe and the associated European Commission on Human Rights provided a framework for discussion of civil liberties within European countries, used against the British government in the early 1970s over both restrictions on immigration and the treatment of prisoners in Northern Ireland. It also promoted cultural and educational exchanges, a function supplemented bilaterally between France and Germany under the terms of their treaty of 1963.

The development of this extensive multilateral framework for intergovernmental co-operation has also carried with it the development of extensive contacts between officials within the domestic ministries of national governments, which again goes far beyond what the American administration has so far experienced (except perhaps during World War II in the very close relations between British and American officials). The displacement of diplomatic intermediaries by direct exchanges between responsible officials from national capitals is a distinctively European phenomenon, facilitated not only by regular multilateral meetings within formal international organisations but also by the ease of travel between European capitals and the spread of an efficient telephone network, with direct dialling between Europe's major cities and secure lines between national capitals.[9] The travelling time between Bonn and Paris is after all no greater than between Boston and Washington. Officials and ministers can and do frequently visit each others' capitals for brief consultations and return home within the same day, keeping their opposite numbers briefed on their own attitudes and often also on the internal conflicts within their own administrations, and leaving their foreign ministries and embassies to keep abreast of their conversations as well as their limited staffs will allow.[10]

Not surprisingly, therefore, academic observers have identified within Western Europe 'a crisis in sovereignty that is likely to worsen appreciably in the coming decades ... attested to in the French case by the great concern with sovereignty in both domestic and international affairs in the 1960s.'[11] Marxist critics of advanced industrial society have seen the European Community and the whole trend towards multilateral intergovernmental co-operation as 'an attempt to overcome within the context of capitalism one of its major "contradictions", namely the constantly more marked obsolescence of the nation-state as the basic unit of international life.'[12] Certainly, the growth of an integrated international economy, the weakening of the state's independent security role, and the emergence of politically significant transnational links have undermined the boundaries of national sovereignty and limited the ability of even the strongest European governments to hold the gate between their domestic political system and foreign policy. Certainly, too, membership of the European Community weakens yet further national autonomy in domestic policy, and is arguably transforming the whole context of foreign policy – as David Allen describes in another chapter.[13] But this does *not* mean that the nation-state is withering away, or that any of these three governments has abandoned the struggle to monitor and control the mass of transactions between their own administrations and those of their partners. 'The contradiction between the impulse to independence and the necessities of interdependence', which one observer identifies as a central tension in French foreign policy since 1958, is a tension shared by the governments of Britain and West Germany.[14] All three governments face the same predicament of interdependence; it is their reactions to that predicament which differ.

Interdependence has not decreased the role of nation-states in international life; on the contrary, it has increased it. 'The symbiosis of state and industry' which J.K. Galbraith noted as a common feature of advanced industrial societies is most evident in France, least evident in West Germany; but the necessities of domestic economic management and international economic co-operation have forced all three governments to extend the boundaries of intergovernmental activity.[15] As a result, 'foreign policy as such – as creative foreign policy – and with it the concept of sovereignty as such, is continuously diminishing in importance. At the same time, however, because of the ever-growing dependence of all domestic politics on international politics, domestic sovereignty is more and more tied to the circle of decision-makers in foreign policy'.[16]

In other words, 'foreign policy is simultaneously losing and gaining importance'.[17] All major ministries in London, Paris and Bonn are involved in the formulation, management and implementation of foreign policy. The disintegration of creative foreign policy based upon centrally imposed co-ordination and centrally orchestrated objectives into bureaucratic politics based upon the particular interests of different ministries and their client groups is an ever present danger. The loss of domestic support for foreign policy, with the consequent loss of leverage on partner governments who find it easy to inform themselves in detail of domestic divisions and hesitations, is as great a threat: requiring governments to pay particular attention to managing domestic opinion, most of all to maintaining close links with groups which have both domestic political weight and transnational connections. And in all this activity, it is the government as a whole which is engaged: not simply

35

each country's foreign ministry and the two or three other departments with long established international responsibilities, but almost all the major agencies of the state.

The patterns of national response

For none of these three states, still possessed of substantial economic and military resources, still ranking among the leading powers in international diplomacy and international economic management, would the response to interdependence adopted by such smaller countries as the Dutch government now be a tempting option. In the 1950s and 1960s the government of the Federal Republic, like the Dutch, had proclaimed its commitment to European integration and its willingness to sink its sovereignty within a larger entity; but the evident and increasingly international weight of the West German economy, the regaining and exercise of West German sovereignty and the arrival of a new generation of political leaders whose only political experience had been of the Federal Republic and who were consequently less convinced of the need to expunge German guilt, left only the rhetoric of this commitment to survive into the 1970s. For Britain and France, 'great powers' at the end of World War II and still possessed of empires, nuclear powers by the 1960s, the process of adjustment to declining international capabilities and increasing interdependence has been more gradual, though perhaps ultimately no less painful than the 'adjustment' forcibly imposed upon Germany after 1945. But in both Britain and France in the mid-seventies neither political leadership nor the public at large regarded the abandonment of sovereignty as desirable or necessary. Rather, they looked to their government (as did their West German partners) to strike the best obtainable balance between the maintenance of autonomy and the acceptance of interdependence. The point at which that balance was struck has necessarily differed from issue to issue, and from country to country; depending upon the framework of assumptions about sovereignty, the role of the state and the pattern of relations with other countries which obtains in each of these three powers.

Certain responses may thus be seen as common to these three medium powers, converging in status and outlook as Britain and France accept their reduced autonomy and West Germany gains a sense of international strength. All three have reacted to the tension between sovereignty and interdependence by strengthening their efforts to control and direct negotiations between their domestic bureaucracies and those of other states, most evidently in their management of policy towards the European Community.[18] All three have extended the role of the state in the economy and in protecting and promoting the international interests of domestic industry: supporting national concentration rather than transnational amalgamation, underwriting national 'champions' and 'flag-carriers' on the international market.[19]

Beyond this, however, responses diverge. Historical experience, political culture, administrative capacity, geographical situation, economic strength or weakness were distinctive patterns. This perhaps is most starkly evident in their different outlook towards relations with the United States, their dominant partner in the security and monetary fields and dominant competitor in industrial and technological matters; in which 'the French have adopted defiance (attenuated but not abandoned since Georges Pompidou replaced de Gaulle), the British compliance, and the West Germans hesitation.'[20] But it is evident more widely in each country's whole approach to the problem of foreign policy, of maintaining coherence and of pursuing independent objectives within an unavoidably interdependent world.

Successive French governments have taken the most self-conscious approach to the preservation of sovereignty and the pursuit of an active foreign policy. The stamp of President de Gaulle has impressed itself so deeply upon the language and ideas of French foreign policy that it is tempting to assign the responsibility for the idiosyncracy of the French response directly to him. Taking office in 1958 under the strain of France's second war of decolonisation in Algeria, he not only successfully reversed policy on Algeria and North Africa, but by 1966 had challenged the American dominance of the international monetary system, interrupted the American 'invasion' of the French economy, summoned his country and his European partners to throw back the technological and scientific challenge posed by the United States, and taken France out of the integrated command structure of NATO. Yet his language and his style found ready echoes on the French left, even while they denounced his domestic policies, which suggests that its roots lay deeper, in the French 'étatist' tradition, in the ethos of the French élite and civil service, and in the absence of any special ties with the United States which might counterbalance the pull towards the reassertion of national independence as the economy recovered and the burdens of empire were shed at last.

Admirers of French foreign policy point to its greater international impact in the mid-seventies than that of its European partners, to the clarity of its objectives, and to the realism with which French negotiators bargain for national advantage, exploiting to the full the limited resources at their disposal. The many critics point rather to the underlying contradictions between its stated aims and its capabilities for their achievement.[21] If 1966 marked the high point of Gaullist foreign policy, the decade since then – it is argued – has witnessed a gradual retreat from the nationalist positions thus adopted towards an uncomfortable and still incomplete acceptance of the limitations of French resources and the need for co-operation with its partners. The grand conception of French defence policy has been exposed as leading to an overconcentration on strategic forces and neglect of conventional forces, by the mid-seventies leading to discontent within the French military. French opposition to American plans for international monetary reform had already been modified under pressure from France's allies before the 'events' of May 1968 undermined the strength of the franc and forced a more conciliatory position; French insistence on the monetarist path towards European economic union, from 1969 on, was undermined in turn by the withdrawal, under speculative pressure, of the franc from the currency 'snake' in January 1974. Resistance to American multinationals had alternated throughout the 1960s with periods of partial co-operation; and after the loss of the 'arms sale of the century' in 1975 to an American competitor it gave way almost completely to a succession of active efforts to strike advantageous bargains with American aircraft manufacturers and high technology firms, to the detriment of France's proclaimed European commitment. The Pompidolian and Giscardian echoes of Gaullist foreign policy seemed largely to consist of grand but insubstantial gestures, activist in their pursuit of international initiatives, but little concerned either with the effect of those initiatives on the interests of their allies or with the detailed negotiation needed to carry those initiatives through into concrete form.

How conscious French policy-makers have been of the contradictions behind a foreign policy the consistency of which they so often proclaimed is likely to remain a matter of dispute. Some critics have seen French Fifth Republic governments as deliberate 'free riders' on the international system, taking advantage of their partners' reluctance to upset the delicately balanced framework which guaranteed collective security and collective prosperity.[22] To pursue such a strategy successfully required clear central direction, clearly defined priorities, and an efficient and united administration – aspects of French policy-making which will be explored further in the next section. Others have identified the root cause of this contradiction between 'the logic of interdependence' and 'the phraseology of independence' in the complex political divisions of French society, and the unwillingness of post-Gaullist governments to swim against the tide of public opinion – a contention to be examined in the section following.[23]

The contradictions within the British response to interdependence have been more muted. 'British foreign policy is marked by pragmatism and an absence of ideology,' behind which 'we can merely guess and argue about the hidden assumptions, the collective prejudices and emotions' which move policy-makers and guide the 'climate of opinion'.[24] In contrast to the preoccupation of successive French governments with the *grandes lignes* of foreign policy and the need to define and redefine France's attitude to international developments, the predominant style of successive British governments has been to avoid too sharp a definition of purpose, to deny the significance of changes of direction even as they were being made. No British statesman has attempted publicly to redefine the strategic priorities of foreign policy since Winston Churchill enunciated the 'three circles' doctrine towards the end of the Second World War. Yet successive and substantial adjustments have been made in the thirty years since then. Britain's privileged 'special relationship' with the United States had been transmuted by the mid-1960s into a much looser sponsor–client relationship while the Heath government of 1970–74 appeared to have moved on from regarding the Atlantic link as the 'first circle' of Britain's international influence, and to have made the European connection its first priority. The transition from Empire to Commonwealth was achieved without suffering the full scale wars or domestic traumas which the French experienced, and with only the 'failure' of Rhodesia and domestic opposition to the immigration policies to which decolonising British governments had committed themselves to count against the record of successful adjustment. By the mid-seventies, too, Britain had not only become a member of the European Community but had carried a decisive majority of its electorate with it in a referendum which may be seen as a test of the public's acceptance of Britain's limited international resources and of its need for partners in an interdependent world.

Perhaps the underlying acceptance by British policy-makers of the essential benevolence of American leadership of the Western world and of their own continuing access to that leadership made a more conscious or deliberate redefinition of priorities unnecessary. Mr Macmillan's definition of interdependence, in the aftermath of the Suez invasion (the greatest trauma foreign policy-makers had experienced since 1945), was after all one of interdependence with the United States far more than with the European continent. In contrast to France, successive Conservative and Labour governments treated American investment in Britain as a welcome benefit and a non-salient issue, for all Mr Wilson's rhetoric in 1966-67 about the dangers of 'industrial helotry'.[25] Yet the ambivalence and imprecision which has marked the style of British policy-makers from one government to another has carried its costs, exposing contradictions which characteristic ambiguities of definition could not hide. Had Mr Macmillan chosen to set out more clearly the implications of accession to the EEC in 1961-62, in particular its consequences for relations with the USA, Britain might have been spared a decade of uncertainty in its relations with the rest of Europe – though at the cost of arousing considerable dissension within his own party, and opposition within the public at large. Had the priorities of British defence policy been more openly debated and clearly defined, it is unlikely that the armed services would have continued expanding their bases east of Suez until a year before the final withdrawal was announced, or that their equipment in the mid-1970s would have been so inadequately adapted for what had then become a purely European role.[26] By the 1970s, however, acute awareness of economic weakness and the constraints which it placed upon foreign policy had created a climate of opinion among British policy-makers that it was pointless to attempt to pursue objectives less immediate than economic and commercial recovery, and that the need to ensure the full co-operation and understanding of its partners in that recovery ruled out such flamboyant and unilateral initiatives as French presidents loved to make.

One might anticipate from the incoherence of objectives a similar incoherence in the management of British foreign policy, a disintegration of central direction into bureaucratic politics. If sovereignty is a concept too theological for most British politicians, and the idea of 'the state' a concept almost entirely foreign, then it would not be surprising if the penetration of the British administration by foreign governments and the differing conceptions of national interests among ministries in Whitehall combined to undermine any attempts to hold the boundary between domestic debate on policy and foreign policy as such. That this does not appear to have resulted directs our attention to the style and ideology of the policy making machinery, to be discussed in more detail below.

The point from which the West German government approached the problems of interdependence was radically different from that of France and Britain. Defeated, occupied, and deprived of formal sovereignty after the Second World War, West Germany was accepted back into the Western international community on sufferance and on conditions. The recreated state was not coterminous with the historical German 'nation', which politicians of all parties were pledged to reunite: there was therefore an air of temporariness about the new government for its first twenty years, a sense of operating as a 'provisional' state with the overriding objective that reunification might be achieved.[27] The West German state was self-consciously a child of the Cold War, immediately aware of its dependence upon the United States for its security and willing to accept the political and economic dependence which went with it. Its leadership reacted to the fanatical nationalism of the Nazi regime and to the continuing distrust of Germany, among its allies as well as its enemies, by committing itself firmly to the idea of European integration, offering to submerge the new German state in a wider and supranational entity. In a sense, then, the first response of the post-war German government to interdependence was to embrace it, seeing in a dual commitment to Atlantic and to European co-operation a means of avoiding the awkward issues of national interest and of a redefined German role in the world.

A number of factors combined during the late 1960s to transform the context of German foreign policy. The most deliberate was the reorientation of policy on German reunification – at once a central issue of German domestic politics, at least in symbolic and rhetorical terms, and the key to much of German foreign policy. The formulation of an active *Ostpolitik*, and Willy Brandt's determined diplomacy both as foreign minister and as Chancellor, succeeded over a period of years in reconciling West Germans to the reality of two German states and in re-establishing a *modus vivendi* with Bonn's eastern neighbours. During the same period progress towards 'union' within Western Europe was first halted by Gaullist opposition to an integrated Community and then tentatively restarted by the agreement at The Hague summit in 1969 to open negotiations on British entry and to attempt an Economic and Monetary Union. Growing awareness of West Germany's economic preponderance within the EC, and of its weight within the Western industrialised world as a whole, gave added confidence to German policy-makers, and made domestic opinion conscious of the international demands made on the German budget and on their carefully stabilised economy. Acceptance of American leadership was weakened first by the Johnson administration's preoccupation with Vietnam and then by the Nixon administration's preference for dealing with the Soviet Union over the heads of its allies. The passing of the 'war-guilt' generation out of positions of responsibility, marked politically by the succession of Herr Schmidt to the Chancellorship, therefore marked also the culmination of a process in which West German policy-makers and public opinion had gradually defined a set of foreign policy attitudes and priorities which limited their acceptance of interdependence by recreating a sense of national interest.

The rhetoric of West German foreign policy makers in the mid-seventies however retained elements of the old doctrines as well as the new attitudes. The commitment to European union was regularly restated, though the unwillingness of

German finance ministers to countenance greater contributions to the Community budget from the German taxpayer, and the failure of German foreign ministers to press for the reforms which they themselves demanded, deprived these restatements of much of their substance. In defence and security matters – still the most sensitive areas of German foreign policy – their governments continued to waver between their American alliance and pressure from France, without attempting much more than a reactive policy to the demands of both. As befitted an economic power of the first order, the West German government was most active in international economic policy, supporting American proposals for Atlantic economic summits in 1975 and 1976, pressing for a common European and Atlantic response to the energy crisis of 1973 and to the international recession which accompanied it. But there were few if any German initiatives within this field, compared to the repeated initiatives of the French or even to the proposals put forward from time to time by the Dutch. The dominant image the West German government presented, within the European Community, in its contributions to European discussions on UNCTAD and on the Conference on International Economic Co-operation, in debates within the OECD and at Atlantic summits on international reflation, was one of reluctant and reactive co-operation: guarding its resources, protecting its domestic interests, but doing little actively to pursue defined objectives of its own.[28]

Here again it is difficult for the observer to disentangle from the pattern of policy-making those factors accounted for by ideology and style, those by administration, and those by public opinion and domestic constraints. There remained in the approach of German policy-makers to international issues, even thirty years after the end of World War II, an awareness of the image of the 'ugly German' (as some of them called it) and a consequent reluctance to press German interests too vigorously in negotiations with their partners. There remained also an unwillingness to admit the principle of an international political role for Germany, even if in relation to such European countries as Spain, Portugal or Turkey the German government was beginning to pursue an active diplomacy. This reluctance was reinforced by the determinedly domestic orientation of public opinion, and its resistance to international commitments which would threaten Germany's economic stability or raise political echoes from the past. It was reinforced also by the hesitant management of West German foreign policy: at its most coherent in international economic issues, but marked in all fields by a stiffness of execution, a concern with detail rather than with broader conceptions, and a repeated failure to follow through proposals in continuing negotiations.

The problem of management

The growth of government involvement in international activity is not simply a consequence of international interdependence. It results also from the growth of government's domestic responsibilities, which then spill over national boundaries into the international domain. In spite of the differing emphases of their national economic policies, Britain, France and West Germany all have substantial government involvement in economic management and industrial planning, partly in response to domestic objectives and demands, partly in response to international pressures. In steel or shipbuilding, for example, the West German government's commitment to a 'social market economy' gave way before the need to protect its own industries and to co-operate with its partners in resisting Japanese imports. In energy, it has followed both France and Britain in promoting the establishment of a 'national' oil company and a national capacity for building nuclear power stations – both of which carried implications for its international relations. Domestic policies on education, employment and social security also carried international implications, as immigrant labour became an important factor in the economies of all three states and as the European Community attempted to lay down rules for free movement of labour within the partly-integrated economy and society of Western Europe. Europe's three largest economies, each with an industrial base which covers the whole spread of politically sensitive industries, from military aircraft and computers to textiles and food processing, require of their governments activity across the entire range of international regulation, rule-setting, import substitution and export promotion. A strategy of selective activity in international discussions, open to smaller states with a more limited range of interests, is not open to them.

The most immediate problem, therefore, is one of overload. The enormous expansion in the range and intensity of consultations among the governments of advanced industrial countries has sharpened what observers twenty years ago had already identified as a problem into what is now in effect the central problem of the nation-state in its international expression: how to select out of the mass of detailed information and activities a sufficiently small number of key issues to enable top policy-makers to absorb a coherent impression and at the same time to impose a sense of direction on the whole, and conversely how effectively to monitor the international actions of dozens of government agencies and thousands of officials without swamping the central machinery in paper and co-ordinating meetings.[29] Yet the ability of central policy-makers to monitor and to steer, and thus to hold the boundary between domestic politics and foreign policy, is crucial to the continued viability of the nation-state. The intensity of this problem for the major European governments is far greater than the challenge which faces the American government: it is this above all which distinguishes the European predicament from that of the United States.

The separation of foreign policy-making from domestic policy has since the emergence of the modern European state been maintained and reinforced by two structural factors: the greater authority retained by the executive in this field than on domestic issues, and the existence of a separate diplomatic service. Historically, the foreign services of Britain, France and Germany shared high prestige both within their own governments and countries and outside: an élite corps within the civil service, more aristocratic in recruitment than the services of domestic ministries, yet with high qualifications for entry.[30] Their professional obligation to spend between half and two-thirds of their career overseas to some extent separated them further from domestic politics and gave them a necessarily more 'internationalist' perspective – and continues to separate them from domestic civil servants in experience and outlook. All three diplomatic services are hierarchical in organisation, with between 3,000 and 3,500 in the administrative grades: large enough to have developed bureaucratic traditions and habits, but not too large to retain some of the old ethos of a small and self-conscious service the members of which knew each other and recognised their common loyalties and expertise.

Yet to conclude from this, following the assumptions of the bureaucratic politics perspective, that like 'every nation's foreign ministry' these three diplomatic services 'will advocate similar patterns of decision-making and policy objectives' would be a considerable oversimplification.[31] Certainly, diplomats in Bonn, Paris and London shared a number of assumptions and interests about the proper role of foreign ministries and embassies in the management of foreign policy: that they above all should be the 'gatekeeper', the agency which monitored the flow of communications between their own government and other governments, and which imposed the distinctive stamp of national interest upon that flow. Certainly, too, they fought similar battles with other ministries, worked in the same way to protect their own spheres of competence and to guard those few areas of foreign policy which remained theirs alone.[32] But beyond that, there are marked differences between their structure, status and ethos which help to account for divergences in the management of foreign policy between the three governments.

The French foreign ministry still, in 1976, drew its authority in relation to other departments of state partly from two Napoleonic decrees setting out his reformed structure for managing the French Empire's foreign policy.[33] Last overhauled in 1945, the rigid divisions between the three 'grand' directorates for political, economic and cultural affairs formed barriers and created rivalries within the ministry itself. For some years their share of the national budget had been held down, and the consequent strains both on staffing and living conditions had adversely affected morale (and led to a mushrooming of trade union activity within the diplomatic service). President de Gaulle's successors followed him in concentrating the direction of French foreign policy in the Elysée, but did not follow his traditionalist acceptance that it should be *managed* in the Quai d'Orsay; a succession of incidents in which presidential initiatives were taken without most responsible diplomats being consulted helped to shake morale further.

Yet the Quai d'Orsay retained very considerable strengths within the French administration. Its large and expert Economic Directorate powerfully maintained the foreign ministry's voice in international economic policy. Its key officials belonged to the same administrative élite as senior officials in other ministries, and shared with them the same concepts of policy, state and national interest. Most important of all, the assumption by politicians and officials alike that foreign policy remained a separate activity, providing the 'political' input into a dialogue with 'technical' ministries, retained for the foreign ministry a clear sense of its own role, which was shared even by the domestic ministries with which it struggled. To

43

reinforce this role, a plan for reform was announced in October 1976 which included in its proposals a strengthening of diplomatic control of overseas missions, an increase over five years in its share of the budget, and an increase in staff.[34]

The British Foreign and Commonwealth Office, in contrast, had been reformed twice since 1964, and was in early 1977 awaiting the report of a third committee of investigation with some disquiet. Although it had reduced its staff by some thirteen per cent since the post-1964 amalgamations, it remained a prestigious and well-staffed ministry which vigorously defended its interests in Whitehall. With a much more flexible internal structure than its French counterpart, it had during the 1960s created a series of new functional departments, to keep abreast of the expanding international activities of domestic ministries, and had begun to pay attention to training some of its officials in economic and technical subjects.[35] Diplomats played a leading role in the negotiations for British entry into the EEC, and the FCO managed to retain a dominant position both in the British representation in Brussels and in the co-ordination of European policy in Whitehall. Staffed by a competent and self-confident corps of officials, the FCO in the mid-seventies suffered however from two external weaknesses: from the general loss of direction in British foreign policy, which had led to public questioning of the need for a diplomatic service and for a distinctive foreign policy effort as such, and from the debilitating effects of economic weakness, which had brought politicians, home civil servants and outside observers to question the possibilities of active engagement in international diplomacy and to begrudge the share of the budget claimed by overseas representation.

The Auswärtiges Amt suffered from the peculiar disadvantage, in relation to its partner ministries, of having been re-established after the war only gradually, re-emerging as a full ministry with West Germany's acceptance into NATO and into the Western community of nations as a full partner in 1955. 'De-nazification' had also hit the German diplomatic service, both in personnel and in self-confidence. Faced with a Chancellor's Office which had in effect directed foreign policy in the immediate post-war period and with powerful domestic ministries which had already established entrenched positions, the Auswärtiges Amt only slowly regained ground.[36] Its rigid internal structure, with powerful directorates which one German official compared to feudal baronies in their proud and formal independence of each other, inhibited adjustment to shifting international patterns; though here too the Economic Directorate had by the mid-seventies markedly grown in size and in influence, supplemented by a number of ad hoc units handling multilateral negotiations which could not be accommodated within its traditional hierarchy. If its strength in the policy-making process was increasing from the late sixties onwards, this was more a reflection of the key position of its minister, as leader of the junior coalition party, and of the growing international responsibilities which economic success was pushing on to Germany, than of the active determination of the ministry itself and of any clear or agreed definition of its role.

Patterns of co-operation and tension between different ministries follow not dissimilar lines in all three capitals. The age-old conflict between finance ministries and foreign ministries, both over the cost of foreign policy and over the determination of foreign economic policy, is evident in the active rivalry between the Trésor and the Quai d'Orsay's Economic Directorate in Paris, and in the undercurrents of mistrust between the Treasury and the FCO in London. The situation in Bonn is complicated by the existence of a large and powerful Economics Ministry alongside the Finance Ministry, adding its own 'social market' interpretation of foreign economic policy to the Finance Ministry's defence of the interests of the German taxpayer.[37] Relations between foreign offices and defence ministries, in contrast, have been generally close, and based upon an acceptance of the foreign offices' leadership in matters of political significance – with the partial exception of France, where for a period in the early seventies the Délégation Ministériel pour l'Armement appeared to be pursuing a policy in arms sales largely independent of the Quai d'Orsay.[38] As the relationship between state and industry spilled out on to the international plane, in civil as well as military industries, the problem of alerting foreign ministries to the political implications of technical negotiations and of educating domestic ministries about the wider context within which their concerns now needed to be placed became more acute. In Britain, for example, Treasury witnesses admitted to a Parliamentary Committee in 1964 that they had not yet given formal authorisation to the Concorde project, on which a binding treaty had been signed two years before; while FCO witnesses to another committee in 1966 denied any responsibility for approving Britain's signature of the convention setting up a European Launcher Development Organisation.[39]

For all three governments, therefore, the problem of management has come to focus above all on co-ordination and coherence: on holding together the threads which tie national policies to international negotiations, and on maintaining an element of steering, of self-direction, amidst the wide and swiftly-flowing current of activity. The problem is most acute for the French, given their determined commitment to maintain sovereignty and 'independence', and least acute for the Germans, given their continuing ambiguity about both those concepts.

The increasing personalisation of French foreign policy-making, from de Gaulle to Pompidou to Giscard d'Estaing, reflected the continuing determination of successive presidents to demonstrate to their parties and their electorate France's capacity to act decisively on the international scene, unhampered by the complexities of detailed negotiation. The smallness of the President's personal staff is striking, amounting in 1977 to two diplomatic advisers in the Elysée, with a third official advising on international economic policy and a fourth responsible for relations with francophone Africa, as well as a small military staff. Significantly, the Secretary-General of the Elysée was also normally a diplomat, marking the pre-eminent role of the President in foreign policy, the *domaine réservée* of the Fifth Republic. Close relations between the Elysée as laying down the *grandes lignes* of policy and the Quai d'Orsay as implementing foreign policy and watching over the political dimension of the state's international activities was ensured by appointing officials as foreign ministers. Pompidou indeed transferred the Elysée's Secretary-General direct to the post of foreign minister, without fundamentally changing his role in policy-making. The Council of Ministers operates as a forum for settling hard-fought inter-ministerial disputes, under the chairmanship of the President; but more often foreign policy questions were determined in *conseils restreints*, with only the responsible ministers attending, or bilaterally between the President and the minister most directly concerned. The Prime Minister's Office at the Matignon was, in contrast, only marginally involved in foreign policy. It arbitrated on minor points of disagreement between ministries, within the strategic lines of policy laid down by the Elysée; while an attached Secretariat was responsible for co-ordinating all 'technical' aspects of French policy towards the EC.[40]

The German Chancellor's Office, as has been noted, had played a decisive role in formulating and managing policy towards the Allies in the years leading up to the restoration of sovereignty to the West German state. This reflected more the dominant personality of Konrad Adenauer as Chancellor in successive German governments than any constitutional grant of authority over foreign policy, and was not maintained to the same degree under succeeding chancellors. The departmental competition which has historically marked German administration re-established itself in Bonn, with each ministry defending its legal competences and resisting direction from the centre. The German Cabinet is therefore the court of last resort in German policy-making, in foreign as in domestic issues, with the Chancellor and the Chancellor's Office asserting their *Richtlinienkompetenz* against the particular competences of the major ministries. In this political forum, the personalities of successive Chancellors and the drive and effectiveness of their advisers has proved a significant factor in the varying importance of the Chancellor's Office in determining the guidelines of foreign policy, most evident in the role of Egon Bahr as adviser to Willy Brandt during the active phase of *Ostpolitik*. The personality of successive foreign ministers, Vice-Chancellors also throughout the last decade, and their varying exploitation of the resources of the Auswärtiges Amt, has been hardly less important. In one sphere, however, the Chancellor's Office has remained central: in 'inner–German relations' on Berlin and the German Democratic Republic, where more than in any other sphere the lines of German policy have been clearly defined and where the ideological commitment to reunification has left a vital area of policy hanging between domestic and international competences.

The growth of the Cabinet Office has been one of the most significant but least remarked developments in British government since the early sixties. Part of the impetus behind this growth has been the need to pull together the different strands of domestic social and economic policies under difficult economic conditions; but the major force for expansion has come from Britain's increasing international commitments. Within a constitutional system based upon Cabinet responsibility and the answerability of each minister to Parliament for his actions, other ministries were increasingly unwilling to leave to the Treasury and the Foreign Office the role of co-ordination on matters which were now of real importance to the government as a whole. A number of new units were therefore established within the Cabinet Office, to assemble intelligence collected by different ministries into a coherent assessment of international developments, to service the structure of inter-ministerial committees concerned with the European Community, and so on.

Yet it would be hard to say that the Cabinet Office played a determining or decisive role in British foreign policy. Formally it had no authority to do so, existing simply to serve the Cabinet and to expedite its business. The position of the Prime Minister, though powerful, was by no means monarchical; he had no particular responsibilities in the foreign policy field, and necessarily devoted a great deal of his time and attention to domestic policy. There was no clearly assigned responsibility in the unwritten constitutional system of British government for determining the guidelines of foreign policy, and no clearly defined guidelines to which officials could work. No unit of the Cabinet Office, significantly, had the authority to produce planning papers on foreign policy: this remained a Foreign Office responsibility, though the FCO did not have the authority to impose agreed strategic objectives on Whitehall. Strong Prime Ministers could from time to time hope to make their own foreign policy initiatives without arousing direct opposition from their own Cabinet; but for most purposes policy emerged from Cabinet decisions, and necessarily emerged (except when major turning points were presented, such as the decisions to apply to the EC for membership) little by little.[41]

If the overriding object of managing foreign policy is to maintain as far as possible the distinction between domestic and foreign policy, and to stamp political objectives onto the mass of technical transactions among governments, then the French machinery must be adjudged the most effective. By separating out the responsibility for determining the *grandes lignes* from day-to-day management, it enables the French presidency to see above the tangle of detail and to concentrate on wider issues. Yet the system has its costs, in the unavoidable contradictions between the simple certainties of grand strategy and the awkward and often unforeseen interdependencies between initiatives in one area and reactions in others. As one British official unkindly and characteristically put it, the Elysée's freedom from concern with detail enabled French Presidents 'to ignore the facts of international life'. But the complications of international life were increasingly being borne in on the French in the mid-seventies, when for example in the aftermath of their failure to sell the Mirage F-1 to a four-country consortium of NATO countries as a 'European' plane they were forced to reconsider their political resistance to organised co-operation in arms procurement, in order to protect the interests of French industry; or when Giscard d'Estaing's enthusiastic espousal of the enlargement of the European Community towards the south was followed by sharp resistance from within the French finance and agricultural ministries, once they had calculated in detail the likely costs of such a political gesture for French political interests. With the steadily increasing percentage of popular support for the opposition parties of the Union of the Left from 1973 onwards, and the approach of the 1978 parliamentary elections, there were many in Paris who doubted whether this essentially Gaullien concentration of power over foreign policy in the Presidency was likely to last much longer.

The British machinery was well adapted to the pragmatic and non-ideological response of successive governments to interdependence. Its search for interdepartmental consensus, and the weakness of its capacity for planning, were after all partly reflections of British governments' commitment to international consensus among the advanced industrialised countries and of their relative lack of concern for grand designs or long term perspectives. The West German government's machinery, while adequate for the low key approach to foreign policy adopted in most areas by West German governments until the end of the 1960s, was less well adapted to the more positive responses of Brandt and Scheel, or of Schmidt and Genscher. Particularly in relations with France, to a lesser extent in relations with Britain and the United States, West German officials failed to adopt the more robust attitudes displayed by their political leaders. Within the EC as within NATO, their diplomats continued to be bound by the formal instructions sent out to them from Bonn, unable to risk reopening the carefully constructed inter departmental compromises around which they had been drawn up.

One cannot therefore argue either that the pattern of administrative politics within these national capitals simply reflected the same unavoidable bureaucratic conflicts, or that it was administrative politics alone which determined the output of foreign policy. Certainly, as has been noted, there were bureaucratic tensions even within Paris, instances where the administration resisted presidential direction or where the clash of perspectives between different ministries was evident. But in no case can the observer safely ascribe the outcome to bureaucratic politics alone. Foreign policy in Paris, Bonn and London, as (one suspects) in most other capitals, emerges out of the continuous interaction between political direction and administrative habit, against the background provided by cultural tradition and constitutional authority.

The problem of consent

Foreign policy-making, 'like all decision-making, requires choices which often cannot please everyone, and in such cases it is safer to displease foreigners who cannot vote, and who often cannot retaliate immediately and directly as an offended domestic interest group would be apt to do'.[42] So, one might expect, given the increasing interconnection between international and domestic politics, the domestic governments of Britain, France and Germany would naturally conduct foreign policy with one eye firmly fixed upon domestic opinion and domestic pressure. Yet close observers of politics in these countries have emphasised 'what a limited role domestic groups play in the making of foreign policy, even in pluralistic Western democracies'.[43] The positive influence of domestic groups on specific foreign policy decisions - except in decisions with a direct industrial or commercial link - is generally limited, both by the weakness of parliamentary intervention in foreign policy and by relative lack of interest among the electorate at large in matters which still appear to them remote. The negative influence of public opinion,

48

as assessed by policy-makers, upon foreign policy is however very considerable. Governments operate within the constraints imposed upon them by the limits of public acceptability, in foreign policy as in other spheres; though in foreign policy none of these governments pays as much attention to the education of the public, to attempting to widen the constraints under which they operate, as they do as a matter of course in matters of domestic policy.

The French government is almost entirely free of formal domestic constraints. Its foreign minister is not a member of the National Assembly, and has only rarely since 1958 been even a politician. The Assembly's Foreign Affairs Commission has had little influence; the Assembly as a whole even less. The debate over foreign policy is conducted between political leaders outside Parliament, largely through the media, and largely in rhetorical terms. The centralisation of control over foreign policy in the hands of the President, and the loyalty and discretion of the administrative machine which serves him, has maintained effective secrecy over such central ambiguities of French foreign policy as the degree of co-operation with NATO or the occurrence of private conversations with the US government. At the same time internal contradictions on foreign policy issues within both the governing coalition and the opposition parties of the Union of the Left have discouraged public debate or the questioning of received opinions. The result, according to one critic, is that 'nothing is said about France's place in the world and the choices in foreign policy with which the world economic crisis confronts it ... The limits of national independence within the Western world are never defined ... and foreign policy continues to be presented as independent of domestic choices'.[44] For President Giscard d'Estaing, an unideological Atlanticist and European, the informal constraints which domestic opinion placed upon his freedom of action were therefore particularly constricting. His Gaullist allies, the largest component of the governing coalition, demanded regular demonstrations of his commitment to national independence. The Communists, within the opposition, actively competed with the Gaullists in their evocation of independence and their suspicion of the United States. The public at large, uninformed about the complexities of France's international predicament, responded to the simplicities of rhetoric; and the President, struggling increasingly desperately to maintain public support, had little choice but to respond to what it seemed the electorate wanted.

The British government is formally accountable to Parliament for its actions in foreign, as in domestic, policy. Parliament has not, however, yet chosen to exert its rights very far, or even to demand from successive governments much information on the conduct and objectives of their foreign policy. There is no parliamentary committee for foreign affairs; debates in the chamber, as in the French National Assembly, are sparsely attended and hardly noticed in the press. The incoming Labour government in 1974 suggested a more open approach, proposing annual statements on foreign policy (parallel to those presented to Parliament on defence) and a fuller provision of information to Parliament and the press; but these proposals were rapidly forgotten under the pressures of office.[45] After long years during which the public's unreadiness to accept what Hugh Gaitskell had called in

1962 'the end of a thousand years of British history', the compromising of British sovereignty by entry into the European Community, the belated referendum campaign of 1975 forced the government and the parties to educate their supporters about Britain's dependence upon international co-operation – receiving in response a decisive majority in favour of continuing membership. But internal differences within the Labour Party prevented the government from capitalising upon this to carry the public into any fuller understanding of Britain's international position, and by the following year ministerial exploration had slipped back into justifications of how they were defending the British position abroad. Within a small élite of business, financial and academic professionals directly concerned with foreign policy issues there was, it is true, a lively debate. But it rarely, if ever, spilled over into Parliament, the political parties, or the wider public.

West German governments had in principle far less cause for concern about the limitations placed upon their acceptance of international co-operation by nationally minded public opinion. They faced a Bundestag with established rights over the provision of information, and with an influential Committee for Foreign affairs. The very vulnerability of Germany's international position, a divided country with an eastern frontier thinly (but visibly) defended by German and allied forces, internalised the foreign policy debate. During the active period of *Ostpolitik*, while West Germans came to terms with the division of their country and established a new basis for relations with their mistrustful eastern neighbours, this fundamental issue became a focus for discussion in parties, in organised groups, and in election campaigns.[46] Yet once that active phase was over, public interest in Germany's international predicament declined, and public commitment to its internationalist stance visibly weakened. With political leaders whose rhetorical commitment to European unity was itself much weaker than that of their predecessors, the preoccupation of the public with economic stability overshadowed wider concerns. The 'burden' of West German contributions to the EC budget, and the threat of additional burdens in proposals for commodity stabilisation funds or international programmes for economic recovery became themes at once in German domestic politics and in foreign policy.

The paradox of increasing governmental awareness of their vulnerability to international developments, and of continuing public resistance to such an awareness, is not easily explained. It does not come easily to a politician, successful at last in scaling the heights of national power, to admit to the voters who have put him there that some of that power is illusory; the national tendency for governments is therefore to emphasise to their public that they are actively defending national interests on the international level, without making it clear that that defence would no longer be possible without extensive and continuing co-operation with their partners. Foreign affairs still seems remote to most voters, less immediate in its impact than the taxes which the government imposes or the laws which it lays down. The national tendency is therefore to attach to the government as intermediary praise or blame for the domestic outcome of international agreements, whether the credit is justified or not. Partly it is also that the tradition of secrecy attaching to foreign policy in European states (in contrast to the United States) has been successfully maintained as activity has expanded: most deliberately in France, least deliberately in Germany. Partly it is also that these still appear to their citizens and their political leaders to be great states, among the ten or so most prosperous countries in the world, among the ten most influential. It is perhaps easier for such smaller countries as the Netherlands or Denmark to appreciate the constraints which a close-knit international economy and the revolutions in communications and technology have placed upon their capacity for independent action. For Britain, France and Germany, still possessed of most of the symbols of national sovereignty and international status, the paradox is far less apparent.

Conclusion

There are a number of immediate parallels between the context and conduct of American foreign policy and that of the major states of Western Europe. But the differences are as striking as the similarities. 'The distinctively European phenomenon of the displacement of diplomatic intermediaries by direct exchanges between responsible officials from national capitals has posed far more acutely for them the problem of maintaining coherence and co-ordination over foreign policy as a whole.[47] Their distinctive governmental and social traditions have limited both the extent of bureaucratic conflicts within the administration and the range of public debate outside. The network of multilateral organisations and agreements through which they operate, in none of which can any of them easily assume itself to be the dominant member, bites far deeper into the process of policy-making than in the United States – even in France, for all its demonstrative assertions of continuing independence.

As medium powers, not possessed of the military resources or security commitments of the United States, it is perhaps less possible to identify in any of these countries a specific and definable field of foreign policy. It might be more accurate to talk (as even French diplomats talk, in private) of an international dimension which covers the whole range of government concerns. The efforts of successive French Presidents to pursue an independent foreign policy have been the most conspicuous attempt to resist this conclusion. But even here, with the exception of the unsuccessful Lebanon initiative of 1976 and the limited support given to Zaire in 1977, the content of such initiatives was becoming increasingly multilateral: suggesting a dialogue between European and Arab governments, sponsoring and playing host to the Conference on International Economic Co-operation, proposing (in the steps of President Ford) regular meetings of the heads of the major Atlantic governments.

Academics will go on arguing for many years about the dominance of domestic or of international factors in foreign policy. Global comparison becomes far easier, of course, if one can assume that equivalent international challenges will meet in different states with an equivalent domestic response. It will be clear from the above, however, that there have been significant differences in the responses of Britain, France and Germany, stemming from such domestic political differences as cultural tradition, administrative ethos and constitutional structure. But it will also be clear that the weight of equivalent international constraints has borne in on each government, limiting how far it can indulge itself and its domestic public and imposing itself upon the direction of policy. The student of foreign policy approaching Western Europe will therefore need a knowledge of both international and comparative politics. He will need, too, an acquaintance not only with the theory of both disciplines, but also with the contextual detail which relates the theories to the countries under study.

Notes

[1] Morton H. Halperin, *Bureaucratic Politics and Foreign Policy*, Brookings, Washington 1974, p. xi.

[2] James N. Rosenau, *The Scientific Study of Foreign Policy*, Free Press, New York 1971, p. 76.

[3] Robert O. Keohane and Joseph S. Nye, *Power and Interdependence: World Politics in Transition*, Little, Brown, Boston 1977, pulls together the threads of much of this academic effort, and analyses both 'the new rhetoric' and the underlying sensitivities of different governments and societies to each other.

[4] Carole Webb, 'Variations on a theoretical theme', chapter one in *Policymaking in the European Communities*, edited by Helen Wallace, William Wallace and Carole Webb, Wiley, London 1977, contrasts the 'integrationist' and 'interdependence' approaches to the study of international co-operation in Western Europe.

[5] John H. Herz, 'The territorial state revisited: reflections on the future of the nation–state' in *International Politics and Foreign Policy: a reader in research and theory* (revised edition), edited by James N. Rosenau, Free Press, New York 1969, pp. 76–89.

[6] John E. Farquharson and Stephen C. Holt, *Europe from below: an assessment of Franco-German popular contacts*, Allen and Unwin, London 1975, provides a useful case-study of these developments. One should, however, note the growth of countervailing pressures within Western Europe towards regionalism and sub-state rationalism; the trend towards greater integration is not the only pressure undermining the solidarity of the state.

[7] Gerald Dorfman, 'From the inside looking out: the TUC in the EEC', *Journal of Common Market Studies*, June 1977, offers a fascinating illustration of how one major union federation learned to use the opportunities the European Community provides to lobby on different levels at the same time and so to increase its overall influence.

[8] There is as yet little published material apart from the press on recent developments among European political parties, preparing for the probability of

direct elections to the European Parliament, or on the support given by social democratic parties to Mario Soares and his followers in Portugal.

[9]   Christopher J. Makins, 'Interdependence: The European Example', *Foreign Policy*, Fall 1976, pp. 139-44, forcefully contrasts the degree of interpenetration between the US Administration and other governments with that which obtains between governments within Western Europe.

[10]   See also William Wallace, 'British external relations and the European Community: the changing context of foreign policy-making', *Journal of Common Market Studies*, September 1973, pp. 28-52.

[11]   Edward L. Morse, *Foreign Policy and Interdependence in Gaullist France*, Princeton University Press 1973, p. 88.

[12]   Ralph Miliband, *The State in Capitalist Society*, Weidenfeld and Nicolson, London 1969, p. 14.

[13]   Ulrich Everling, 'Zur Verflechtung der Nationalen und der Gemeinschaftlichen Politik', in *Regionale Verflechtung der Bundesrepublik Deutschland*, Oldenbourg, Munich 1973, pp. 39-92, and Pierre Gerbet, 'L'élaboration des politiques communautaires au niveau national français', in *La France et Les Communautés Européennes*, LGDJ, Paris 1975, pp. 379-98, discuss the interconnection between Community policy and domestic policies in these two countries.

[14]   Morse, *Foreign Policy and Interdependence in Gaullist France*, p. xi.

[15]   J. K. Galbraith, *The New Industrial State*, Penguin Books, London 1967, p. 51.

[16]   Arnulf Baring, 'The Institutions of German Foreign Policy', in *Britain and West Germany: Changing Societies and the Future of Foreign Policy*, edited by Karl Kaiser and Roger Morgan, Oxford University Press 1971, p. 152.

[17]   Ibid.

[18]   Helen Wallace, *National Governments and the European Communities*, Chatham House/PEP, London 1973, describes this common trend within the French and German administrations, and its adoption by the British as they approached Community membership.

[19]   See the contributions on Britain, France and Germany in *Between Power and Plenty: Foreign Economic Policies of Advanced Industrial States*, edited by Peter J. Katzenstein, special issue of *International Organization*, Autumn 1977.

[20]   Roger Morgan, 'The role of medium powers in world politics: the case of Britain', in *Britain and West Germany* (note 16).

[21]   See, for instance, Alfred Grosser, *La Politique Extérieure de la Cinquième République*, Seuil, Paris 1965, particularly chapters 6 and 7; or, more recently, Marie-Claude Smouts, 'Du Gaullisme au néo-atlantisme: les incertitudes françaises', in *Les Politiques Extérieures Européenes dans la Crise*, edited by Alfred Grosser, FNSP, Paris 1976, pp. 81-114.

[22]   Andrew Shonfield, *International Economic Relations of the Western World, 1959-1971*, Oxford University Press, 1976, vol. I, p. 104.

[23] Marie-Claude Smouts, 'French foreign policy: the domestic debate', *International Affairs*, January 1977, pp. 36-50.

[24] Joseph Frankel, *British Foreign Policy 1945-1973*, Oxford University Press, 1975, pp. 2-3. A similar argument about the classic 'indirection' of British foreign policy had been made eight years before by Kenneth N. Waltz in *Foreign Policy and Democratic Politics*, Little, Brown, Boston 1967.

[25] Michael Hodges, *Multinational Corporations and National Government: a case-study of the United Kingdom's experience, 1964-70*, Saxon House, Farnborough 1974, provides an interesting discussion of the Wilson government's policy in this area.

[26] Philip Darby, *British Defence Policy East of Suez, 1947-1968*, Oxford University Press 1973, traces the long history of indecision in this area.

[27] Arnulf Baring, *Aussenpolitik in Adenauers Kanzlerdemokratie*, Oldenbourg, Munich 1969, explores the idea of Bonn as a 'provisional' state.

[28] Klaus Otto Nass, 'Der Zahlmeister als Schrittmacher?', *Europa Archiv*, 10, 1976, pp. 325-36, provides a critical survey of the German government's stance within the European Community.

[29] As Lord Strang remarked in *The Foreign Office*, Allan and Unwin, London 1955, p. 133, 'Absolute centralization of control is not yet a physical possibility, since the sheer bulk and growing importance of international affairs have largely offset the factor of improved communications . . .'.

[30] Paul G. Lauren, *Diplomats and Bureaucrats*, Hoover Institution, Stanford, California 1976, traces the emergence of modern foreign services in France and Germany in the years before and after the First World War.

[31] Michael K. O'Leary, 'Foreign policy and bureaucratic adaptation', in *Comparing Foreign Policies: theories, findings and methods*, edited by James N. Rosenau, Wiley, New York 1974, p. 61.

[32] William Wallace, 'Political Co-operation: procedure as substitute for policy', in *Policy-making in the European Communities*, edited by Helen Wallace, William Wallace and Carole Webb, Wiley, Chichester and New York 1977, pp. 231-2, notes the highly protective attitude these diplomatic services adopted towards a new multilateral mechanism which seemed to be rightfully theirs alone.

[33] Maurice Delarue, 'La réforme du Quai d'Orsay', *Le Monde*, 1 June 1976.

[34] *Le Monde*, 13 and 15 October 1976. In the spring of 1977 there was however a certain amount of scepticism in Paris as to how far these proposals would be implemented during a period of public austerity.

[35] William Wallace, *The Foreign Policy Process in Britain*, Royal Institute of International Affairs, London 1976, especially chapters 2 and 6.

[36] Baring (note 27), p. 339, notes the dominance of the Chancellor and the Chancellor's Office in German foreign policy from 1949 to the early sixties.

[37] Helen Wallace (note 18), pp. 28-32, notes the Economic Ministry's successful 'seizure of the initiative', for example, in co-ordinating policy towards the EC.

[38] On defence/foreign ministry relations in Britain, see William Wallace (note 35), ch. 5; in Germany, see Helga Hafterdorn, *Abrüstungs und Entspannungspolitik*

Zwischen Sicherheits befriedigung und Friedenssicherung, Bertelsmann, Dusseldorf 1974.

[39] Wallace (note 35), p. 146.

[40] Elijah B. Kaminsky, 'The French Chief Executive and Foreign Policy', *Sage International Yearbook of Foreign Policy Studies*, 1975, pp. 51–80, provides an excellent introduction to this area. See also Jean Massot, *La Présidence de la République en France*, Documentation Française 1977, especially pp. 124–8.

[41] This argument is developed at greater length in William Wallace (note 35), chs. 2 and 3.

[42] Karl W. Deutsch, *The Analysis of International Relations*, Prentice-Hall, Englewood Cliffs, NJ 1968, p. 55.

[43] Arnulf Baring (note 16), p. 160.

[44] Marie-Claude Smouts (note 23), p. 43.

[45] William Wallace (note 35), p. 281. For a fuller discussion of the domestic debate in Britain, see ibid., ch. 4.

[46] On this, see Roger Tilford (ed.), *The Ostpolitik and Political Change in Germany*, Heath, Farnborough, Hants 1975, and Geoffrey K. Roberts, 'The West German Parties and the Ostpolitik', in *Government and Opposition*, Autumn 1972, pp. 434–49. On the role of the Bundestag and of the parties in the foreign policy field in general, see the chapters by Ernst Majonica and by Heino Kaack and Reinhold Roth in Hans-Peter Schwarz (ed.), *Handbuch der deutschen Aussenpolitik*, Piper, Munich 1975.

[47] Christopher J. Makins, 'Interdependence: the European example', *Foreign Policy*, Fall 1976, p. 140.

3 High politics in the Low Countries

A study of foreign policy-making in Belgium and the Netherlands

JAN DEBOUTTE AND ALFRED VAN STADEN

Introduction

There seem to be good reasons for comparing the making of foreign policy in Belgium and the Netherlands. Not only have the inhabitants of both countries studied each other a great deal, but more importantly, in the past Belgium and the Netherlands have demonstrated some undeniable differences in intellectual style and approach, as far as the conduct of international affairs is concerned. The Dutch approach has been frequently described in terms of legalism and moralism.[1] It has been described in terms of *legalism*, because of a strong preference for the creation of international judicial structures and institutions (sometimes considered a substitute for foreign policy itself),[2] and in terms of *moralism*, because of a tendency to judge the deeds of other peoples by the elevated ethical standards of its own, and in addition the display of an anti-power politics attitude in general. On the other hand, the traditional Belgian mode of policy-making might be characterised best as a *pragmatic-bargaining* one, based upon the belief that, within their own context, international problems can and should be solved by the give and take of diplomatic negotiations. In the Belgian approach, elements of conciliation and mediation, and in that connection the rejection of extreme positions, play an essential part.[3]

Whilst the Belgian policy-maker, to put it most simply, is supposed to be more interested in what is possible than what is 'right', his Dutch colleague is said to be preoccupied with the preservation of principles, relatively free from considerations of practical policy outcomes. Perhaps indicative of the atmosphere in Belgian-Dutch official relations (and also explaining in part the rather slight progress made in the context of Benelux co-operation), the proverbial Belgian quest for finding compromises on the international scene (and especially in the setting of the European Community) has been depicted by Dutch diplomats some years ago as a typically Belgian *maladie de compromis*.[4]

Unquestionably, both styles or approaches reflect different foreign policy traditions (a passive versus a more active brand of neutrality before World War II) and divergent religious influences (Calvinism and Mennonism versus Catholicism), as well as varieties in national character. With regard to this last point, Etienne Davignon, the successful Director-General for European Integration and Political

Co-operation at the Foreign Ministry in Belgium, was quoted by a Dutch news correspondent in the early seventies as saying:

> Our Dutch friends and ourselves just do not always have the same temperament, nor always the same interests or the same objectives . . . Our temperament is more pragmatic. We lie in wait for every possibility to take a step forward. Of a tiny step forward we make an enormous success, whereas it is a defeat to the Dutchmen, because they have not got more. We are more *bon vivants* than you, more opportunist or if you do not like that word, more optimistic.[5]

Observations like this could be supplemented by many others of a more anecdotal nature. However, this is not the place to delve further into the idiosyncrasies of the peoples of Holland and Belgium. This study is focused upon three basic aspects of foreign policy-making in the Low Countries, namely (1) organisational framework, (2) external constraints, and (3) domestic sources. Our assumption is that, generally speaking, state actions may be seen to a certain extent as the results of relatively deliberate choices made by top government officials. But, at the same time, as political decisions are not reached in a social vacuum, we also assume that those actions cannot be fully explained or understood, without a profound consideration of the structure of the decision-making apparatus within which the foreign policy of a nation is taking shape and, equally, of the political forces operating in the decision-makers' environment, abroad as well as at home.

1 The organisational framework

We will start off by raising a preliminary problem. In the international relations literature, some divergent views have been advanced as to the influence of 'size' on the foreign policy-making of states. Maurice East, for example, hypothesises that 'there are likely to be some important differences between large and small states in the style and techniques used when processing and reacting to foreign policy issues'.[6] Taking the line that in small states fewer resources are available for allocation to the foreign-affairs sector and that fewer persons will be involved in monitoring international events and executing foreign policy-decisions, East believes this is bound to have two consequences. In the first place, being unable to cope adequately with the total range of international issues facing them, small states must emphasise certain functional and geographical areas and ignore others. Secondly, these states are believed to be slower in perceiving events and developments in the international system.

In contrast, in their interesting research report on departmental decision-making in Norway, Nils Ørvik and his associates warn that one should not exaggerate the differences between great and small nations.[7] According to this group of scholars, foreign policy-making in a country of less than five million people has many traits in common with that in a country of more than fifty million.[8]

We are inclined to share this latter view and, more specifically, to take the position that there are only *gradual* and no *qualitative* differences on this matter. Anticipating the exposition below, we submit that even in small countries the apparatuses dealing with foreign policy-making are rather complex bureaucratic organisations with differing sectional interests and perspectives, and with problems of co-ordination and competence, of which merely the frequency and intensity are probably less than in great countries. The decision-makers of either country (great and small) are facing domestic and international pressures, and are often required to give quick, unprepared responses to sudden and unexpected challenges posed to their nations. Arising out of informational uncertainty and ambiguity, the foreign policy actions of both small and large states often lead to unforeseen and undesired reactions and situations.

Certainly, in large countries more people are engaged in gathering, processing and analysing foreign policy information. However, whether this means (as East suggests) that small states are likely to be slower in perceiving events and developments, seems contestable. For example, in 1976 the Netherlands had diplomatic representatives in no less than ninety countries. Dutch diplomats were accredited, in addition, to many other neighbouring countries, so that it is by no means true that there would be any information inadequacy through lack of overseas representation.[9] Moreover, a state's perception of early warning signals indicating important policy shifts depends on many factors other than numbers of people. In this connection, one might think of the susceptibility of the top decision-makers to discord and to 'unpleasant' information, the willingness and courage of subordinates to transmit such information, the lack of informational distortions, the flexibility in the lines of communication, the absence of competing signals, etc. In the light of several of these matters 'bigness' in foreign policy intelligence might equally well be a liability as an asset.

The anatomy of the Foreign Ministries

The organisational structure of the Ministry for Foreign Affairs in the Netherlands bears the marks of functional rather than of geographical criteria (see Figure 3.1). Of over 1,400 persons staffing the department in 1976, only 53 were employed in the purely geographical divisions Europe, the East, Africa and the Middle East, and the Western hemisphere, forming part of the Directorate-General for Political Affairs (113 officers in total). The largest of the three Directorates-General is the Directorate-General for International Co-operation (420 officers), which deals with United Nations and disarmament affairs, and for the most part with development assistance to the Third World. The smallest is the Directorate-General for European Co-operation (43 persons), mainly engaged in problems connected with the European Community. Next to the personnel of the department (the home officers), in the same year 1976 over 2,000 persons (about 450 of whom were diplomats and consular officers) were working in the Foreign Service, raising the total number of

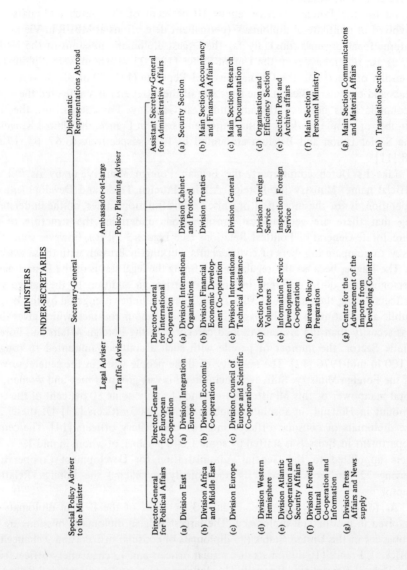

Fig. 3.1   Structure of the Netherlands Ministry for Foreign Affairs

Source: *Staatsalmanak voor het Koninkrijk der Nederlanden 1975*, Staatsuitgeverij, The Hague, 1975.

men and women employed by the Dutch Ministry for Foreign Affairs to almost three and a half thousand.[10]

As for the Foreign Service, about 10 per cent of the Dutch diplomats were involved in multilateral diplomacy (permanent delegations at MBFR in Vienna and international organisations). By far the largest diplomatic missions of the Netherlands are its embassies in the United States (122, 27 of whom were diplomats or consular officers) and the German Federal Republic (112, 20 of whom were diplomats and consular officers). The large size of the latter embassy reflected the strong economic links between Holland and West Germany. For comparison, the total number of people working in the Dutch embassies in France, the United Kingdom, the Soviet Union and Belgium amounted in 1976 respectively to 67, 65, 17 and 48.[11]

Like, its Dutch counterpart, the Belgian Foreign Ministry, or by its full and official name, Ministry for Foreign Affairs, Foreign Trade and Development Co-operation, is for the most part organised along functional lines, on the understanding that there are geographical considerations underlying the structure of the Directorate-General of Political Relations (see Figure 3.2). It is however somewhat risky to compare numbers of civil servants working in Brussels with those working in The Hague, because the regulations defining the legal status of the Department's personnel are quite different in both countries. In addition to the category of officers having the status of civil servant, a large number is engaged by the Belgian public administration on the basis of an ordinary labour contract, which gives them less security than the aforementioned category. In the Foreign Affairs and Foreign Trade Sector, the number of people with such a contract amounted to roughly 1,100 in mid-1976.[12] The majority of these people work in the general services of the Foreign Ministry. Still, even including this vast group of men and women, the total manpower of this Ministry corresponds to only some 80 per cent of the total amount in Holland, in absolute numbers about 2,800 officers.[13] Of these, 395 are diplomats or consular officers and 162 chancellery officers.[14] The central department in Brussels is staffed by some 1,040 persons, of whom in mid-1976 313 were appointed to the General Administration for Development Co-operation, leaving 727 to work in what is traditionally considered the Foreign Relations Sector.

As for the Foreign Service, about 13 per cent of the Belgian diplomats are involved in multilateral diplomacy. The largest Belgian diplomatic missions are the embassies in the United States (25 diplomats or consular officers and 9 chancellery officers), France (16 diplomats or consular officers and 12 chancellery officers) and the Federal Republic of Germany (16 diplomats or consular officers and 8 chancellery officers).[15] For comparison, the Belgian embassy in the Netherlands includes 10 diplomats or consular officers and 5 chancellery officers, whereas the Belgian embassy in the Soviet Union is staffed by 5 diplomats or consular officers and 2 chancellery officers.[16]

The Netherlands Ministry for Foreign Affairs has a considerable number of political appointments at the most senior level. At present, the Minister for Foreign

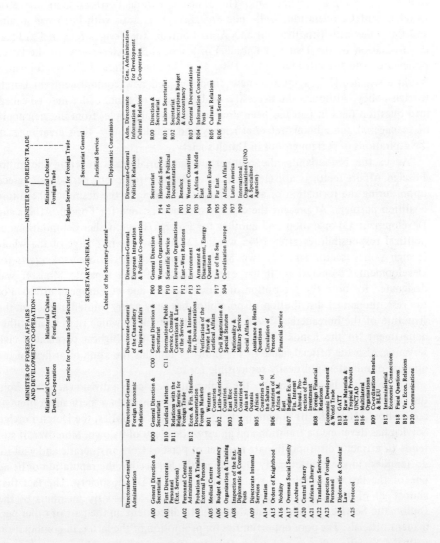

Fig. 3.2   Structure of the Belgian Ministry for Foreign Affairs, Foreign Trade and Development Co-operation

Source: Unpublished paper of the Ministry of Foreign Affairs, Foreign Trade and Development Co-operation, Brussels.

Affairs, who officially heads the Ministry, is joined by a Minister without Portfolio and two *Staatssecretarissen* (Under-Secretaries or Junior Ministers) the last mentioned not having a Cabinet rank. The Minister without Portfolio is in charge of Development Co-operation, while one *Staatssecretaris* deals with European affairs and the other with Disarmament and Arms Control. The designations in 1973 (on the formation of the Den Uyl Cabinet) of a special *Staatssecretaris* for the latter policy-area and the introduction in 1965 of a Minister without Portfolio for Third World assistance,[17] symbolise new directions and new commitments in Dutch foreign policy. Although the necessity or desirability of either office may be called into question (and in fact has been doubted by several people) from the viewpoint of managerial and administrative efficiency and political unity, their creation met the aspirations of certain groups in Dutch society.

As in the Netherlands, the number of ministerial posts covering the entire Foreign Affairs sector is not clearly fixed in Belgium for a long period, but agreed upon during the formation of a new Cabinet according to the desires of the future coalition partners. At present there are two Ministers: one for Foreign Affairs and Development Co-operation and another for Foreign Trade. Other delimitations of political responsibilities after 1945 were: (1) one Minister in charge of the whole foreign policy sector and (2) two Ministers and one special *Staatssecretaris* for Development Co-operation. It has even happened that a separate Minister was designated for both the promotion of Dutch Culture and of European affairs. For the rest, the actual distribution of portfolios has only a very limited impact on the structure of the bureaucracy itself, the smooth running of which is, as in any other department, in the hands of one Secretary-General (the highest permanent civil servant). Also the official name of the ministry remains the same regardless of the number of ministers politically responsible for it.

At the Dutch Foreign Ministry the Diplomatic Service is a division separate from the other departmental divisions, a situation which has been a 'permanent bone of contention'.[18] Like its counterparts in many other countries, the Dutch Foreign Service has developed a tradition and an *esprit de corps* of its own. Moreover, it still tends to attract a disproportionate number of persons from aristocratic and well-to-do families. In the eyes of many Dutchmen, the Service has the reputation of being one of the last strongholds of social conservatism in Dutch society. The fact that almost all of the Department's top positions are occupied by members of the Diplomatic Service has understandably aroused discontent on the part of other permanent officials. The poor opportunities for promotion of the latter, in combination with the objection that most Foreign Service officers, by getting the opportunity of working in the department only once or twice during their thirty years of service, become estranged from their home country, have set a movement in motion for amalgamation of the Foreign Service with the other divisions of the Department since the resignation of Mr. Joseph Luns as Foreign Minister in 1971. However, the intra-departmental discussions on the creation of a so-called joint Foreign Affairs Service have dragged on for several years and at the time of writing the establishment of such a service has not as yet been realised. It is true that in the meantime possibilities for Foreign Service officers to serve at home, and home officers to serve abroad, have been expanded somewhat.

Even though the Belgian Diplomatic Service is not a strictly separate division as in Holland, this certainly does not involve the absence of some kind of *esprit de corps*. Neither does it mean that the Belgian Service, any more than the Dutch Service, mirrors the country's social composition. Besides, the home officers have the same grievances as their Dutch colleagues with regard to the occupation of the Department's top positions. Belgian Diplomatic Service officers, however, are offered more opportunities to work at the Ministry in Brussels. As a matter of fact, at any particular time almost 100 of the 395 diplomats are stationed in the Belgian capital.[19] On the other hand, although possibilities for home officers to be appointed to a diplomatic post do exist, most of them do not make use of that and prefer to remain at home.[20]

Recruitment and political influences in the Civil Services

At the Netherlands Ministry for Foreign Affairs the system of recruitment is not quite uniform. The Diplomatic Service has entrance examinations of its own, which, as Peter Baehr puts it, 'are formal and supposedly more strict than the usual application procedures for the remainder of the department's divisions'.[21] The recruitment procedures for Belgian civil servants have been regulated by law. Almost all of the appointments of public officers have to pass through the *Vast Wervingssecretariaat* (Permanent Secretariat for Recruitment), a service directly under the Prime Minister. It is this service which organises both the entrance examinations for the Diplomatic Service and the examinations for the remainder of the department's services. As in the Netherlands, the examinations for the Diplomatic Service are more formal and more strict than the procedures for the recruitment of the other civil servants working at the Foreign Ministry.

In Belgium and Holland most people entering the Diplomatic Service or one of the departmental divisions (at policy level) have a university background in law or economics, and the greater part of them will not switch to jobs outside the ministry they originally opted for. In general, the mobility of persons between the Foreign Ministry (including the Diplomatic Service) and other departments, universities, industrial circles, banking and trade, in both countries is very small indeed. This has given cause, rightly or wrongly, for complaints of official parochialism and professional deformation.

The Civil Service in the Netherlands has a long established tradition of political neutrality and political appointments of civil servants are in fact the exception rather than the rule. The bulk of Dutch civil servants see themselves as the personification of the general interest and feel superior to narrow party interests. Also the officials of the Foreign Ministry take pride in their loyalty and dedication to the political leadership, irrespective of whether it comes from the political left or right. This seems to be more than rhetoric or flattery. The coming to power in 1973 of the left-dominated [22] Den Uyl Cabinet might be considered a test case. For the

63

first time in Dutch history a socialist, Max van der Stoel, became Foreign Minister, while another socialist, Jan Pronk, known to have more radical views than Mr. Van der Stoel, was appointed Minister without Portfolio in the Foreign Ministry. Despite various rumours to the contrary which were circulating in leftist circles some time ago, experience so far does not indicate a display of politically inspired recalcitrance or even obstruction on the part of the civil servants with regard to the political aspirations of the incumbent Ministers. (Self-evidently, this assessment does not alter the fact that civil servants, wittingly or unwittingly, are *always* exercising some political influence.) In this connection also some importance might be attached to the fact that Minister Van der Stoel did not feel in need of the enlistment of special, politically like-minded advisers, let alone of the creation in his Ministry of a so-called political or ministerial cabinet, a kind of 'spoils-unit' detached from the regular apparatus.

The situation in Belgium is somewhat more complicated. Officially, as a consequence of the operative merit system, there is no political interference in the recruitment of civil servants, who furthermore – as in the Netherlands – are supposed to be the loyal and neutral executors of the choices and decisions made by the politicians. In practice, however, on the basis of a tacit understanding between the major political parties, powerful political forces are operating within the Belgian public administration. Especially when high-level civil servants have to be appointed, it is customary to take care that each traditional party comes into its own.[23] Being at the head of such a politicised department, it is natural that a Belgian Minister feels a certain mistrust of the ulterior motives of his assistants, on whom he has to rely in the elaboration of his policies. He is bound to suspect undesired and hidden value-orientations in the policy alternatives suggested by them. Hence, he will surround himself in his ministerial cabinet with aides from inside or outside the Civil Service, who sympathise with his political ideals. It is this ministerial cabinet which constitutes in every Belgian ministry the link between the civil servants and the political leadership.[24]

The above picture of the Belgian Civil Service as a politicised organisation is, however, an overall picture. For this study it is of course relevant to note that the Foreign Ministry in Belgium is in a lesser degree exposed to political influences than most of the other departments in this country.[25] This limited degree of politicisation of the Foreign Ministry is largely due to the high standards of recruitment on the one hand, and to the historical conviction that the conduct of foreign policy should be a continuous national enterprise, uninterrupted by 'accidental' seizures of power, on the other.

Incrementalism and beyond

By many theorists and practitioners as well, Braybrooke's and Lindblom's well known picture of normal policy-making as a process of 'disjointed incrementalism', characterised by an endless chain of small changes and adjustments under conditions of low understanding and information,[26] has been declared highly applicable to the context of foreign policies. In the opinion of many people, the relative irrelevance of grand designs, the near absence of long term policies and the impossibility of anticipating major international changes are inherent in the complexities and the volatility of this policy sector. There are, however, also more optimistic persons, according to whom it might be possible to improve the control and the quality of foreign policy by the introduction at the Foreign Ministries of special planning units and the use of planning methods. The latter idea also has its supporters in Holland.

Perhaps to the surprise of many persons outside Holland, recurring complaints were raised in the sixties on the allegedly non-imaginative, improvising, and *ad hoc* character of Mr Luns' foreign policy. Such complaints, coming not only from Mr Luns' most vehement opponents, were connected notably in the Dutch parliament with pleas for the establishment of a policy-planning staff or bureau at the Netherlands Ministry for Foreign Affairs. Dutch top officials (both Ministers and civil servants) were said to be overburdened and too much occupied with daily routine and short term affairs, to be able to apply themselves to policy preparation and long range thinking.

At first, Minister Luns firmly resisted the idea of a special policy planning staff in his Department. The argument for his initial rejection was based upon three considerations: (1) the establishment of a planning agency might complicate rather than benefit the process of policy-making, (2) the risk of short-circuits between such an agency and the other departmental divisions, and (3) the fact that experiences with policy planning in other countries were anything but favourable.[27] (As to the latter, it was likely that the Minister especially had the United States in mind, where experiences in the field of foreign policy planning have indeed been less than encouraging.)[28] Nevertheless, by the end of his career as the Netherlands Foreign Minister, Mr Luns announced that considering 'the increasing comprehensiveness and complexity of present-day international problems' the creation of a planning bureau at his Department was under way.[29] Emphasising again that he did not expect any use of planning in the sense of setting long term courses of action, the task of the bureau in his opinion had to be limited to undertaking explorations relative to future policy-areas. We shall follow Mr Luns literally here:

I am still of the opinion that the tracing out of a future policy, that is to say the committing to the attainment of precisely defined foreign policy objectives, is an impossibility for a country like the Netherlands. It is even questionable whether nowadays any power can fix a long term policy, with a reasonable chance of being able to carry out such a policy. What to my mind there is a need of, is the exploration of the areas to which the Government's policy will extend in the forthcoming years, and the setting up of guide-posts which could be taken account of in answering the everyday policy questions. In that sense, planning is also significant and feasible in the Netherlands.[30]

In mid-1972 (about one year after the departure of Mr Luns from Holland) a new organisation unit for policy planning was officially established by Mr Luns' successor at the Foreign Ministry, Norbert Schmelzer (like his predecessor belonging to the centre Catholic People's Party). The new unit, consisting of a so-called policy planning adviser and some aides, was placed hierarchically just below the highest permanent civil servant, the Secretary-General (see Figure 3.1). This disposition of the political top layer of the Ministry enabled the policy planners to have an overall view of different policy developments simultaneously. At the same time, this step apparently signalled to all foreign policy officers the need to take the planners seriously. The policy planning staff was instructed to provide the Foreign Minister (and the Minister of Development Co-operation as well) with advice concerning long term policy developments and, if possible, to formulate policy alternatives. In order to ensure smooth relations and concerted action with the other department's divisions, the planning adviser was allowed to be present at all official policy meetings at the Ministry. The giving of advice, furthermore, may occur either at the request of the department's head, or – in consultation with that head – at the adviser's request.[31]

It is hard to say whether foreign policy planning in the Netherlands is about to become, or has already become a success story. The time is far too short for any clear-cut judgement. Moreover, the passing of judgement is hindered because by their instructions Dutch policy planners act as an internal advisory group; for that reason, they will not step into the limelight. Their advice, just as the department's other advice, is strictly secret and inaccessible to outsiders, even to Members of Parliament.

In Belgium, up until now, no policy planning unit has been established, even though discussions have been held frequently on this matter. A first opportunity arose when in the 1965–67 period the return to Brussels of various French-speaking diplomats coincided with attempts to strengthen the Flemish-speaking element in the decision-making organisation. However, the wish of some people at the Ministry to utilise these diplomats by forming from their ranks the embryo of a planning bureau, led to nothing. As indicated in the organizational chart (Figure 3.2), a Study Service does exist in the Belgian Foreign Ministry, but it is merely engaged in documentation activities. In the recent past, policy planning, combined with other occupations, has been done within the Directorate-General European Integration and Political Co-operation, and, less explicitly, within the different ministerial cabinets.

Problems of policy co-ordination

Although still by far the most relevant and the most dominating, the Foreign Ministries in Belgium and the Netherlands are definitely not the only departments involved in either country's foreign relations. We all know that foreign policy in the traditional Rankean sense hardly exists any more, even though it might be true that 'the belief that foreign policy remains a separate matter dies hard'.[32] Formerly typically domestic policy–areas have continuously been 'internationalised'. Foreign policy in modern times is becoming more and more intertwined and interwoven with other sectors such as monetary and trade policies, defence policy, environment policy, international transport and traffic, and development co-operation. Ministers and civil servants engaged in these different sectors often negotiate directly with their foreign colleagues. Also in the countries under discussion and particularly in the Netherlands, the question has arisen as to which of the ministers concerned should bear the primary responsibility for the country's foreign relations and which should have the right to co-ordinate different policy views in order to ensure an appearance at international fora.

Since especially within the context of the European Community many policy concerns come together, it is not surprising that it has given rise to numerous disputes of competency. Of all such disputes in the Netherlands, the frictions between the Ministry for Foreign Affairs and the Director-General Foreign Economic Relations of the Ministry for Economic Affairs have been the most persistent and the most damaging, but also other bureaucratic units were (not unlike Allison's bureaucratic politics model)[33] behaving as quasi-independent kingdoms, fighting for their own small interests. The consequences of the conflict of interests between the ministries in Holland made their influence felt in the size of the official Dutch delegations at international conferences. Van der Beugel, a former Under-Secretary for Foreign Affairs himself, sneers at the size of these delegations which according to him was exceeded only now and then by 'a phalanx of file-wielding Italian ambassadors'.[34]

However, some years ago the prolonged insistence of the Dutch Foreign Ministry on the supervision or co-ordination of discussions or negotiations at the European level was crowned with success. In a formal letter to the Second Chamber of the Dutch Parliament (which is far more important than its First Chamber) the then Prime Minister, Barend Biesheuvel, declared in March 1972 that the Minister for Foreign Affairs was to be responsible for the formation of a co-ordinated policy in all matters regarding the European Community, as well as for a 'co-ordinated execution of this policy'.[35] True, by that declaration all the troubles of the past were certainly not removed immediately, but in any case it meant an important step in the direction of a more effective European policy of the Netherlands.

Historically, the situation in Belgium has been different as to the shaping of European policies. As already indicated above, in contrast to Holland, foreign trade here has always been a responsibility of the Belgian Foreign Ministry. But at this Ministry, the non-existence of an integrated, high level European directory made possible a mode of decision-making 'based on subjective data and elements resulting from discussions between personalities having personal contacts'.[36] To avoid this risk, within the Ministry a Directorate-General European Integration and Political Co-operation was established in November 1975. To that end, the former Directorate-General Policy was partitioned (see Figure 3.2). Apart from the necessity for co-ordinating the actions of all units involved in the European integration process, this decision was justified by another reason. The former Directorate-General was said to have been too big a task for one civil servant to run, especially in view of the multitude of new duties emanating from the European Community. As Foreign Minister, Renaat van Elslande, stated in an interview:

It is simply because this matter (i.e. policy) has become too extensive, so that it cannot be done by one person any more. Look at the Netherlands. There you have one Directorate-General Europe and one for the other foreign problems. In most of the countries this is experienced as being too large a Directorate-General for one person.[37]

In the same interview, however, the Minister did his best to allay the impression that his decision was directed against the incumbent Director-General of Policy, the French-speaking Viscount Etienne Davignon, who according to some people was more influential than the Minister himself. Whatever the truth of this charge, it certainly makes sense to consider splitting the Directorate-General, also in the light of efforts to limit the personal influence of Davignon and the power of the traditional French-speaking diplomats in general. In this connection, it is interesting to note that during the parliamentary debate of the 1976 foreign affairs budget the opposition parties did not hesitate to relate the new structure of the Foreign Ministry to the Wallonian-Flemish strife.

In this section we must also enquire into the foreign policy role of the Prime Minister in Belgium and the Netherlands. This role has been strengthened recently among other things by the European Council of Heads of Government, created at the Paris Summit Conference of the European Community (December 1974) for the stated purpose of achieving more effective decision-making in the Community. In Holland, where – as in Belgium – according to political and constitutional traditions the Prime Minister is not hierarchically superior to the other Ministers (actually, he is only Chairman of the Council of Ministers), the establishment of the new political institution met with some suspicion. Not only did many interested people apprehend that its functioning was to reduce the already existing European institutions to the second rank, but there was equally a concern about a possible weakening of the position of the Foreign Minister, also in view of his accountability for the European policies to the Dutch Parliament.[38]

One may say that generally speaking the relationship between the head of Government and the Minister for Foreign Affairs is characterised by a certain ambiguity, because many a head of Government feels that foreign policy is too important a field to be left to the discretion of one single minister. Since this relationship has never been well defined or regulated, it is largely determined by personal understandings and ambitions. Yet, against this we should report that especially in Belgium traditionally a high degree of independence was granted to the Foreign Minister. Mark Grammens, writing on the European policy of the Belgian Prime Minister Leo Tindemans, remarks:

The Belgian tradition of independent Ministers of Foreign Affairs is rather an exception and does not apply to Great Britain, France, the Federal Republic of Germany, the USA, the Soviet Union, China and most of the other countries, though perhaps it applies to the Netherlands.[39]

But, of course, it does also happen in the Low Countries that the Prime Ministers (and other ministers as well) try to influence the course of the nation's foreign policy and this is not surprising as it is in the Cabinet that the Foreign Minister regularly gives oral reports on the international situation and the policies of his department. If important matters are at stake, these reports are usually followed by discussions giving the Foreign Minister's colleagues the opportunity to take part and to exert influence. As a matter of fact, neither in the Netherlands nor in Belgium is it conceivable that any major foreign policy decision could be made by the Foreign Minister without prior approval of the entire Cabinet. Foreign policy is increasingly Cabinet policy, even though in the countries under discussion the Foreign Minister remains in this respect the leading figure [40] and even though attempts at clipping his wings formally have so far failed.[41]

2 External constraints

One can take it for granted that because of its growing interdependence the structure of the present day international system (whether labelled loose bipolar, tripolar or incipient multipolar), though it by no means dictates specific policy-choices, sets fairly narrow limits to the implementation of the foreign policies of such small and open countries as Belgium and the Netherlands. Yet, one might ask, to what extent is this basic reality recognised? In answering this question, we hasten to say that *official* policy-makers in both countries are quite realistic as far as their nations' international influence is concerned. In general, they do not indulge in a quest for national *grandeur* and realise very well that this influence is bound to be modest and that the fate of a small and open state is largely determined by outside developments and conditions. And they also see that ignorance or disregard of international power realities would make any policy fruitless in practical terms, however interesting it might be theoretically. Still, tensions may occur here because, in the words of Dutch Foreign Minister Van der Stoel, the makers of foreign policy should take account of two elements:

> On the one hand, there is the objective international situation, which shows the Netherlands as a relatively small, vulnerable country, strongly dependent on foreign trade, and which makes compelling demands and imposes limitations. On the other hand, there is the subjective way in which we Dutchmen perceive, interpret and appraise that international situation. Both elements, the 'exterior' and the 'interior', play their parts in the preparation and the implementation of foreign policy.[42]

It is evident that tensions in fact must arise, if the international images of the attentive public (the people involved and interested in foreign policy matters) deviate from those of the official decision-makers, as is the case in Holland at present.[43]

For the realisation of their foreign policy objectives the Low Countries necessarily depend on co-operation with other states. The most fundamental aspect of

Belgium's and Holland's foreign policy orientation is the close connection with NATO and the European Community, springing from strong military and economic interests. Even though the membership of these international organisations gives both countries a certain degree of access to the decision-making apparatus of the larger countries and therefore a modest opportunity to influence world events in an indirect way, at the same time that very membership also implies a certain constraint. Since neither Belgium nor the Netherlands can afford to run a completely independent political course, both nations continuously have to consider the views held by more powerful partners. Consequently, the formulation of foreign policy in the Low Countries is a subtle process of reconciling national preference to international reactions, whether anticipated or not. The overall responsiveness of the Netherlands, be it in a lesser degree during the last years, and of Belgium to the wishes of notably the United States made the exercise of crude forms of pressure by the latter superfluous. Even so, it would be rather naïve of course to presume that political coercion on the part of the USA or other countries is completely absent in Belgian and Dutch foreign policy.

Especially as far as Belgium is concerned, its reputation as a loyal partner in the Atlantic Alliance on the one hand and its traditional cultural and economic links with several East European countries on the other, enabled it to play an important role in the field of *détente* in the sixties, as shown for example by the so-called Harmel exercise on the future tasks of NATO.[44] Still, it should be stressed that Belgium could perform its bridge-building and mediating activities only with the explicit knowledge and agreement of the United States. To this situation the Belgian policy-makers who, as mentioned before, traditionally took a pragmatic line, accommodated themselves willingly.

In the recent past, however, Belgium has fallen out with its major West European partners on the occasion of President Ford's invitation to the heads of Government of Canada, Japan, France, Great Britain, West Germany, and Italy for an economic summit in Puerto Rico at the end of June 1976. When this invitation was accepted by the bigger EC countries without prior intra-European discussions, the Belgian Foreign Ministry protested in the most vigorous manner possible and asked for urgent consultations between the Ministers of the Nine and the European Commission.[45] Its position was that the matters to be discussed at Puerto Rico fell within Community competence and that the dialogue with the United States should respect the Declaration on the European Identity, which had been ceremoniously signed by all EC members in 1973. During the 10 June meeting of the Nine in Luxembourg, Belgium made a proposal to the effect that both the president of the Community's Council of Ministers and the president of the European Commission be allowed to participate in the Western summit conference. This Belgian proposal, however, could not be adopted. The French government, which incidentally had not been particularly averse to the idea of select big power meetings in the past, refused to promise not to accept Puerto Rico type invitations in the future, while the Dutch and the Danish Government wanted guarantees on this point. The result was that no Community delegation went to Kingston at all and the Belgian efforts had been of little use.

The above example illustrates the relative powerlessness of a small state by focusing on their impotence to influence other powers' intentions: it does not, however, show the external influences that small states are subject to, as the following two cases with regard to the Netherlands demonstrate. The first case, strongly affecting a sensitive part of Dutch foreign policy in recent times, is related to the Declaration on the Middle East, signed on 6 November 1973 by the Foreign Ministers of the European Community countries (including the Netherlands) after the Israeli–Arab War of October 1973. One of the basic points in this declaration – the first tangible result in the effort to harmonise the foreign policies of the EC members – was the pressure on Israel to end 'the territorial occupation which it has maintained since the conflict in 1967'. This formulation clearly suggested the need for a *complete* withdrawal by Israel from Arab territories. Until then, the Dutch government's interpretation of the famous Security Council Resolution 242 left open the possibility for a *partial* Israeli withdrawal. And only three weeks before, namely on 13 October, the Netherlands government (again in company with Denmark) had stopped a proposal of having France and Great Britain appear as the spokesmen for the entire Community at a session of the Security Council dealing with the Arab–Israeli conflict, because they were apparently afraid of too much French and British leniency towards the Arabs.

Despite this and despite the traditional Dutch firmness of principle, the Dutch government changed its tack, to the undisguised disappointment of the Israeli government and the pro-Israel groups in Holland. What made the Dutch government do so? By the end of October, the Netherlands (along with the USA and Portugal) had been singled out by the Arabs as the target for an oil embargo. For this action the Arab states gave many reasons; amongst other things reference was made to an official Dutch declaration issued three days after the start of the Yom Kippur war stating that Egypt and Syria had unilaterally broken the truce in the Middle East observed since August 1970 and calling upon the belligerents to return to the *status quo ante*. This declaration was taken by the Arabs as a hostile act. The Dutch government and particularly Foreign Minister Van der Stoel took great pains to refute the Arab accusations and, not accepting the official Arab explanations of the embargo against the Netherlands, he tried to convince the Dutch people that, in reality, the Arab states were out to put pressure on the Western European economy as a whole by hitting the important oil refining capacity of Rotterdam.

In any case the embargo had far-reaching consequences for the economy of the Netherlands and in a bid to overcome its energy problems the Dutch government appealed strongly to the solidarity of the other EC members (which, as it turned out later, failed to materialise). In these circumstances, it saw no other choice but to bow indirectly to the Arab pressure and to join reluctantly the accommodating, if not capitulationist, position of the European Community. Clearly, the Netherlands was unable to swim alone against the political stream.[46]

The second example concerns Dutch defence policy. In the Spring of 1974 some of Holland's NATO partners (including the USA and West Germany) levelled a sharp critique at the defence plans of Dutch Defence Minister Henk Vredeling (like his

71

colleagues Van der Stoel and Pronk a member of the Labour Party). This critique was not completely surprising, since the plans – fixing Dutch defence policy for the next five to ten years and to be published in a special white paper (*nota*) – involved cutbacks in military spending, which would inevitably affect the Netherlands' contribution to NATO. In particular, objections were aimed at the plan to reduce Dutch army troops unilaterally, that is to say regardless of whether the MBFR talks would lead to results or not. Influenced by the rebuffs of its allies, the Dutch government made some concessions in the final version of the white paper that became public in July 1974. Nonetheless, NATO headquarters at Brussels, afraid of a proliferation of military cutbacks in other member states, persisted in a number of objections. And again, the Dutch government (also under the pressure of the centre coalition partners) felt compelled to undo a part of its original proposals. In so doing, it incurred the displeasure of those radical followers (*achterban*), who claimed that the Dutch government had passed under the NATO generals' yoke. The Dutch government had overplayed its hand.

Of course, one might speculate on the question of what would have happened if the Netherlands had not partially backed down. Apart from angry faces, probably nothing, for, strictly speaking, the NATO countries are free to revise their commitments to the alliance, which in formal terms are not binding agreements but unilateral promises of the states concerned. And after all, some years earlier Denmark had made even more far-reaching defence reductions than the Netherlands, without being punished at all. Still, it stands to reason that political reality is somewhat more complex. For a better understanding of the situation it may be pointed out that the Dutch government badly needed the allies' support for its ideas of a better division and specialisation of military tasks in NATO, as well as of a reduction of the role of nuclear weapons in Central Europe. These ideas had been strongly pushed and advertised on the home front. By completely ignoring the wishes of its partners in the matter of its own military efforts, the Dutch government was bound to lose its credibility and to risk its general prestige within the alliance. It is likely that this unpleasant prospect constrained it to a large degree in its ultimate decisions on the future Netherlands defence policy.[47]

3 Domestic sources

It has become a commonplace to say that states cannot be seen like billiard balls bumping against each other under the impact of external influences only. The behaviour of nations, as is now being more and more frequently emphasised, is also influenced by efforts to satisfy domestic needs and wants. Some authors even go so far as to state that if these needs and wants are strong enough, no nation is going to be constrained at all. Dealing with this subject in their empirical study of foreign policy behaviour in dyadic relationships between 130 states (or 'national societies', as the authors called them), Rosenau and Hoggard found that the potency of internal factors as sources of state actions and interactions was clearly greater than the potency of external factors.[48]

72

Yet, in the countries under discussion the so-called billiard ball model of international politics was certainly not unrealistic over a very long period. Until recently, foreign policy in Belgium and the Netherlands was mainly the domain of an intimate circle of professional specialists who used to watch exclusively the events and developments located *outside* the national borders, which incidentally was the job they were supposed to do. Next to this narrow and official circle the number of people aware of and interested in the way foreign policy was formulated, was negligible. Among the larger political parties a broad consensus existed with respect to the principal foreign policy objectives and instruments; as a matter of fact, foreign policy was depoliticised for the greater part. (An exception in both countries was constituted by the decolonisation issue with respect to the former overseas territories.)

Continuity in Belgium

As far as Belgium is concerned, the above picture is to a large extent still valid. Foreign policy continues to stir up little public interest, as shown among other things by parliamentary behaviour. Just like its counterpart in Holland, the Belgian Parliament (consisting of a Chamber of Representatives and a Senate) is entitled to subject foreign policy matters to debate at any time. However, in contrast to the situation in Holland a discussion with the government is seldom arranged other than the annual debate on the budget; the latter, by the way, always taking place in an almost empty chamber.[49] International treaties, which according to constitutional provisions have to be ratified by both the Chamber of Representatives and the Senate, are immediately forwarded to both bodies' Foreign Affairs Committees and in fact only scrutinised in the seclusion of those places.[50]

Furthermore, one can hardly say that Belgian parliamentarians firmly insist on their rights. In Holland, many Members of Parliament continually express their concern about an erosion of parliamentary control over foreign policy because, especially as a result of the process of European integration, ever more important decisions are made at the international level over the heads of the members of the national decision-making organs. Indeed, they have pledged themselves to block any further step on the path to European unification, unless the powers of the European Parliament are strengthened. On the contrary, there are only a few Belgian MPs who seem to be worried about the partial transfer of national sovereignty without adequate political control.

Likewise the Belgian parliament as a whole is anything but alert with regard to the information it receives from the government. It often happens that the Parliament is informed only at the moment when the decision has already been made and when a formal obligation has already been entered into. The arguments used by the Belgian government to justify its position in such cases are the traditional ones: the need for secret diplomacy and the necessity for quick action. One of the most illustrative examples of this was given by the former Foreign Minister, Pierre Harmel, in the Chamber of Representatives on the occasion of the discussion of the transfer of NATO headquarters to Belgium in 1966. In reply to a question about whether or not this transfer had already been made, the Minister said:

> Believe me, it will frequently come to pass that we will be obliged during the lifetime of this Government, when in diplomatic matters I will be facing international conflicts, that I will have to make decisions before informing the Parliament. I cannot ask the Fourteen or Fifteen [i.e. NATO member states] to wait until the Parliament has finished the deliberations of this matter, to permit them to start the international deliberations. This is not possible.[51]

Significantly, instead of expressing their dissatisfaction with such an exclusion of the national parliament, the majority of the Belgian Chamber acquiesced in Harmel's course of action.

Another indication of the prolonged absence of a real public interest in foreign policy is the attitude of the Belgian political parties. Even the most internationalist of them relatively speaking, the Belgian Socialist Party, is only marginally involved in this policy sector. In a valuable study, Hubert Lyben finds that of the total debating time of this party's congresses held since 1945 only 14 per cent was related to international affairs.[52] For the other political parties in Belgium, this figure is probably not higher. The main reason for this limited interest seems to be the fundamental agreement between the parties on the basic principles of Belgian foreign policy, which in turn might be attributed to the fact that the three traditional and largest political parties (the Catholic Christian People's Party, the Liberal Party for Freedom and Progress, and finally the Socialist Party) are still strongly integrated in the country's public life. This integration is the result not only of having a carefully balanced number of their members in the civil service (see above), but also of the various party-linked cultural and social organisations.

Change in Holland

Contrary to Belgium, far-reaching changes have taken place in the Netherlands since the late sixties. Stimulated by a recurring and extensive news media exposure, public interest in foreign policy issues and especially those related to Third World problems has dramatically increased. This induced the Netherlands Parliament to relinquish gradually its rather defensive and passive attitude *vis-à-vis* the Foreign Minister by trying to exert more influence upon the formulation and implementation of Dutch foreign policy. And despite Mr Luns' claim that he spent more time attending parliamentary debates than any of his foreign colleagues, Members of Parliament regularly complained that the information they received was insufficient for an effective control of his policies.[53] On several occasions the Parliament and the Foreign Minister also clashed on more substantive points, above all regarding the position to be taken with respect to American military actions in Indo-China. For example, against the explicit will of Mr Luns, the Second Chamber adopted a motion in August 1967 appealing to the Dutch government to convey to the

American government its conviction that the air bombardments of North Vietnam should be stopped unconditionally. And three years later, in May 1970, uneasiness and concern prevailed in the same body when the government refused to dissociate itself from the large scale American and South Vietnamese military operations in Cambodia. Mr Luns was obliged to defend his attitude in a special memorandum. Meanwhile, Portugal's role in Africa also caused conflicts between a majority of the Dutch parliament and its Foreign Minister.

Since 1970, domestic pressures on the successive Dutch governments (the centre-right Biesheivel Cabinet 1971-73 and the left-centre Den Uyl Cabinet 1973-77) to reconsider its foreign policy priorities have mounted more and more. As Heldring (a prominent opinion leader in Dutch society) points out,[54] in parliamentary debates in Holland more time was devoted to the situation in Vietnam, Angola, South Africa, Greece, Chile, etc., than the problems of European integration and Atlantic co-operation. In April 1975 Foreign Minister Van der Stoel was embarrassed when an extraordinary congress of his own political party, the dominant Dutch Labour Party, carried a resolution expressing the opinion that the Netherlands should withdraw from NATO, if certain conditions were not fulfilled in the near future. Revealing the increased importance of foreign policy especially within the biggest political party of Holland, this congress was practically entirely devoted to problems of peace and security.

Previously, a smaller coalition partner of the Labour Party, the new Radical Party (a meeting place of, for the greater part, idealistic youngsters disappointed about the allegedly conservative character of the existing religious parties) had already pronounced itself in favour of such a withdrawal without reservations. It is also in the ranks of this party that the feeling of identification with the developing countries is strongest. Its political leader, Bas de Gaay Fortman (born in a prestigious Dutch Calvinist family), believes that the Netherlands is pre-eminently qualified to show to other countries the way to a better and happier world. His conception of the Netherlands as a *gidsland* ('guide-land' or 'moral exemplar') links up with older Dutch foreign policy traditions.[55]

The role of promotional groups

A peculiar and also relatively new phenomenon in Belgium and the Netherlands is the conspicuous manifestation in the foreign policy arena of a welter of so-called *actiegroepen* ('action groups'), to be distinguished from more long standing and established goal organisations, such as the European Movement, the Atlantic Committee and associations supporting the United Nations, as well as economic interest groups. *Actiegroepen* usually attract young people, focus on the poor countries and espouse far-left ideas; they are rather small and informal pressure groups of a more or less idealistic nature, which often try to influence the foreign policy of their own government (and indeed that of other governments) by unorthodox methods outside the normal institutional channels (for example the occupation of foreign embassies or consulates). Although one should certainly not over-estimate these groups' ability to demolish the cornerstones of Belgian and Dutch foreign policy, particularly in the Netherlands they have unmistakably succeeded in making their influence strongly felt in the public debate on international affairs and in contributing to the formation of the present day foreign policy mood of this country in a way which is out of proportion to their scanty following.

A striking example of a successful domestic attempt at thwarting a major Government decision in Holland was the case of the projected building of two nuclear reactors in South Africa. This case is highly illustrative of the difference in atmosphere between the Low Countries, because one could hardly imagine that a comparable affair would stir up so many emotions and publicity in Belgium as it did in the Netherlands in the Spring of 1976. An important point at issue was the employment of thousands of workers at a Dutch concern which was in economic difficulties and was therefore trying to get a large share in the building of the reactors. But also at issue was the credibility of the South Africa policy of the Netherlands government, which had been based upon a strong political commitment to the cause of anti-apartheid for a long time. At first, there were certain indications that the government, worried by rising unemployment figures, was willing to lend its assistance to the business deal and to provide the required credit guarantee that the Dutch concern had asked for. However, the nearer the deadline for this decision came (including whether the whole transaction would go ahead or would be cancelled altogether), the more protests against a possible Dutch share in the building (which was said to buttress the policy of apartheid at least indirectly) were articulated. In this chorus of protests some *actiegroepen* (united in the Anti-Apartheid Movement in Holland) played a leading part. Since the protests were also echoed in the political parties participating in the government, the Cabinet was being put under massive pressures. Oscillating between economic consideration and ideological principles, the sharply divided and stalemated Cabinet was not able to reach a final conclusion in time, so that the Dutch firm missed out on the project. In the eyes of Dutchmen on the political right the result of this affair meant that vital national interests had been sacrificed to irresponsible *Prinzipienreiterei*.

It is hard to avoid the impression that – for better or for worse – Belgian policy-makers take fuller account of the promotion of economic interests in their policy formulations. Apart from differences of political culture, this tendency may also be explained in terms of the influence of domestic economic pressure groups on Belgian foreign policy. One Belgian observer even implies their influence is so great that they are in a position to veto certain foreign policy decisions.

> . . . it seems that our diplomacy is also and perhaps especially, at the service of our foreign trade. . . . The industrial and financial groups directly affect our foreign policy. It is assumed that they exercise even a relatively effective control of it. . . . To a certain extent, we could even go so far as to say that our Foreign Minister has freedom to act provided his policy is not opposed to our business groups, or at least as long as he does not meddle with them.[56]

The promotion of the Belgian export industries abroad is effected not only via the normal diplomatic channels, but also via the Belgian Service for Foreign Trade, a quasi-governmental institution which is under the custody of the Minister for Foreign Trade. Its most spectacular activity consists of the organisation of special trade missions, headed by the Minister for Foreign Trade himself or sometimes even by Prince Albert, King Baudoin's brother. Although the Dutch are not averse either to the exploitation of royalty for commercial reasons (think of Prince Bernhard's role!) and though likewise the Dutch Minister for Economic Affairs now and then heads foreign trade missions, no official export promoting agencies have been created in Holland so far, in contrast to the Belgian situation.

The role of the press

In the preceding pages we have already hinted at the role of the media, as far as the increased public interest in the Netherlands was concerned. Conversely, it is natural to relate the absence of such an increased interest in Belgium to a low media exposure there. Fortunately, we can use the results of a quantitative study in order to substantiate our hunches.[57] This study shows that the Belgian press indeed pays very little attention to information and comment on Belgian foreign policy. Of the total news and editorial space an average of only 0·51 per cent is taken up by this subject. Even per two-week period this percentage is never more than 1. On the other hand, it often happens that during the same period the Dutch newspapers denote much more than 1 per cent of their news and editorial space to information and comments on Dutch foreign policy. Furthermore, it turned out that in Holland, far more than in Belgium, editorials in particular are devoted to the country's foreign policy.[58] On the basis of our own observations, too, we do not have any difficulty in endorsing the author's conclusions that there seem to be no big controversies concerning Belgium's foreign policy and that the Belgian public in general does not participate in the making of foreign policy.

Not surprisingly, this non-participation corresponds to a lack of interest and knowledge regarding foreign policy problems. A cross-national survey, organised by the European Community in Brussels, indicated that on one of the keystones of Belgian foreign policy, i.e. European integration, no less than 46 per cent of the interviewed Belgians had no interest in the problems of the European Community, whilst only 9 per cent of them were able to mention the nine member countries of the Community. True, the latter figure was not higher for the Netherlands, but the interviewed Dutchmen did indicate far more interest. It is perhaps equally significant that 41 per cent of the Dutch respondents were prepared to make a personal sacrifice for the complete realisation of the Community, compared with only 27 per cent of the Belgian respondents.[58]

Final considerations

The preceding analysis leads to the conclusion that in the Low Countries the making of foreign policy is broadly the same as far as the impact of external constraints is concerned, even though at this moment the Dutch Government finds it more difficult than the Belgian to comply in all circumstances with the policies of both countries' major military protector, i.e. the United States. Nor are there striking differences regarding the organisation of the foreign policy process in the two countries, at least no differences of such an extent that they have caused distinctly different courses of action. It might be added that whatever the structures, standard operating procedures, and routinised processes within the Belgian and Dutch Foreign Ministers, a lot will depend on the leading persons involved. Indeed, during the Luns era (1952–71) foreign policy-making in the Netherlands was highly personalised, and so was Belgian policy-making during the last ten years, because of the paramount influence of Viscount Etienne Davignon. The dimension in which Belgium and Holland differ greatly is the importance of the domestic sources factor – in Belgium less important, in the Netherlands, on the other hand, more. How can this difference be explained? No explanation whatsoever seems possible without reviewing the total political context in either country. Despite the division of Belgian and Dutch society into a number of distinct and self-contained segments or blocs, both countries succeeded in bringing about a high degree of political stability during a great part of this century.[60] The secret of this success was the so-called politics of accommodation (in Dutch *pacificatiepolitiek*), characterised by over-arching co-operation at the élite level, a strong deference of the rank-and-file to the bloc leaders, as well as a great deal of political passivity and non-participation on the part of the general public.

In Belgium, this model of the politics of accommodation still fits the present political situation to a large extent because political developments did not keep pace with the social changes of the sixties. It was as late as May 1969 that the then President of the Belgian Socialist Party, Leon Collard, formulated the proposal for the forming of a progressive front (in Dutch *progressieve frontvorming*), calling for a new political movement based upon an alliance of the Socialist Party and the left wing of the Christian Democrats. However, the leadership of the Christian Democratic Party, to whom the appeal was addressed, turned down this proposal completely. Also other less spectacular 'renewal movements', such as 'All power to the workers' and 'Political alternative', drew only a very slight response.

In Holland, on the other hand, radical religious and social changes that started in the mid-sixties did not fail and challenged the foundations of the old political order. The social cleavages between the blocs began to lose their sharpness; many leaders rejected the system of overarching co-operation; deference and indifference were on the wane; and, most important of all, the Dutch political system began to show clear signs of political instability.[61] The ultimate outcome of this process of political transformation was the complete collapse of the politics of accommodation. This collapse produced an explosion of political activity, accompanied by demands for more political participation and efforts to expose and accentuate political contrasts and differences.

It is likely that these tendencies have disturbed the familiar foreign politics scene as well.[62] The Vietnam war, colonial oppression and racism in Africa, and hunger and poverty in the Third World in general, the dramatic impressions of which were to belong to the salient environment of nearly every conscientious citizen as a result of intensive media coverage, constituted easy levers for political action. Whereas the objective scope for the accentuation of domestic political differences remained restricted because of a continuing welfare state consensus, because of an unremitting necessity for coalition formation, and last but not least as the result of the strong economic dependence of Holland on other countries, burning international problems did seem to offer some political parties a welcome opportunity to stand out from the rest.

That, actually, the margin for change in the field of international politics was equally small (or perhaps even smaller) than in the domestic domain was better recognised in Belgium than in the Netherlands. Many Dutchmen, especially outside official policy-making circles, seem to overlook the fact that a small nation's foreign policy inevitably tends to be pitched at the level of purely verbal actions, without practical consequences.

Notes

[1]   See, for example, J. C. Boogman, 'Enkele aspecten van het Nederlandse natiebesef in historisch perspectief', in *Oost–West*, V (3), March 1966, p. 79.

[2]   See E. H. van der Beugel, *Nederland in de Westelijke Samenwerking: Enkele aspecten van de Nederlandse beleidsvorming*, E. J. Brill, Leiden 1966, p. 8.

[3]   Speaking on the general approach of his country to international problems, an anonymous Belgian diplomat remarks that in the General Assembly of the United Nations the attitude of the Belgian Government mostly constituted the highest common denominator of the extreme positions of France and the United Kingdom on the one hand, and the Netherlands and Denmark on the other. See his article on the role of a small country in the world organisation, in *Tijdschrift van het Ministerie van Buitenlandse Zaken, Buitenlandse Handel en Ontwikkelings-samenwerking*, no. 4, Autumn 1975, p. 11.

[4]   See A. van Staden, *Een Trouwe Bondgenoot: Nederland en het Atlantisch Bondgenootschap*, In Den Toren, Baarn 1974, p. 155.

[5]   *NRC Handelsblad*, 20 November 1972.

[6]   Maurice A. East, 'Size and Foreign Policy Behaviour: A Test of Two Models', in *World Politics*, XXV, July 1973, pp. 58-9.

[7]   Nils Ørvik and associates, *Departmental Decision-Making*, Oslo-Bergen-Tromsö 1972, p. 11.

[8]   Ibid.

[9]   See for this conclusion Peter R. Baehr, 'The Foreign Policy of the Netherlands', in R. P. Barston (ed.), *The Other Powers: Studies in the Foreign Policies of Small States*, George Allen & Unwin Ltd, London 1973, p. 71.

[10] Figures from *National Budget 1976*, chapter V, Foreign Affairs, Appendix I and II.

[11] *National Budget 1976*, chapter V, Foreign Affairs, Appendix II.

[12] Furthermore, at the same time more than 1,700 persons were working in developing countries on the same basis. This number is not included in the figures presented.

[13] Information given by the Belgian Foreign Ministry to the authors.

[14] In Dutch official statistics this category does not show up as a separate category.

[15] Besides, a mission consisting of 3 diplomats and 1 chancellor is stationed in West Berlin.

[16] Information given by the Belgian Foreign Ministry to the authors.

[17] The introduction at the Foreign Ministry of a Minister without Portfolio was not a novelty. From 1952-56 Mr Luns also served in that rank under Foreign Minister Jan Beyen. However, at that time the task of the Minister without Portfolio did not concern development aid.

[18] This is Peter Baehr's formulation. See Baehr, *The Foreign Policy of the Netherlands*, p. 69.

[19] Information given by the Belgian Foreign Ministry to the authors.

[20] Ibid.

[21] Baehr, *The Foreign Policy of the Netherlands*, p. 69.

[22] Of the sixteen Cabinet seats, ten are occupied by representatives of the left parties (Labour Party, Radical Party, and Democrats '66).

[23] See Luc Huyse, 'Patronage en makelarij in het Belgisch benoemingsbeleid', in *Civis Mundi*, XIII (11-12), November-December 1974, pp. 222-9, and the same author's 'De plaatsbezorgers: politici en partijpolitieke benoemingen in België', in *De Nieuwe Maand*, XVIII (8), October 1975, pp. 465-74.

[24] See Hugo van Hassel, 'Politics and Public Servants in Belgium', in *Res Publica*, IX (3), 1967, p. 550.

[25] See André Molitor, *L'Administration de la Belgique*, CRISP, Brussels 1974, p. 64.

[26] David Braybrooke and Charles E. Lindblom, *A Strategy of Decision: Policy Evaluation as a Social Process*, The Free Press, New York 1963, pp. 61-79.

[27] *Proceedings Second Chamber 1961-1962*, p. 612, and *Proceedings of the Standing Committee for Foreign Affairs of the Second Chamber of Parliament 1967-1968*, p. B54.

[28] See for a very devastating evaluation, for example, Robert L. Rothstein, *Planning, Prediction, and Policy-Making in Foreign Affairs: Theory and Practice*, Little, Brown & Co., Boston 1972. See also the *Report of the Commission on the Organization of the Government for the Conduct of Foreign Policy*, the so-called Murphy report, Washington DC 1975.

[29] *National Budget 1971*, chapter V, Foreign Affairs, Explanatory Memorandum, p. 6.

[30] Ibid.

[31] See *Jaarboek van het Departement van Buitenlandse Zaken 1972-1973*, Staatsuitgeverij, The Hague, September 1973, pp. 165-6.

[32] William Wallace, *The Foreign Policy Process in Britain*, London 1975, p. 271.

[33] Graham T. Allison, *Essence of Decision: Explaining the Cuban Missile Crisis*, Little, Brown & Co., Boston 1972.

[34] Van der Beugel, *Nederland in de Westelijke Samenwerking*, pp. 23-4.

[35] *Proceedings Second Chamber 1971-1972*, no. 11743, Brief van de Minister-President, Minister van Algemene Zaken, 9 March 1972.

[36] Jules Gérard-Libois, 'La politique extérieure de la Belgique', in *Politique Belge '68*, Institut Belge des Sciences Politiques, Brussels 1969, p. 227.

[37] Published in *Spectator*, 3 April 1976.

[38] See for example C. Th. Smit, 'Minister-President en Buitenlands Beleid', in *Internationale Spectator*, XXX (2), February 1976, pp. 84-9. As for the European Council, under pressure of some member states (including Holland) the European heads of Government ultimately agreed that the Foreign Ministers would be allowed to join their Premiers during the Council's sessions. However, in practice it has not quite worked out that way. At two of the Council's sessions (Paris, December 1974, and Rome, December 1975), in the course of which the hectic discussions ended in a deadlock, the Foreign Ministers were rudely sent off.

[39] Mark Grammens, 'De Europese politiek van eerste-minister Tindemans', in *Tijdschrift voor Diplomatie*, I (3), 1974-75, November 1974, p. 127.

[40] Gérard-Libois, for example, stresses that the Belgian Foreign Minister still is 'Premier' in his field. Gérard-Libois, *La politique extérieure*, pp. 223-34.

[41] In October 1967 (when in Belgium a so-called ministerial committee for foreign policy co-ordination was created), the then Prime Minister Paul Van den Boeynants did not succeed in changing the competencies and traditional positions of the Foreign Ministry in favour of himself.

[42] Foreign Minister Van der Stoel in an address to the *Verbond van Nederlandse Ondernemingen* (Netherlands Confederation of Industries) entitled *Taken van Nederland in de internationale samenleving* (Tasks of the Netherlands in international society) and delivered 26 November 1975.

[43] For an authoritative view on this phenomenon, see former Foreign Minister Schmelzer's speech *'Enkele gedachten over de spanning tussen het wenselijke en het mogelijke in de buitenlandse politiek'* (Some thoughts on the tension between the desirable and the possible in foreign policy), printed in *Internationale Spectator*, XXVIII (7), 8 April 1974, pp. 217-21.

[44] See on Belgium's role F. Govaerts, 'Belgium, Holland and Luxembourg', in O. de Raeymaeker, et al., *Small Powers in Alignment*, Louvain University Press, Louvain 1974, p. 362.

[45] Angry Belgium seeks EEC talks on Ford Summit, in *The Times*, 10 June 1976.

[46] For a critical account of the Dutch position with respect to the conflict in the Middle East, see H. A. Schaper, 'Nederland en het Midden-Oosten: Het regeringsbeleid in de jaren 1967-1973', in *Internationale Spectator*, XXIX (4), April 1975, pp. 229-42.

[47] See on the international aspects of the Netherlands defence proposals, J. W. van der Meulen and S. Roozemond, 'De defensienota - enkele internationaal-

politieke facetten', in *Internationale Spectator*, XXXVIII (15), 8 September 1974, pp. 489-94.

[48] James N. Rosenau and Gary D. Hoggard, 'Foreign Policy Behaviour in Dyadic Relationships: Testing a Pre-Theoretical Extension', in James N. Rosenau (ed.), *Comparing Foreign Policies: Theories, Findings, and Methods*, John Wiley & Sons, New York 1974, pp. 177-249.

[49] During the 1976 parliamentary debate of the Foreign Affairs budget the official reporter Nothomb (a member of the Chamber and president of the French-speaking Christian Democrats) said: 'We should be honest, our discussions on Foreign Policy do not attract large crowds'.

[50] See Herman Van Impe, 'De Parlementaire behandeling van Internationale Verdragen in Belgie', in *Res Publica*, VIII (3), 1966, pp. 321-7.

[51] *Proceedings Chamber of Representatives, 1965-1966*, 16 June 1966, p. 43.

[52] Hubert Lyben, 'De partijcongressen van de BSP sinds de tweede wereldoorlog. Proeve tot analyse naar frekwentie en besluitvorming', in *Res Publica*, vol. XV (1973), nr. 4, pp. 701-24.

[53] See Peter R. Baehr, 'Parliamentary Control over Foreign Policy in the Netherlands', in *Government and Opposition*, IX (2), Spring 1974, pp. 173-4.

[54] Jerome L. Heldring, 'Die Konstanten der niederländischen Aussenpolitik', in *Europäische Rundschau*, IV, 1975, p. 17.

[55] See Heldring, op. cit., pp. 11-19.

[56] Luc Desmedt, 'M. Harmel et M. Spaak: Dix années de politique étrangère belge. Deux hommes, une même politique', in *Res Publica*, XVI (5), 1975, p. 615.

[57] Herman Van Wolputte, *Het Belgisch Buitenlands Beleid als strijdpunt: Een onderzoek naar de ruimte in de pers* (unpublished master's thesis, Catholic University of Louvain, Faculty of Social Sciences 1972), 108 pp.

[58] Van Wolputte, op. cit., pp. 99-100.

[59] See *België in de Europese Gemeenschap*, Dossiers van het centrum CRISP 1975, 18 pp. + ann.

[60] See for Holland, Arend Lijphart, *The Politics of Accommodation: Pluralism and Democracy in the Netherlands*, University of California Press, Berkeley, 2nd and rev. ed., 1975, and for Belgium, Lucien Huyse, *Passiviteit, pacificatie en verzuiling in de Belgische politiek: een sociologische studie*, Standaard, Antwerpen/Utrecht 1970.

[61] Lijphart, *The Politics of Accommodation*, 2nd ed., pp. 197 ff.

[62] For a similar opinion, see Heldring, *Die Konstanten*, pp. 16-17.

4   The making of Italian foreign policy

DONALD SASSOON

The study of Italian foreign policy has received little more attention in Italy than in the rest of the world. The development of foreign policy studies as a separate discipline has had its main impetus in the United States and has been characterised by model-building strongly influenced by positivist conceptions. Positivism as such had been subjected in Italy to the dual attacks of Crocean idealism and Italian marxism. Foreign policy studies have been left to historians specialising in diplomatic history. For better or for worse American political science has made little headway in Italy and has had little impact on Italian social science, which in any case has paid scant attention to foreign policy.

This particular cultural setting is familiar enough to students of Italian politics and culture. But there are other reasons for this lack of interest: the fact is that foreign policy as such has never been considered by the policy-makers themselves as an area in which Italy should or could be particularly active. If it is not surprising that foreign policy studies have been a 'growth' discipline in a country such as the USA, which has an international role embracing the entire globe, it should not be surprising either that a relatively marginal country such as Italy should not have contributed to the field. It could be argued that an examination of Italian foreign policy should focus on those variables which constrain Italian decision-makers at the international level. If we want to use the familiar metaphor of nation–states as 'actors' on an international stage, we should state at the outset that the Italian actor has a role which is potentially of great importance but that, due to the establishment some time ago of rigid casting, it has never been able or willing to engage in anything more than a walk-on part in which it repeated more or less the same lines.

The role of the executive

An adaptation of the 'bureaucratic model'[1] would suggest that one of the reasons for the relatively static nature of Italian foreign affairs lies in the structure of the foreign office administration. After all, the Italian civil service has often acted as a corporative body engaged in the defence of its self-interest rather than as an efficient machine designed to carry out instructions from the executive, and there is little reason to assume that this general inefficiency does not apply to the foreign office as well. But this is by no means certain. R. E. M. Irving has asserted that the Ministry of Foreign Affairs is 'probably Italy's most efficient central government department' and Cesare Merlini claims that it is the only department well-equipped to deal with EC matters.[2] This may well be the case, but one should also add that not only has the 'Farnesina' (where the ministry resides) the possibility to contrast, facilitate or even sabotage the policies of the minister in charge,[3] but that it has also developed a particularly oligarchical nature. Rampant nepotism allied with the tradition of diplomacy as a family career has made the Farnesina not only a bastion of conservatism,[4] but one of a special type: its fundamental tendency has been towards *immobilismo* and is therefore undoubtedly a contributory factor to the absence of an active Italian foreign policy.[5] This is not to say that the foreign office administration has made a conscious choice, but only that its 'natural' vocation simply to exist admirably fits the conscious choice of foreign policy makers to delegate to foreign powers and principally to the USA the task of conducting Italian foreign policy.[6]

Formally, of course, the supreme executive authority in matters of foreign policy is the Council of Ministers. Within the Council the Prime Minister and the Foreign Minister have the dominant role with the Foreign Minister in a subordinate position. But the formal appearance is supremely irrelevant in this context. The marked factionalisation of Italian politics suggests that foreign policy outputs (as any other) are subject to a long process of negotiations which often is initiated within a faction of the ruling Christian Democratic Party (DC). These negotiations take the form of compromises covering a wide field involving also agreements between the coalition parties and, increasingly, the Communist opposition. These negotiations involve partial package deals where foreign policy issues are dealt with as units of account to be exchanged for the acceptance of certain measures in the domestic sector. The indications are that 'pure' foreign policy issues (that is issues which cannot be linked directly to other social or economic issues) rank very low.[7] Thus the linkage between domestic and foreign policy is established at the outset.

Foreign policy and the political parties

The actual limited parameters within which Italian foreign policy can be located are set by two major policy choices which have remained substantially unchanged since 1947–50: these are what R. E. M. Irving has aptly named the 'twin pillars' of Italian foreign policy: the Atlantic Alliance and a commitment towards European integration.[8]

The boundaries of organised political parties, however, do not coincide with their foreign policy positions. There is a considerable amount of overlap. If we take one of the two pillars of Italian foreign policy, Atlanticism, we can distinguish three basic positions: the intransigent Atlanticist, the temperate Atlanticist and the neutralist response. The political forces which correspond to these positions have considerably shifted in the course of the past three decades and we do not find the same names in the same pigeon-holes. In the period of formation of NATO, all these tendencies were very much in the forefront of Italian politics. We can roughly define them in the following manner.

The intransigent position, adopted by the right wing groups of the DC, by the Liberal Party and by a section of social-democracy, conceived of the division of Europe into two spheres of influence as a more or less permanent feature of international affairs and assumed that the only threat to this stability would come from the Soviet Union and from their 'main agents' in Italy, the Italian Communist Party (PCI). It therefore entailed support for the Cold War and a conception of NATO as a purely military pact. The 'intransigents' were quite happy to delegate to the USA all foreign policy decisions and had a conception of Italy as a subordinate international actor.

The temperate position saw in NATO not simply a military pact but also an organisation which could be made to act in a social direction and to contribute towards the unification of Europe and towards a new relationship between the 'West' and the countries of the Mediterranean. This position saw NATO as an unfortunate necessity but it also assumed the possibility of initiating a process of *détente* which could lead to an eventual decrease in international tension.

The neutralist response, never a dominant one in Italy, presents a variety of ideological motivations. In its pacifist socialist version it advocated an active type of neutrality outside any alliance; it did not advocate a new bloc, nor an 'Italian place in the sun' but attempted to identify a specifically independent national interest different from and often opposed to that of the USA. This position, which was essentially that of the Italian Socialist Party (PSI) until its entry in the governing coalition in the early sixties (it then became the position of the left of the PSI which eventually split away), came to be shared by the Italian Communist Party. However, in 1974, the PCI officially accepted Italy's NATO membership but from a standpoint which cannot be reduced to 'moderate Atlanticism' and yet is no longer 'neutralism'.

Also in the neutralist camp but identified with a different tradition is the Christian pacifist position with fairly deep roots in Christian Democracy.

This overlap between Socialists, Communists and Catholics on a major foreign policy issue was not unprecedented. When the old *Partito Popolare* was recreated in 1943 under the name of Christian Democracy, its programme coincided in many ways with current thinking among Communists and Socialists. Both the DC and the Left were against monopolies, in favour of agrarian reform and some form of workers' control in industry. The DC was also in favour of autonomous regions, a demand which was later incorporated in the Constitution and consistently supported by the PCI.[9]

In the immediate post-war period Pietro Malvestiti's group was the only DC faction which was an outspoken supporter of European federalism. De Gasperi was far from being enthusiastic. It was only when the European issue became part of the Cold War that De Gasperi embraced it.[10] Malvestiti's position was then pro-European and anti-Atlanticist since he considered that only an independent Europe could be a united Europe. But not all the members of the DC left held that position. Giovanni Gronchi, for instance, who was originally close to Malvestiti, felt that Italy should take no part in the Cold War and should not be in any military alliance, but he was not a convinced European and rejected the idea of a federalist Europe.[11] The important Dossetti faction grouped around the journal *Cronache Sociali* was also in the neutralist camp. They too had originally hoped that Italy could remain neutral between the USSR and the USA. Dossetti's rejection of Atlanticism was part of his conception of Europe as a 'Third Force' between rival power blocs. Europe, in order to find its truly independent voice had to avoid becoming entangled in a system created for the defence of US interests.

The DC was not the only party which was seriously divided over NATO. The Italian Social-Democratic Party, which had split from the PSI because it considered the socialists too close to the PCI, was far from being the intransigent pro-Atlantic lobby it eventually became. Its left-wing faction understood that an acceptance of NATO would reduce the chances of its eventual re-unification with the PSI. A majority, however, voted in favour of NATO and soon the Social-Democratic Party became an enthusiastic adherent of the Atlantic Alliance.[12]

In a very real sense however the opposition to NATO from within the DC was doomed from the start. The Atlantic choice was intrinsically linked with a domestic one. Once the DC decided to break up the post-war coalition with the PCI and the PSI, it could not fail to become the champion of capitalist interests. This was linked to a corresponding choice in foreign affairs. Once the DC left lost its battle for the continuation of the tripartite coalition it could not expect to win the battle for neutralism. De Gasperi was able to use his remarkable talents to keep his party united and to have his own way.

This foreign policy victory was not only determined by the factional balance within the DC. De Gasperi was throughout able to rely on two powerful allies: the USA and the Vatican. This is not the place for an extended discussion on the degree and impact of US interference in Italian politics nor on the power of the Vatican in Italian life.[13] Concerning the latter, however, one should point out that immediately after the war the DC had practically no political organisation of its own. Its best cadres were the priests in the villages. Its connection with the Vatican ensured a constant supply of votes. As long as it could be seen to be the party of the Catholics, it could also continue to be the ruling Italian party.

Characteristically, in his speeches advocating Italian membership of NATO, De Gasperi chose themes which would eventually become part of the rhetoric of 'moderate Atlanticism'. Rather than emphasising the 'Soviet threat' and the military aspects of the alliance, he stressed the economic advantages which would be derived: NATO would guarantee continuing economic aid for development, it would assure continued Italian emigration and would not interfere with trade with the USSR.[14]

After the failure of the European Defence Committee project, the DC embraced the cause of the EEC and took part in the negotiations leading to the Rome Treaties. The parliamentary debates which followed revealed a split between the Communists and the Socialists: the Communists voted against both treaties while Nenni's Socialists voted in favour of Euratom and gave their benevolent abstention to the EEC. This provided the first major instance of a process of diversification

86

between PCI and PSI, a process partly determined by the revelations of the Twentieth Congress of the Communist Party of the Soviet Union and by the Hungarian events of 1956 and which indirectly contributed to the formation of centre-left coalition government (DC, PSI and other minor centrist parties).

It is with the formal ratification of the Rome Treaties that the 'twin pillars' can be said to have been finally erected. Italy was now both in a military alliance dominated by the USA and in an economic treaty which would pave the way, or so it was thought, to the integration of Western Europe in a single capitalist bloc, a bulwark against communism.

The period of the creation of the EEC coincided with the collapse of the neutralist position within the DC. Giovanni Gronchi, after being elected to the Presidency of the Republic in 1955 (with Communist help) had shifted his position and embraced the moderate Atlanticist cause. This also entailed the advocacy of a new relationship with the countries of the Mediterranean and in particular with the Arab countries. This, of course, corresponded to the interests of the powerful state hydrocarbons company, ENI, and to the particular objectives of its chairman Enrico Mattei.[15]

A similar shift of position also characterised Fanfani's career: once in control of the *Direzione* of the DC he abandoned his previous neutralist stand and acted decisively against some of his former friends. Thus the possibility of the development of a strong and relatively permanent anti-NATO tendency within the majority party was eliminated. Fanfani's purges of the early fifties in practice condemned to political isolation all the leading neutralists.[16]

Fanfani's passage to moderate Atlanticism in fact signalled his attempt to construct a foreign policy which would diverge in some respects from that of the USA. These efforts were facilitated by the advent of Gaullism. In the years 1959–62 the Christian Democratic leader began a series of symbolic moves directed towards increasing contacts with Third World countries. There followed other gestures which, in Italian eyes, had a distinct Gaullist hue: during the Berlin crisis of 1961 and the Cuban missile crisis of 1962 Italy took a cautious stand and failed to identify itself totally with the USA position.[17] During the Middle East war of 1967 Fanfani attempted to hold a position of 'equi-distance' from the warring parties.[18]

All these attempts failed because of the 'Atlantic taboo'. The anti-Gaullist backlash led by the right wing of the DC was in fact a cover for re-affirming the unconditional allegiance of Italy to NATO.[19] The dispute over Gaullism was in Italy essentially a dispute between two factions, one consisting of moderate Atlanticists like Fanfani, the other led by the traditional right of the DC allied with some sections of social-democracy and of the Liberal Party.

Fanfani was never able to control the large centre faction of the DC, the *Dorotei* (from the convent of Saint Dorotea where it had been founded), but, significantly, this faction took little interest in foreign affairs except in order to give general support to pro-European and pro-Atlantic policies. Thus with the right balancing the left and the centre conspicuously absent from the international scene it is of little surprise if the foreign policy of the Christian Democratic Party (and hence of Italy) was largely an immobile affair.

The only time when it could have been argued that Italy's pro-NATO position was remotely threatened was in the course of the debates leading to the formation of the centre–left government in the early sixties. Here, however, one could say that it was more a case of a foreign policy issue used completely for internal consumption. The right wing of the DC (Mario Scelba and others) opposed the entry of the PSI in the ruling majority on the ground that Italy's foreign policy would have to change because of the Socialists' convinced neutralism. But this was clearly an argument for keeping the PSI out as no one in Italy seriously doubted that Italy would remain in NATO.[20] There were fears in the US Department of State (not shared by Kennedy) which were finally overcome with the appointment of Averill Harriman as Under-Secretary for Political Affairs in the Spring of 1963.[21] Nenni's socialists dropped their objections to NATO fairly quickly: the price of the governmental participation was paid at the altar of NATO.

It is significant that some concessions were made by the DC as well. In the November 1963 programme presented by Aldo Moro, now leader of the DC, the references to NATO were kept to the minimum. The 1964 government programme, again drafted by Aldo Moro after extensive negotiations, practically never mentioned the Atlantic Alliance. This was, of course, pure ritual. As Italy's loyalty to NATO was not in doubt, the government could afford to give symbolic concessions in the interests of maintaining the unity of the coalition.

Although the issue of NATO and of the EEC were closely connected in Italian foreign policy the division lines within the DC were not so firm as to make anti-Atlanticism necessarily result in an automatic anti-EEC position. The disputes were usually about interpretations. Thus the neutralist position conceived of the EEC as an interventionist body which could plan rationally the development of Western Europe from a social and economic point of view on the basis of some form of central planning. This reformist conception of Europe (which would eventually be embraced and rigorously and consistently supported by the PCI) could not only be adopted by the neutralist but also by some tendencies within 'the temperate Atlanticist' camp. The intransigent Atlanticists were pro-European too, but their view of Europe was one based on an uncritical acceptance of the free market system and on the assumption that the major task of the EEC was the removal of all impediments to the market mechanism. This tendency, always weak in a country where the power of the leading party was based on the systematic intervention of the state in the economy, saw its power base decrease drastically as the Church and big business moved away slowly but consistently from the positions of intransigent anti-communism they had previously held. Intransigent Atlanticism, however, kept its influence in the middle and higher echelons of the diplomatic corps and of the military bureaucracy and maintained contacts with the most obscurantist elements in the papal Curia.

On the whole the right wing of the DC attempted from the very beginning to interpret the EEC in the same way as it had interpreted NATO (but with less justification): as a bastion against communism and the left in general.[22]

Thus in the early 1960s the EEC and NATO issues were quickly internalised in the heated debates which led to the formation of the centre-left government. While the PSI was distinctly cool over NATO and accepted it unenthusiastically, its attitude towards the EEC had always been relatively positive. Traditionally the major difference between the PSI and the DC on the issue of Europe lay in the fact that the PSI insisted from the beginning on the need to have a proper representative system at the European level and fought to transform the European Parliament into a genuine representative institution.

It is true that the official policy of the Christian Democratic governments after 1958 also consisted in demanding the enlargement and democratisation of the EEC. Generally speaking, however, these were subordinated to a greater if contradictory aim: the defence of the EEC *status quo*. Whenever this was threatened Italy would fairly consistently avoid demands for democratisation and enlargement.[23] In these circumstances although Italian foreign policy *vis-à-vis* the EEC was often at odds with that of De Gaulle, Italy usually backed down under French threats of veto, withdrawal and boycott.

This was particularly visible in the course of the negotiations for British entry. Italian foreign policy here once more followed that of the USA, although in this case the linkage between American and Italian interests was more apparent that usual. For different reasons both countries wanted the UK to be in the EEC as a counter to De Gaulle's pretension to dominate Europe through a 'special relationship' with Bonn.

The knowledge that democratic guarantees were the best defence for a relatively weak country which could not negotiate as equal with the stronger economies of France and Germany meant that there was a material reason for Italy's insistence on the democratisation of EEC institutions. But it was again Italy's economic and political weakness which pre-empted a forceful advocacy of democratising measures such as a directly elected European Parliament.

Whilst successive Italian governments supported the general principles of European economic integration and whilst they showed great interest in EEC developments which directly related to domestic matters they took little note of the wider problems of the European Community. Thus, for example, they practically ignored the Fouchet plan of 1962 which was concerned with De Gaulle's proposal for the political union of Europe, the French veto of 1963 on the UK's admission to the EEC, even though the Italians were on the whole fervent supporters of British entry, and the 1965-66 EEC crisis.

In 1962 while the controversy over De Gaulle's proposals about political union was raging throughout the EEC, Italy did not seem at all concerned.[24] There was no serious examination of the role of Italy within the EEC and little analysis of how changes in European integration could affect Italy. Instead, the major foreign policy debates were mainly concerned with NATO questions, questions which Italy could not hope to affect substantially. It was as if Italian political leaders had decided that 'real' foreign policy was not a matter of great concern, and that it had to be invoked only for domestic purposes. In this sense foreign policy disputes had little impact on foreign policy simply because they were about domestic issues.

Again, as Vannicelli shows,[25] the EEC crisis of 1965-66 was little debated, whilst the Vietnamese war and the recognition of China were very prominent. However, what is not always realised is that these, far from being esoteric subjects used only for the purposes of scoring internal debating points, were central to the development of foreign policy in Italy. In order to explain this, one should make a few general remarks.

The central issue of Italian foreign policy revolves around a question which at first sight may seem philosophical: what sort of foreign policy should Italy have? While this issue is debated 'real' Italian foreign policy remains in a state of sleep and undisturbed, that is, it remains anchored to the choice originally made in 1947-50, the 'choiçe of civilisation', i.e. NATO, and that of 1955-57: EEC. Within this twin pillared policy, the room for manoeuvre is limited unless either a radical revision of the interpretation of the twin pillars or the elimination of one or both of these pillars is achieved. The day to day decisions can be left safely to the bureaucracy or to the executive. The latter is sufficiently paralysed by the requirements of coalition making and party unity for this to constitute a sufficient guarantee against any major change.[26]

Given this position of immobility it is thought that until Italy develops a general view of what sort of foreign policy it should have, it will find it difficult to intervene vigorously and immediately on major EEC questions. The question is precisely the creation of this general view: how can Italy achieve an independent foreign policy? Can this be done outside a European context? What sort of European context is required? What could Italy do to contribute to this context? These are questions which are of a general character and which permit the continuous emergence of a 'philosophic' dimension in foreign policy. Thus the debates over apparently esoteric issues such as US intervention in Vietnam represent in fact the discussion over questions of independence from the USA. Italy's position on *détente*, and a new relationship with the Third World, is part of a solution to the problems posed by the international position of Italy (and Europe) in a bipolar world.

One may suggest that these discussions could have chosen more 'concrete' symbols such as the 1963 French veto crisis on the UK admission. A debate on this question could also have dealt with problems such as the relation between Europe and the USA, but general policy questions are better approached through symbolic issues which pose more clearly questions of principle. For this reason Vietnam was a better symbol than the 1963 veto crisis.

This would tend to corroborate Vannicelli's affirmation derived from James Rosenau's model that 'External issues can be utilised at the national level for their symbolic significance apart from their actual substantive importance, thus resulting in the "internalisation" of international developments.'[27] This is not only a result of the conjunction b̀etween the birth in 1948 of the Christian Democratic regime and the integration of Italy in an anti-communist West but it is also a result of the growing integration of Italy in the international economic system.

Just as 'men make their own history, but not of their own free will; nor under circumstances they themselves have chosen but under the given and inherited circumstances with which they are directly confronted'[28] so nation–states cannot behave as 'free actors' but exist in a complex system of international and national determinants which may allow them little room for manoeuvre.

This is all the more evident in the case of Italy confined in the strait-jacket of its twin pillars policies. Yet the international economic constraints which act as determinants of Italian foreign policy are not simply the economic consequence of the twin pillars. Eugenio Peggio has argued that Italian economic development could also have been achieved through a planned and rational expansion of the home market rather than what has been an excessive reliance on export-led growth favoured by the expansion in world trade.[29] For example, if successive governments had given Italian agriculture the proper encouragement and if its rationalisation had been among the priorities of the Christian Democratic regime then this would have resulted in a coherent overall agricultural policy and would have led the Italians to a more active participation in the shaping of the Common Agricultural Policy. If a different path had been chosen, some of the existing constraints on the Italian economy, which act as so many obstacles to the development of an independent foreign policy, might not have been as severe.

There is, of course, an international constraint which affects all countries: the contemporary phase of international economic development characterised by a generalised trade contraction. This crisis hit Italy in a particular way because of the high level of economic interconnection with other economies. If we take the sum of imports and exports as a percentage of gross national product as an index of the international component of the Italian economy we obtain the following figures (see Table 4.1).

Table 4.1

Foreign trade as a percentage of gross national product

Year	Import as a percentage of GNP	Export as a percentage of GNP	Total as a percentage of GNP
1958	11·6	10·6	22·2
1970	18·0	17·2	35·2
1974	29·8	23·7	53·5

If we compare these data with the equivalent figures for 1974 of other major industrial nations we can conclude that Italy (with the UK) is in a special category of countries which are particularly subject to variations determined by changes in world trade. In contrast the corresponding figure for the USA is 14·2 per cent of GNP, for Japan it is 30·5 per cent, while for West Germany it was 41 per cent and, for France 42·1 per cent. Only the UK had a foreign trade percentage higher than Italy (60·5 per cent).[30]

Another economic constraint which must be faced by any Italian foreign policy maker is represented by a deteriorating balance of payments. Traditionally Italy has had a surplus in its balance of trade: thus a surplus existed from 1958 to 1972 (except in 1963). After 1972 a deficit appeared and increased at a rapid pace: the 1972 surplus of 1,168·5 thousand million lire changed into a deficit of 1,472·5 thousand million in 1973 which increased in the following year to the level of 5,067 thousand million.[31]

It is obvious that a sizeable proportion of this deficit is due to the increase in primary commodity prices in general and in oil prices in particular. This fact alone would require a particular posture towards the oil producing countries. In other words it is a question of deciding whether to establish a new relationship with the oil producing countries in co-ordination with the other EC countries or to delegate, once more, the task of establishing this new relationship (with the stick or the carrot) to the USA on the behalf of the West.

It should be added, as evidence of a strict linkage between domestic development and foreign policy, that the necessity of this choice in foreign policy is not determined by 'natural' conditions alone (e.g. the lack of major domestic energy resources) but also by the fact that the polarised form of economic growth which had taken place in Italy, that is an uneven development between an industrialised North and an underdeveloped South, has made the country even more vulnerable than it would otherwise have been to the sort of economic changes represented by the oil crisis.

A third major economic constraint, possibly the most obvious, is created by the size of Italy's external debt. Traditionally Italy has always been a gold-hoarder and the size of its reserves has always been greater than the size of its debts to other countries.[32] Since 1973 this position has changed. By August 1976 Italy's foreign debt had reached the all-time record of 17 billion dollars including 7 billion dollars borrowed on international capital markets, 3 billion from the International Monetary Fund, 4 billion from the EEC and 2 billion dollars from West Germany. The gold reserves plunged to 5·23 million dollars by the end of June 1976 compared to 6·7 million dollars a year earlier.[33]

This external debt, which is constantly on the increase, makes Italy particularly open to foreign pressure of a political nature. These pressures have become all the more public in the current political situation characterised by the growth of the Italian Communist Party and of the Eurocommunist parties. Remarks made by Helmut Schmidt in Washington on 19 July 1976 revealed that the possibility of using foreign loans as a pressure on the domestic policies of the Christian Democratic Party had been discussed at the economic summit in Puerto Rico in June 1976. Such pressures were aimed against the possibility of the Italian Communist Party entering a coalition government.

Constrained within its twin pillars policy, limited by the hard realities of economic and political dependence, Italy's foreign policy has at times attempted to establish the possible range of options available within the relatively rigid parameters we have tried to describe. Italy's verbal commitment to the EC and NATO have not corresponded to its actual behaviour. This is the result as we have seen of a precarious equilibrium between factions and parties in which a consensus on the fundamental loyalty to NATO and the EC hides a divergence on the interpretations to be given to these commitments. The growth of the PCI's electoral support and its formal acceptance of European integration and of the Atlantic Alliance may accelerate the development of a coherent foreign policy, though in the short term at least its acceptance of the twin pillars can be seen as a contributory factor to further *immobilismo*.

Policy towards Europe

In examining the commitment towards Europe, it has become commonplace to note Italy's failure to send distinguished civil servants to Brussels, its inability to agree on a President of the Commission in 1967 when Jean Rey of Belgium had to step in [34] and its failure to fill vacancies in the Italian delegation to the European Parliament for a number of years until 1969. Even on matters of tax co-ordination within the EEC Italy has been slow: it was the last country to adopt the VAT system.

In the currency crisis of 1973 Italy abandoned EC rules on a common exchange rate policy and floated the lira. In fact Italy holds the record for the number of infringements of the EEC Treaty.[35] Often, however, Italy's relation to the EEC exhibited a passivity which runs counter to its interests. Thus it was the then Commissioner for Regional Affairs, George Thomson who, in October 1974, pointed out that Italy, as the member country with the most massive regional problem was in a position of disadvantage with respect to the other countries in receipt of regional subsidies. In fact, from 1954 to 1972 Italy received 26·4 per cent of all subsidies for the regions with a population representing 29 per cent of the EEC.

The question raised is whether this is to be attributed to the inefficiency of Italian bureaucracy or to the unfairness of EC policies. As the survey of the Istituto Affari Internazionali points out, both elements have played a role.[36] While Italy's disastrous public administration system has not been able to take advantage of all the opportunities membership of the Community has produced, it is also true that many of the financial instruments of the EC have been tailored to fit other economies. For instance, the European Agricultural Guidance and Guarantee Fund (FEOGA) seems built for French agriculture and thus, while Italy obtains about 24·5 per cent of the FEOGA fund, her agricultural population represents 40 per cent of the EC agricultural population. High protection against non-EEC imports was granted for the sort of products Italy imports (e.g. cereals, dairy products and meat) while low duties on extra-EEC imports were established on those agricultural products Italy could export (oleaginous products, tobacco, citrus, etc.).[37] Thus while Italy, with the weakest agriculture in the Europe of the Six, ran large deficits on the guarantee section of FEOGA, France and Holland were accumulating vast surpluses:[38] an instance of the poor subsidising the rich. Paradoxically Italy developed a modest surplus in the guidance fund of FEOGA but has failed to take advantage of it partly because of the lack of a comprehensive policy for the rationalisation of Italian agriculture. The failure to develop an agricultural strategy at the European level is paralleled by Italy's passivity in the field of EC regional policies.[39]

It is true that in the Europe of the Six Italy was practically isolated in advancing a regional policy. There was no partner with similar objective interests and thus there was no possibility of a co-ordination of policies similar to that which occurred between Germany and France who, with their strong economies, could also impose their will on the others. It was only with the entry of the UK in the EC (supported enthusiastically by all Italian political parties) that regional policy became one of the fundamental issues of the EC.

In the course of the negotiations for the new regional policy which occurred after the Commission proposals of July 1973, Italy had maintained a close relationship with the UK. The West Germans' new conception of the regional fund was that it should be quite simply a small fund designed to transfer resources from the richer nations to the poorer ones. France, being a 'rich' nation would have been excluded from the fund's recipients in spite of its own regional problems.

Here the Italian government had two options: it could, on the one hand, propose a new conception of regionalism thus challenging the West German suggestion (which in practice condemned Italy to a permanent subordinate position) by formulating an entirely new approach to regionalism. The other option open was to try to obtain a better deal for the Italian economy by making a number of technical proposals.[40] Needless to say the burden of an absence of international vision and strategy had once again its price: Italy limited itself to proposing a special quota within the fund to be reserved for the countries with particular regional problems. Thus Italy tried to obtain the biggest possible share of the cake while avoiding any community control on the ways in which the money was spent, thus safeguarding the plans of the *Cassa per il Mezzogiorno* as well as the clientele system of the Christian Democratic Party which partly depends on the *Cassa*.

All evidence points consistently to the fact that Christian Democratic decision-makers have been reluctant to develop new European policies not only because of a limited vision of the international possibilities of Italy, real constraints and internal divisions, but also because a new international stand would weaken considerably the positions of privilege which backward and parasitic groups have achieved and on which an important section of the Christian Democratic Party must rely.

It is partly for these reasons that one would tend to agree with Vannicelli's comment: 'Rhetoric notwithstanding, in practice Italy placed its rigid determination to maintain solid NATO links before its commitment to European unification. Its objections to French EEC policies stemmed from the fear that an autonomous Europe, under French influence, would move away from the Atlantic relationship'.[41] But even this loyalty, as Vannicelli himself admits, has been verbal rather

94

than actual. From the military point of view, Italy can hardly be considered a bastion of the Atlantic defence; its contribution in relation to GNP has been among the lowest in Europe.[42]

The armed forces

Furthermore Italy's entry in NATO coinciding as it did with the establishment of the Christian Democratic regime entailed a particular selection in the armed forces with criteria which relied more on political loyalty than on military efficiency. Thus a systematic purge began of officers with left wing connections.[43] This was accompanied by the reconstruction of an armed force which would be loyal to the regime. The consequence has been the tendency towards frequent promotions and a top-heavy military. Thus, for instance, by 1968 Italian admirals and generals amounted to 927 while the French armed forces had only 40 generals and admirals.[44] For the most important appointments a previous consultation with NATO command was considered necessary. As a result, in so far as the higher echelons of the military have any influence on defence decisions affecting foreign policy, the voice of NATO and hence of the USA has another powerful channel of pressure. The acquisition of weapon systems is more determined by what the USA is prepared and willing to sell to the Italians than by the requirements of Italian defence. As a result not only would Italy be unable to conduct any extensive military operation (whether defensive or offensive) on its own, but it would have to rely on US guidance at every stage.[45]

Whenever there has been a state of pre-alarm or alarm at the NATO bases in Italy it has always been NATO headquarters which decided. For instance when the Warsaw Pact countries invaded Czechoslovakia it was General Parker of the NATO headquarters who pushed the button for 'standby', that is, the pre-alarm signal for all air forces.[46]

The politicisation of the army is exemplified by DC control over the Ministry of Defence; this has been practically uninterrupted with a few exceptions.[47]

The well known inefficiency of the Italian armed forces has never caused serious concern in NATO circles. This is, of course, a different problem from the question of the availability of naval bases in Italy for the US Navy. Italy's commitments are important *per se* but not for any real contribution it makes from the military point of view.

It has been fashionable to consider Italy as a pawn in a huge game of chess played by two super-players across the world. The Italian pawn has indeed been a relatively unimportant one and until the early seventies its impact on the international scene was better characterised by Nixon's remark: 'Italy, a country to forget about'.[48] Recent rapid changes occurring in the Mediterranean as well as the development of the Communist Party as a credible coalition partner, led the USA to develop a more active interest. Greece was taking a negative position towards NATO while Turkey began a dialogue with the rest of the Islamic world.

Spain was beginning to move towards a new political system. The establishment of democracy could make Spain more European and less pro-American while democratic freedoms could only facilitate the growth of a Communist Party, closely aligned with the Italian CP. Portugal too could no longer be automatically relied upon to be subservient to American interests and Yugoslavia was moving towards a difficult situation, as Tito's long life was visibly coming to an end. In this context the stability of the Italian peninsula was becoming of greater importance for the USA. Frequent American interferences in the internal affairs of the Italian Republic met only with timid reactions from the Italian government; for the Christian Democrats, frightened at the constant advance of the Communist Party, systematically put party interests before any attempt to establish at least a shadow of national independence. Another instance of the subordination of foreign policy to internal politics.

The basis of Christian Democratic thinking seems to be that the economic and political weakness of Italy is their major strength because the Germans and the Americans have no interest in allowing the Italian economy to decline further. Every new loan is used not to solve any of the major structural faults of the Italian economy, but simply to delay the moment of decision, while there is a growing acknowledgement that divine providence in the shape of dollars and Deutschmarks is no substitute for policies. The Italian crisis can, after all, drag down the other advanced industrialised nations.[49]

At no time was the absence of a political strategy more evident than during the oil crisis which followed the decision of the OPEC countries in October 1973 to increase the price of oil. A number of proposals and plans were put forward. The IMF had suggested the creation of an 'oil facility' system whereby a fund would be created in order to finance the balance of payments deficit of oil-importing countries due to the rise in oil prices. A substantially similar plan was suggested also by the British Chancellor of the Exchequer, Denis Healey. These suggestions were partially frustrated by the resistance of the USA, leaving the oil facility fund of the IMF with the meagre sum of 5,000 million dollars in 1975 (while the Healey plan involved sums of the order of 30,000 million dollars). Following an earlier French plan clearly divergent from American intentions, in 1974 President Giscard d'Estaing proposed a tripartite approach, that is a conference with the representatives of the oil producers, oil consumers and of the non-oil producing developing countries.[50]

It would seem from a simple glance at Italy's scarcity of energy resources and at the hard currency gained through the refinement of crude oil that Italy would have been compelled to assume an important role in the wave of proposals and counter-proposals.[51] Geographically and economically Italy could not afford to remain a passive spectator. Yet to a large extent it did, as its response to the Kissinger proposals show.

The Kissinger plan on the oil question (October 1974–January 1975) proposed the establishment of a sort of North Atlantic 'energy community' on the basis of a 'minimum price' for oil. It was an undisguised and brutal attempt to re-establish an integrated front of the advanced countries under American leadership.

This American move necessitated some sort of Italian answer, and this, inevitably, could not but be highly ambiguous. As long as new general foreign policy guidelines were not established, the DC-controlled Italian government would be careful not to appear to tread on American toes, particularly as it needed all the foreign support it could obtain for the impending local elections of 1975.

Officially the Italian position was against any confrontation with the OPEC countries and at the same time one of support for the American position. Thus even though the Italian government was the first to give a positive answer to the Kissinger plan, it did so in a highly ambiguous manner.[52] But in the early part of 1974, before the definite formulation of the Kissinger plan, the Italian government had manifested its opposition to the establishment of 'an antagonist front directed against the producing countries'.[53] In February 1974 Aldo Moro had declared that Italy would continue bilateral negotiations while favouring an EC management of all problems concerning oil supplies to the community members, but he excluded the possibility that a 'collective organism would take over the tasks of supply and distribution'.[54] After Kissinger's declarations of October and November 1974, the Italian government decided to welcome them without modifying its previous position. Thus it declared its satisfaction with the proposals of the American Secretary of State and at the same time interpreted them as entailing the necessity to begin a 'constructive dialogue' with the oil producing countries on the basis of the recycling of petro-dollars and of the establishment of new ways to render financial assistance to the developing countries.[55]

It has also been suggested that this extreme caution was partly due to the fact that a consortium of American banks was negotiating a major loan to the Italian government.[56] This illustrates another characteristic of Italian foreign policy, namely the subordination of long term objectives to short term ones, a characteristic which follows naturally from the absence of long term perspectives and the inability to establish definite guidelines.

The relative *immobilismo* of Italian foreign policy, even in the course of a crisis which touched the nation's interests as closely as the oil crisis did, must not obscure a tendency towards change. Without challenging the twin pillars, there are now attempts to examine the possibility to acquire an area of autonomy within membership of NATO and the EC. These are made possible by the toning down of internal ideological divisions in matters of foreign policy. In fact if Italian foreign policy has been determined by the balance of forces among the various factions and parties, it should follow that the considerable growth of communist influence should also have an impact in foreign affairs. This has been facilitated by the PCI's ability to delineate a new approach to the EC which, in accepting the inevitability of greater economic integration, is both novel and realistic, and by its official declaration that it will not demand Italy's withdrawal from NATO in the event of it being asked to enter into a coalition government.[57] In so doing the PCI eliminated the two most divisive issues in the field of foreign policy. The establishment of this new consensus was acknowledged in July 1976 by Giulio Andreotti who, when asked to form the first government since 1948 in which the indirect support of the PCI was formally sought and granted, declared that there was a vast consensus on foreign policy 'among the various political parties on basic points . . . Not only the Atlanticist and European issues are not contested, but also the policy of *détente* and the North-South policies (that is, the relations with the developing countries) . . . are included in this vast area of consensus'.[58]

This position was undoubtedly in part the result of the large increase in Communist votes (34.4 per cent in June 1976) and of the ever-growing realisation that Italy could no longer be governed without some form of Communist support.

However, there was increasing evidence of a growing consensus on foreign policy even before the elections of June 1976.

On Vietnam, for instance, both government and opposition demanded an end to the US bombing of North Vietnam in December 1972.[59] In the following January, the Italian Foreign Minister sent a message to the US Embassy saying that the government was 'dismayed' at the continued bombing of North Vietnam. By March 1973 the Italian government had officially decided to recognise North Vietnam. The motions presented by the DC and by the PCI and PSI showed a remarkable similarity in their concrete proposals in spite of the diversity of motivations.[60]

When the then Prime Minister Mariano Rumor presented his programme for a new government to the Chamber of Deputies on 16 July 1973 he stated that the fundamental elements of his foreign policy would not only be support for the EC and for NATO but also support for East–West *détente* and 'solidarity' with the Third World countries. Like the PCI, he demanded once more an extension of the powers of the European Parliament and he offered Italy's support to the European security conference and to a conference on security and co-operation in the Mediterranean.[61] Clearly on most of these policies there was and is ample room for consensus with the communist opposition. This growing convergence explains the similar stand which the PCI and the DC took over the *coup d'état* in Chile. Both condemned it and the government refused to recognise the Pinochet regime. But even more remarkable is the similarity in their respective analyses of the causes of the *coup*. The spokesman for the DC, Flaminio Piccoli, a representative of the moderate right wing faction, suggested that the Allende government should have tried to compromise with the Chilean DC.[62] This point also figures prominently in Enrico Berlinguer's own considerations on the Chilean events in which he put forward for the first time the proposal of an 'historic compromise' between the three main traditions of Italian society Communist, Socialist, and Catholic.[63]

A general degree of consensus has also been achieved on the Middle East. Again at a formal level the positions of the Communists and the Christian Democrats are practically identical. Both recognise the right of Israel to exist and both re-affirm the right of self-determination of the Palestinians. Traditionally the DC has tended to emphasise the pro-Israeli element, while the PCI has often re-affirmed its solidarity with the Palestinians. Since the October 1973 war and hence after the oil embargo, the Italian government has shifted its ground. The tones used by senior

Italian decision-makers have acquired a distinctive note of impatience towards Israel. The 'unacceptability of territorial acquisition by force' is often reiterated coupled with the affirmation that 'it is not possible to deny the right of the Palestinians to have a fatherland.'[64]

It is, of course, difficult to foresee the eventual stages and turning points towards the development of a bi-partisan foreign policy. The determinant elements will be both the evolution of the historic compromise and the relations between Europe and the USA and hence the development of European integration. What is apparent, however, is not so much the erosion of the Atlantic pillar of Italian foreign policy but rather a willingness to put more emphasis on the European pillar.

This process is characterised by great caution, but it is also in continuous development irrespective of the actual formal political 'colour' of the government. Thus, during the centrist coalition government led by Andreotti in 1973, the conservative foreign minister Medici declared that there was a need to review the relationship between Europe and the USA and that consequently there was a need for Europe to acquire greater strength *vis-à-vis* the USA. He pointedly noted that, after all, the USA derived considerable benefits out of its overseas investments and, at the same time, was able to maintain a chronic deficit in its trade balance.[65]

After the reconstitution of the centre-left government, Aldo Moro, now foreign minister, affirmed that Italy 'wanted a European union also because it would allow us to have good and dignified relations with our major ally',[66] a diplomatic way of saying that only within a united Europe could Italy hope not to be bullied. Significantly Moro did not hide his annoyance at the lack of consultations which featured so prominently during the 'pre-alarm' declared by Nixon in mid-1974 over the Middle East: 'The allies must consult each other in time and with frankness on events which, even if they take place in areas outside the competence of the Alliance, can touch on matters of common interests'.[67]

These new developments are always made in the context of reassertions of Italy's loyalty to NATO and of denials that there could be 'an antithesis between a "European" Europe and an "Atlantic" Europe'.[68] This tends to substantiate Vannicelli's comment that '. . . the fundamental issue regarding Italy and the EEC is not whether the country is sufficiently committed to European integration but to what extent regional unification can be accomplished without eroding the Atlantic Alliance.'[69]

What has emerged from this analysis of Italian foreign policy is not merely a fairly static foreign policy. The twin pillars, because they now seem to be accepted by all political parties, are apparently more unshakeable than ever. But under this appearance there are new political realities. While for the entire post-war period Italian foreign policy was 'northern oriented' or 'European' the tendency in recent years has been the development of a 'Mediterranean vocation'. The preoccupation with Europe had, of course, profound prewar roots; this, coupled with Italy's relative exclusion from the scramble for colonies, was undoubtedly an important factor in pre-empting a more southern oriented policy. The determinant factor, however, must have been the close link between the choices for Europe and the Atlantic Alliance and domestic political and economic choices.

The rise of the strength of the Third World countries in establishing some say in the price of primary products and especially the importance of the oil producers, by causing a reorganisation in the relations between states, has permitted Italy to take the first, if timid, steps, towards the development of a Mediterranean role which fits more logically with its geographical and cultural position.

As this analysis has tried to show, these new developments are so closely connected with internal developments, and principally with the new foreign policy of the Italian Communist Party, that Italy must be considered as an extreme case of the subordination of foreign policy to domestic politics once the major 'choices' of 1947–50 were made.

As we have tried to show, the Italian system exhibits a high degree of linkage between internal and external developments. This would seem to suggest that Rosenau's 'linkage model' would be one of the most fruitful in its application to the Italian context.[70] Of the three basic types of linkage processes delineated by Rosenau, in fact, at least two can be easily discerned in the Italian situation: the 'penetrative process' and the 'reactive process'.[71] However, unless a far more organic theoretical framework can be established, the usefulness of the model will remain condemned to the confines of descriptive categorisation.

The weakness of this type of model building is that it simply lists categories into which empirical data can be fitted. It does not and cannot offer a set of related criteria with which the relations between the data can be organised.

Refreshingly the contributors to Rosenau's *Linkage Politics* make disarmingly modest claims: 'Is it self-defeating to propose research based on impressionistic and overlapping categories that have not been derived from a theoretical model and that may thus prove more misleading than helpful?'.[72] 'Given the highly speculative nature of the propositions offered here, any conclusion must be tentative';[73] 'The lack of rigorous control in the research is freely admitted';[74] 'But there are some significant limitations in the present paper which must at least be noted';[75] and, finally, 'We must again warn the reader that our conclusions are to be regarded as tentative and speculative'.[76] Clearly we can only wait, remembering, with Marx, that 'there is no royal road to science, and only those who do not dread the fatiguing climb of its steep paths have a chance of gaining its luminous summits'.

Notes

[1]   Graham T. Allison and M. H. Halperin, 'Bureaucratic Politics: A Paradigm and some Policy Implications', *World Politics*, vol. 24, Spring 1972. See also M. H. Halperin, *Bureaucratic Politics and Foreign Policy*, Washington DC 1974. Halperin's generalisations are dubious as they are based entirely on the US decision-making process, and his assumption that '. . . all governments are similar to the US government as we have described it . . .' (p. 311) is, to put it mildly, preposterous. For a critique of the Allison–Halperin model see Lawrence Freedman, 'Logic, Politics and Foreign Policy Processes', *International Affairs*, vol. 52, no. 3, July 1976.

[2]   See R. E. M. Irving, 'Italy's Christian Democrats and European Integration', *International Affairs*, vol. 52, no. 3, July 1976, p. 402, and C. Merlini, 'Italy in the European Community and Atlantic Alliance', *The World Today*, April 1975, p. 163.

[3]   Thus Sergio Segre, in charge of the Italian Communist Party's foreign affairs department, complained in Parliament that the diplomats in Lisbon were supporting right wing circles while the official policy of the Italian government was in total support of the democratic movement; see the text of the debate in the Foreign Affairs Commission of the Chamber of Deputies in *Bollettino delle Commissioni*, 1 August 1974, p. 10. The socialist leader Riccardo Lombardi made a similar point (p. 9) widely documented in the Italian press.

[4]   Jean Meynaud defined it as '. . . the most conservative of all Italian ministries' in *Rapport sur la classe dirigeante italienne*, Lausanne 1964, p. 91.

[5]   L. Graziano, *La politica estera italiana nel dopoguerra*, Padova 1968. For a descriptive account of the formal decision-making process in foreign policy see also G. Negri, *La Direzione e il controllo democratico della politica estera in Italia*, Milan 1967.

[6]   As N. Kogan pointed out, writing in 1962, 'Italy has been the most loyal, uncritical, if not subservient, of American allies, at least as far as official policy goes', in *The Government of Italy*, New York 1962, p. 170.

[7]   The tendency towards 'issue linkage' is a general one and not merely confined to Italy. See William Wallace 'Atlantic Relations: Policy Co-ordination and Conflict: Issue Linkage Among Atlantic Government', in *International Affairs*, vol. 52, no. 2, April 1976.

[8]   R. E. M. Irving, *op. cit.*, p. 400. This view is accepted by practically all students of Italian foreign policy, see Roy Willis, *Italy Chooses Europe*, New York 1971, and Primo Vannicelli, *Italy, NATO and the European Community*, Harvard Studies in International Affairs, 1974. See also G. P. Orsello (ed.), *L'Italia e l'Europa*, Rome 1966, and Bino Olivi, *L'Europa difficile*, Milan 1964. For a Christian Democratic view see Paolo Taviani, *Solidarieta atlantica e communita europea*, Florence 1967, and, for a left socialist position, see V. Orilia, *Imperialismo atlantico*, Padova 1969.

[9]   See R. Orfei, *L'occupazione del potere. I democristiani '45/'75*, Milan 1976, pp. 29–36.

[10]   Willis, op. cit., p. 225. See also P. Canali, *Alcide de Gasperi nella politica estera italiana*, Milan 1953, pp. 30ff.

[11]   Willis, op. cit., p. 261.

[12]   US archives recently opened revealed that the Italian social-democrats received from the very beginning the necessary funds to carry out anti-communist activities. See R. Taenza and M. Fini, *Gli Americani in Italia*, Milan 1976, pp. 214–21. The document in question is State Department Paper 86500/9–347 (the first five digits indicate the serial number for 'Italian political affairs', the second part indicates the date: September 3 1947).

[13]   One should resist the temptation to see the entire history of Italian foreign policy as being manipulated from Washington. It has often been the case that

intervention from Washington has been actively sought and guided by the Christian Democratic Party.

[14] See speech by De Gasperi in the Senate on 27 March 1949, quoted in Kogan, op. cit., p. 167.

[15] See P. H. Frankel, *Mattei: Oil and Power Politics*, New York 1966.

[16] For A. Fanfani's position in the first part of the fifties see his *La DC e i problemi internazionali*, Rome 1957.

[17] R. Sandri, I. Trevi and D. Pelliccia, 'La crisi della Nato: dibattito in "occidente" ', *Critica Marxista*, vol. 4, no. 3, May–June 1966, p. 37.

[18] Graziano, op. cit., pp. 149–50.

[19] Note Vannicelli's perceptive comment: 'Italy's resistance to Gaullism has been portrayed as a defence of supranational integration; but De Gaulle's Europe would have signified a radical alteration of the status quo away from the Atlantic link, and as such it was perceived as threatening to Italy's political system', in op. cit., p. 48.

[20] Note N. Kogan's comment: 'What we have here is the attempt to use foreign policy commitments as instruments of domestic politics', in op. cit., p. 172.

[21] See Arthur Schlesinger, *A Thousand Days*, pp. 747–51.

[22] Vannicelli, op. cit., p. 14.

[23] Irving, op. cit., p. 408.

[24] Vannicelli, op. cit., pp. 16–17.

[25] Ibid., p. 31.

[26] This should not be read as implying that actual foreign policy decisions are taken by the bureaucracy. 'Bureaucratic politics' does not operate to the extent Allison and Halperin (op. cit.) seem to indicate. The Italian bureaucracy – in the field of foreign policy – has real influence only in the interpretation of routine decisions. Besides, it is itself a mirror of the factionalised DC.

[27] Vannicelli, op. cit., p. 20 based on James N. Rosenau, 'Pre-theories and Theories of Foreign Policy' in R. Barry Farrell (ed.), *Approaches to Comparative and International Politics*, Evanston 1966.

[28] K. Marx, 'The Eighteenth Brumaire of Louis Bonaparte' in Marx, *Surveys from Exile*, Penguin, Harmondsworth 1973, p. 146.

[29] E. Peggio, *La crisi economica italiana*, Milan 1976, pp. 35–6. The following analysis relies heavily on Peggio's essay.

[30] Ibid., pp. 38–40.

[31] Source: Bank of Italy.

[32] In 1974 Italy had 2,500 tons of gold in its reserves, the fifth largest amount in the world; see Barclays Bank Group Economic Intelligence Unit, *Country Report: Italy* of 27 August 1974. Since then Italy has used its gold as collateral for loans on a market-price-related basis.

[33] See Barclays Bank Group Economic Intelligence Unit, *Country Report: Italy* of 16 August 1976. Italy repays its debts promptly but only to contract new and bigger ones.

[34] Irving, op. cit., p. 405 and p. 407.

[35] See Gisele Podbielski, *Italy: Development and Crisis in the Post-War Economy*, Oxford 1974, p. 197 and p. 200.

[36] Istituto Affari Internazionali (IAI), *L'Italia nella politica internazionale, anno terzo: 1974/1975*, 1975, p. 412.

[37] Podbielski, op. cit., p. 199.

[38] Luigi Marras, 'Le vicende della politica agricola comunitaria' in Istituto Gramsci-CESPE, *Il capitalismo italiano e l'economia internazionale*, vol. 2, Rome 1970, p. 111.

[39] Note these justified, but severe, remarks of an Italian specialist of foreign affairs: 'Italy lacks an international political idea as regards the European Community . . . In these conditions Italy no longer even knows what to ask at Community headquarters: regional policy . . . industrial policy and social policy, the triptych of Italy's major interests, have received no serious proposals or entreaties from the Italian government', in Introduction to the Yearbook *L'Italia nella politica internazionale (1973-4)* reprinted in *Lo Spettatore internazionale*, vol. IX, no. 34, July-December 1974, pp. 148-9.

[40] IAI op. cit., pp. 442-3.

[41] Vannicelli, op. cit., p. 43.

[42] Ibid., p. 23.

[43] See A. Boldrini's documentation in 'Le forze armate e i comandi militari nello stato italiano e nella NATO' in *Critica Marxista* vol. 6, no. 2, March-April 1968, p. 107.

[44] Ibid., p. 109.

[45] Italian military thinking followed closely the twist and turns of US strategic doctrines, from Dulles and Maxwell D. Taylor to Kissinger, see the 'classical' expositions of M. D. Taylor, *The Uncertain Trumpet*, New York 1959, H. Kissinger, *Nuclear Weapons and Foreign Policy*, New York 1957 and R. E. Osgood, *Limited War*, Chicago 1957.

[46] A. Silvestri, 'L'occupazione della Cecoslovacchia', *Rivista areonautica*, March 1969, p. 463.

[47] This has tended to make the political influence of the army negligible: Italian generals or admirals owe their position to powerful government leaders. See Jean Meynaud, op. cit., p. 62.

[48] IAI, op. cit., p. 603.

[49] See Stefano Silvestri and Cesare Merlini, 'Politico-Military Evolution in the Mediterranean Area and the Southern European Situation', *Lo Spettatore internazionale*, vol. X, no. 2, April-June 1975, p. 91.

[50] IAI, op. cit., pp. 204-5.

[51] Note Italy's heavy dependence on petroleum:

Sources	Consumption as % of total consumption
Hydro-electric	6·5
Nuclear	0·5
Solid fuel	7·5

Sources	Consumption as % of total consumption
Natural gas	10·5
Petroleum	75·0

Source: Ministry of Energy

In 1974 75 per cent of the trade deficit was accounted for by imported energy resources. Eighty-five per cent of all energy requirements has to be imported (November 1975). The government has drafted a comprehensive energy plan: the share of oil as a source of energy is to decline to 56 per cent in 1985. Its substitute will be natural gas until nuclear energy is available in the 1980s. Needless to say the development of nuclear energy is entirely dependent on the development of an organic energy policy at the EEC level. This will involve various strategic political questions, as well as facing the fact that the international market for some of the material needed for nuclear plants is controlled by the USA.

[52] IAI, op. cit., p. 297.

[53] Aldo Moro, then Foreign Minister, to the Foreign Affairs Commission of the Senate on 23 January 1974 in *Sedute delle Commissioni*, no. 156, p. 30.

[54] Statement to the Foreign Affairs Commission of the Chamber of Deputies, 28 February 1974, in *Bollettino delle Commissioni*, no. 318, p. 3. A similar position was taken, after a change of government, by the Prime Minister Mariano Rumor in his inaugural speech to the Chamber of Deputies on 21 March 1974 in *Atti Parlamentari*, Camera dei Deputati, no. 232, pp. 13,730-1.

[55] See reports in the *Corriere della Sera*, 17 November 1974.

[56] IAI, op. cit., p. 298.

[57] For an analysis of the Italian Communist Party's foreign policy see my 'The Italian Communist Party's European Strategy', *The Political Quarterly*, vol. 47, no. 3, July–September 1976.

[58] See *Il Corriere della Sera*, 23 July 1976. Even before then, however, as Cesare Merlini pointed out, foreign policy was 'incredibly absent from the labour pains which customarily accompany the birth of a new government', op. cit., *Lo Spettatore internazionale*, vol. IX, no. 34, July–December 1974, p. 146.

[59] Declaration of Undersecretary of State Pedini, on behalf of the government, to the Foreign Affairs Commission of the Chamber of Deputies on 21 December 1972, in *Bollettino delle Commissioni*, no. 103, p. 2.

[60] See the PCI and DC motions presented on 15 March 1973 in the Chamber of Deputies, in *Atti Parlamentari*, no. 103, pp. 5,902-3.

[61] See *Atti Parlamentari*, no. 141, pp. 8,120-1.

[62] See *Atti Parlamentari*, no. 155, pp. 9,168-73. Piccoli was particularly bitter with the 'extremist' component of the Unidad Popular (i.e. the Chilean Socialist Party) which impeded an agreement with the Chilean DC, while singling out for praise the Communist leader Luis Corvalan (p. 9,170).

[63] See Enrico Berlinguer, 'Riflessioni sull'Italia dopo i fatti del Cile' in *Rinascita*, no. 40, 12 October 1973.

[64] See the then Foreign Minister Aldo Moro's declarations to the Foreign Affairs

Commission of the Chamber of Deputies on 1 August 1974 in *Bollettino delle Commissioni*, no. 400, p. 7 and, as Prime Minister, to the Chamber of Deputies on 2 December 1974 (*Atti Parlamentari*, no. 306, pp. 18,130-1).

[65] Speech to the Foreign Affairs Commission of the Senate on 16 May 1973 in *Sedute delle Commissioni*, no. 94, p. 36.

[66] Speech to the Foreign Affairs Commission of the Chamber of Deputies on 28 February 1974 in *Bollettino delle Commissioni*, no. 318, p. 5.

[67] Speech to the Foreign Affairs Commission of the Chamber of Deputies on 1 August 1974 in *Bollettino delle Commissioni*, no. 400, p. 7.

[68] See Prime Minister Mariano Rumor's speech to the Chamber of Deputies, 21 March 1974, in *Atti Parlamentari*, no. 232, p. 13,730.

[69] Vannicelli, op. cit., p. 44.

[70] Vannicelli's book is certainly a very good example of such application.

[71] A 'penetrative process' is when 'members of one policy serve as participants in the political processes of another' while a 'reactive process' is brought about by responses in one country which are determined by activities in another country without any direct participation of one in the political processes of another; see J. Rosenau (ed.), op. cit., p. 46. See also his 'Pre-theories and Theories of Foreign Policy' in op. cit., pp. 65-71. Instances of the 'penetrative process' in Italy are the activities of the US Department of State in splitting the Italian Socialist Party and the trade union movement in the late forties or, more recently, the bribes Lockheed Corporation paid to some leading Italian ministers. An instance of a 'reactive process' could be the reaction of the PCI to the Chilean events: the proposal of an 'historic compromise'.

[72] James Rosenau, 'Towards the study of National and International Linkages' in *Linkage Politics*, p. 60.

[73] Douglas A. Chalmers, in ibid., p. 90.

[74] William G. Fleming in ibid., p. 121.

[75] Ole R. Holsti and John D. Sullivan in ibid., p. 194.

[76] Robert T. Holt and John E. Turner in ibid., p. 235.

5 Foreign policy making in Scandinavia

IB FAURBY

Introduction

A major problem in the study of foreign policy concerns the selection of explanatory variables. No commonly agreed upon theory of foreign policy exists and the field of foreign policy studies exhibits a wide variety of ways in which to explain the foreign policies of states. In particular the question of how many and which independent variables to include in the analysis continues to be a problem. Many theoretical formulations - frameworks for analysis - from Richard C. Snyder's influential framework outlined in the middle of the 1950s [1] to the latest attempt by Andriole, Wilkenfeld, and Hopple [2] to create a framework for the comparative analysis of foreign policy, are large taxonomies of potentially important variables. Such frameworks, although often imaginative, do not furnish the student of foreign policy with theoretically justified criteria for selecting the crucial variables. If the researcher does not himself supply additional criteria of relevance these frameworks lead to explanations which are highly overdetermined, meaning that the necessary and sufficient causes have not been revealed. The empirical literature is full of examples of overdetermined explanations of foreign policy behaviour.[3]

The opposite problem, that of underdetermination, is equally common. It arises from a one sided concentration on one explanatory variable which is so general that it does not contribute to the understanding of the specific policies of individual countries. Examples of such concentration on a single factor can be found in the history of the study from the geopolitical school, via the power theorists to neomarxist theory. But no matter whether the factor chosen is geographical location, power, or economic structure, single factor analysis leads to either very abstract or banal explanations and is not able to give us a detailed understanding of how and why foreign policy is made.

'Most similar systems'

One possible method by which to reduce the number of variables is comparative analysis. Comparing the foreign policies of two or more countries or the foreign policies of the same country at different times by itself forces the researcher into some selection of variables since it is not practically possible to include as many variables in this type of analysis as in the study of a single case. However, the mere contrasting of different cases does not in itself add up to a genuinely comparative method.

106

What constitutes a or the comparative method is a much disputed question. According to one conception there are three scientific methods: the experimental, the statistical, and the comparative.[4] The experimental and the statistical methods are superior to the comparative method, but the comparative method must be used when the control of variables required by the experimental method is not possible or the number of cases is too small to allow for the use of the statistical method.

In the study of foreign policy we often have to deal with a situation where there are only a few cases but a large number of possible variables. In the particular conception of comparative method used here, the 'most similar systems design' or 'the comparable cases strategy', cases are selected which are as similar as possible.[5] The number of operative variables are reduced by the similar variables being left out of the analysis or treated as non-varying parameters. The variance in behaviour is thus explained in terms of the remaining, operative, variables.

Applied to the comparative study of foreign policy this conception of the comparative method implies that we should select cases from countries which have a high degree of similarity on a number of the independent variables often considered relevant in explaining foreign policy, such as economic structure and resources and characteristics of the political system and the political processes. Differences in foreign policy must thus be explained in terms of the variables which are not identical.

In this essay, an attempt will be made to discuss the making of foreign policy in the three Scandinavian countries in a way which, although not rigorously 'scientific', has at least been informed by the arguments for a 'most similar systems design' in the comparative study of foreign policy. Undoubtedly, the three Scandinavian countries – or all five Nordic countries, though to a lesser extent – provide a particularly good field for the application of this approach to the study of foreign policy. One problem with 'most similar systems' is that they often do not show sufficient variation in behaviour (dependent variable) for this approach to be used, but that is not the case as far as the foreign policies of the three Scandinavian countries are concerned. In spite of their similarity on a large number of variables often used in explaining foreign policy, their foreign policies in relation to the most important issues differ considerably. Sweden is neutral and a member of neither NATO nor the European Community; Norway is an original member of NATO but not a member of the EC (membership having been explicitly rejected in a referendum and a decision by Parliament). Denmark is a full member of both these organisations. These differences, especially if one posits that questions of security and foreign trade are the two most 'salient' foreign policy issues for the three countries, are remarkable as they are found together with a high degree of co-operation and co-ordination between the three countries on domestic as well as other foreign policy issues.

Within the limits of this essay we cannot discuss all aspects of the foreign policies of the Scandinavian countries. Instead the discussion will be centred on the apparent paradox: why do these countries, so similar in many respects, situated within the same region, having extensive co-ordination of domestic policies and co-operating on a number of foreign policy issues, have such fundamentally different foreign policies when it comes to the two most important foreign policy issue–areas?

Framework

Any meaningful comparison must be based upon some idea of what is relevant to compare and what is not. Suffering from the lack of a general theory of foreign policy we are left with a number of more or less persuasive frameworks and 'pre-theoretical' formulations on which to base our discussion. In the following passage some of the ideas of James N. Rosenau will be used to structure the presentation, though none of his frameworks has been used to the fullest extent possible.

In his well known pre-theory Rosenau [6] claimed that all explanations of foreign policy behaviour could be grouped into five categories. Later he reduced the number to four:[7] systemic variables (i.e. phenomena pertaining to the international system), societal, governmental, and individual variables. Rosenau went on to categorise states according to size (large/small), development (developed/developing), and political system (open/closed). Combined they make eight nation types. The pre-theory then consists of an ordering of the four (five) categories of independent variables according to assumed relative potency in explaining the foreign policies of each of the eight different types of states. Following this line of thought, the three Scandinavian countries, which are all small, highly industrialised, and democratic, belong to the same category and for this particular category Rosenau's ranking of the explanatory variables is: 1   systems, 2   societal, 3   governmental, and 4   individual variables.

The hypotheses of the pre-theory are of a speculative nature and were not, when originally formulated, based upon systematic empirical research. The pre-theory has been criticised by several authors,[8] yet when trying to explain the foreign policies of the three Scandinavian countries, the ranking of explanatory variables seems, *prima facie*, to be correct. However, it is important to note that the pre-theory only lists categories of variables, not specified variables. The actual variables must still be selected since it is inconceivable that every variable at, for example, the systemic level is more potent than all variables at lower levels.

The major part of the following chapter will thus be arranged as a discussion of the phenomena within each of Rosenau's four levels or categories thought to be most important in explaining the differences in the general foreign policy posture of the three countries. The 'variables' will be stated in rather broad and general terms, and, quite deliberately, many of the nuances which would have been considered in a more detailed case study, will be disregarded.[9]

Finally, since there is no single general process of foreign policy making the chapter is concluded by a short discussion of policy making within three broadly defined issue–areas in order to show the different impact of the variables outlined.

Systemic level

According to the 'pre-theory' the most important factors explaining the foreign policies of small, developed, and 'open' states are to be found at the systemic level. This, nevertheless, leaves us with a practically unlimited number of possible explanatory factors. In the following, the systemic factors will be further divided into three sub-categories: 1 Global and Atlantic, 2 Western European, and 3 Nordic. Within each of these again only the most general factors contributing to an understanding of the main differences between the three countries will be mentioned.

Global and Atlantic

In the immediate post World War II period the Scandinavian countries tried to follow a policy of so-called 'bridge-building' between the great powers. They did not want to conclude any exclusive alignments and they strongly emphasised the role of the newly created United Nations Organisation and the need to make it strong. However, the growing antagonism between the two superpowers and the subsequent emergence of a tight bi-polar international system made a foreign policy based on 'bridge-building' and a strong UN increasingly unrealistic. In particular the coup in Czechoslovakia and Soviet pressures on Finland made a strong impression.

The Swedish government in 1948, partly diverging from its established policy of non-alignment, proposed the creation of a Scandinavian Defence Community. Negotiations between the three countries followed, but in the end Norway could not accept the Swedish precondition of a completely neutral Scandinavian arrangement. Denmark followed Norway when the Scandinavian solution proved impossible.

Several factors contributed to this development, and we shall return to some of them in later sections. One factor had to do with the different strategic position of each of the three countries. Although within the same region, important strategic dissimilarities exist. Military analysts agree on the strategically favourable location of Sweden not making its territory of direct importance to the major powers. Denmark's position at the gate of the Baltic and as an appendix to Central Europe and Norway's extended west coast and, in later years, its desolate northern regions along the waterway to Murmansk and bordering on the Soviet Union give these two countries a greater strategic importance. Furthermore, specific problems arose from Norway's possession of Svalbard and Jan Mayen and from Denmark's possession of Greenland and the Faroe Islands – areas which are of special interest to the superpowers. The negotiations for a Scandinavian Defence Community were complicated by the fact that Sweden was unable to share responsibility for these distant territories, and the strong American wish to maintain bases on Greenland.

Another factor particularly influencing the Norwegian decision to join NATO was the lack of enthusiasm in Britain and the United States for an independent

Scandinavian security arrangement. Both Denmark and Norway needed larger supplies of arms than Sweden was able to furnish. However, the United States was not willing to guarantee such supplies to members of a neutral Scandinavian alliance and indicated that its primary obligation was to its own allies.

The breakdown of 'bridge-building' and of the negotiations for a Scandinavian Defence Community and the decisions of Norway and Denmark to join NATO illustrate the influence of external factors on the making of foreign policy. Space does not permit a detailed chronological description of how further developments in superpower relations in the following years shaped the framework within which the Scandinavian countries had to formulate their foreign policies. However, the bipolar nature of the international system has been reflected in the Nordic sub-system. This can be seen most clearly in alliance policies, but also in the basic attitudes towards economic integration and to other foreign policy issues.

Denmark and Norway are members of NATO; Sweden is neutral. Finland is also neutral but has a treaty of friendship and assistance with the Soviet Union. Whilst these differences in alliance policy are important, they should not be overemphasised. Finland is not an ally of the Soviet Union; culturally and politically it belongs to the western world – as, of course, does Sweden. Although never mentioned by Swedish politicians, an important precondition for Swedish neutrality has been an implicit understanding that Soviet dominance was unacceptable to the West. Furthermore, Denmark and Norway, although full members of NATO, maintain a so-called 'low posture' within the alliance. This refers primarily to their ban on stationing of foreign troops and nuclear arms on their territory (except on Greenland) in peace time. These modifications, combined with a high degree of similarity in the world views held by political leaders and the public in all four countries, indicate that Nordic security policies are not quite as divergent as formal alignments seem to indicate.

This situation has given rise to the concept of 'the Nordic balance', which posits that there is an interdependence between Soviet policy towards Finland, Swedish neutrality, and Danish and Norwegian behaviour within NATO. If all parties concerned follow moderate policies there will, according to this concept, be a stable balance in the region serving the interests of all. However, further steps towards Danish and Norwegian integration in NATO, or westward changes in Swedish policy could lead to increased Soviet pressure on Finland and vice versa.

The concept of 'Nordic balance' has been subject to prolonged academic as well as political discussion.[10] Whilst much has been written in its favour, the basic disagreement is on the relative importance of considerations relating to the 'balance' compared to other considerations entering into the policy-making process in the relevant countries. The disagreement, in other words, is on the automaticity of the 'balance'. References to it can serve as a useful argument in some political debates but will be neglected in others. It would, for example, be difficult to find situations where an evaluation of the consequences for Finland has entered directly into the making of Danish foreign policy, whereas such considerations do carry considerable weight in debates over Swedish policy.

110

1 Europe

But it is not only at the global level that we find important systemic factors influencing the making of foreign policy in Scandinavia. Such forces are also at work at the regional levels in the wider European region and in the more limited Nordic region.

The political and economic development in Western Europe has profoundly influenced both foreign and domestic policies of the three countries. Through the Marshall Plan and the creation of first OEEC and later OECD they were drawn into close economic co-operation with the other countries of the Western world. Most important, however, was the political-economic co-operation between the original six members of the European Community. The creation of the Economic Community gave rise to a number of problems for the Scandinavian countries. The Six, and in particular West Germany, were a most important market for Scandinavian exports, and particular problems were created for Danish agricultural exports as the EC developed its common agricultural policy. The dilemma for all three countries was that their largest trading partner, Great Britain, was outside the new grouping, but their second largest customer, West Germany, was inside. Furthermore, the political goals of the EC dampened the interest of all three countries in joining the EC and for Sweden, in particular, it raised the question of the compatibility of neutrality and EC membership. The Scandinavian countries all favoured a broader and politically less binding type of co-operation and supported the British approach for a wider free trade area in the Maudling negotiations of 1957-58. When these attempts failed they joined Britain in EFTA. Sweden was very active in the creation of this organisation, whilst Denmark, concerned about her agricultural exports, was the least enthusiastic. Whilst EFTA never meant much for Britain, it had profound influence on inter-Scandinavian trade which grew rapidly, causing Sweden to replace West Germany as the second most important trading partner for Denmark and Norway.

Since the creation of the EC, the single most important development in Western Europe viewed from the perspective of the three Scandinavian countries involves Britain's relations with the EC. When Britain opened negotiations for membership with the Six in 1961 the Danish application followed the very same day, whereas the Norwegian application only followed after some hesitation. In Sweden the British application led to a debate which resulted in an application for association with the Community. But when General de Gaulle blocked British membership the applications of the three Scandinavian countries were no longer valid. The same pattern could be seen following the British 1967 application: Denmark followed suit, Norway after a little hesitation, while Sweden applied for an unspecified 'comprehensive, close, and durable' relationship. Again a veto by the General on British membership immediately depoliticised the issue in the Scandinavian countries. Finally in 1970, following the resignation of General de Gaulle and The Hague summit, negotiations for British membership were resumed. At that time the four

Nordic countries (Iceland did not participate) were negotiating the creation of a Nordic Economic Union (Nordek). Negotiations had proceeded quite far, but the new development on the European scene brought the negotiations to a halt. Denmark and Norway claimed that membership of Nordek would be compatible with membership of the EC or that Nordek could serve as a stepping stone to the EC. Finland, however, could not accept this view and maintained that a Nordic Economic Union should be independent and that Finland was unable to participate in a union where two members were seeking full membership of the EC.[11]

The Nordek negotiations were broken off and each of the four countries started their separate negotiations with the Six, Denmark and Norway for full membership, Sweden and Finland for a trade agreement. Where Sweden in 1967 had asked for a relationship with the EC which should be specified through negotiations, the Swedish government in 1970-71 soon found membership incompatible with its foreign policy.

British membership of the EC solved the problem of the separation of the British and West German market, which, particularly as far as agriculture was concerned, was important from a Danish point of view. Due to the success of EFTA, a new problem had, however, arisen: Sweden had become a much more important trading partner for Denmark and Norway and had replaced West Germany as the second most important market for industrial goods. This problem was solved in the final Swedish trade agreement and the Danish terms of entry.

In the end Denmark became the only Nordic country to become a member of the EC. Finland and Sweden got a free trade agreement with the Community, and so did Norway after the referendum when the electorate turned down membership on the terms negotiated by the government.[12] Although a relationship with the EC had thus been defined for all the four countries, the political and economic development within the EC continues, though in different ways, to be the most important regional phenomenon influencing their foreign policies. This is obvious in the Danish case, but the other Nordic countries are in many areas just as dependent upon decisions made by the EC. It is, for example, an open question whether Sweden, already conducting more than 50 per cent of her foreign trade with the EC, will be able to retain the degree of economic independence necessary to make its neutrality credible.

2 Nordic area

Finally, at the systemic level there are the factors relating to the Nordic region. We have already seen how the global bipolar system has been reflected within the Nordic area in what has been called the 'Nordic balance'. Likewise we have seen how the development of economic groupings in Western Europe has influenced and divided the region. In this section we shall take a quick look at the particular Nordic factors and their influence on the policies of the three Scandinavian countries.

Besides the three countries dealt with in this essay the Nordic region includes Finland and Iceland. The nature and extent of co-operation among the five countries has often been misunderstood by outside observers and not seldom by the inhabitants of the Nordic countries themselves. This is partly due to the lack of supranational institutions and partly to the spectacular failures of the more ambitious attempts at Nordic co-operation such as the plan for a Scandinavian Defence Community and the attempts in the 1950s at creating a Nordic Customs Union, and in the late 1960s at establishing an Economic Union (Nordek). However, these grandiose failures should not lead to a total dismissal of the importance of Nordic co-operation which has been and continues to be quite substantial in the so-called 'low politics' areas. Here integration sometimes has gone further than between any other group of states – the EC included.

The present institutional structure for Nordic co-operation has its roots at the beginning of the 20th century, at the parliamentary level in the Nordic Parliamentary Council founded in 1907 and at the governmental level in the regular meetings of ministers, starting with the foreign ministers in 1914.

The Nordic Council was created in 1952 on a Danish initiative and partly as a reaction to the failure of the defence negotiations. Finland, however, did not join until 1956 for reasons having to do with its particular international position. The Council consists of eighteen representatives from each of the national parliaments, though only six from Iceland, plus government ministers *ex officio* without voting privilege. There are five national secretariats under the Council, but since 1971 the Presidium has had its own secretariat. The Council can only make recommendations to the member countries, and security and defence policy is, as a matter of principle, excluded from the deliberations of the Council.[13]

The weak institutional structure and the exclusion of the core of 'high politics' is a characteristic feature of Nordic co-operation. The fact that it took almost twenty years before the Council got a non-national secretariat illustrates the sceptical attitude towards supranational institutions. However, in later years there has been a greater willingness to discuss the creation of such institutions and in a few cases even moves beyond discussing it. In the abortive Nordek negotiations for a Nordic Economic Union in 1969–70 the four countries went further in the acceptance of supranational institutions than ever before. And although the negotiations failed, some of the institutional proposals were nevertheless implemented, although for the most part they consisted of no more than the formalisation of existing practices, such as the creation of a Nordic Council of Ministers.

But the most important side of Nordic co-operation is not the institutional set-up but the actual co-operation and co-ordination of policies which takes place outside the 'high politics' area. Examples of this functional 'integration' can be found in many areas such as the common labour market (including the professions), equal social security treatment of each other's citizens, passport-free travel within the Nordic area, and the Scandinavian Airline System. And in spite of the acknowledged lack of institutional machinery there is in fact quite a large number of functionally specific inter-Nordic organisations both at inter- and non-governmental levels. One of the latest creations is the inter-governmental Nordic Investment Bank, established with Danish participation after Denmark's membership of the EC.

Besides the amount of co-operation which can be measured by the number of treaties or agreements entered into by the governments, there is an extensive amount of informal co-operation which must be taken into account, although its effects are difficult to measure and evaluate. It takes place between ministers and civil servants, and between political parties and interest organisations. One example is the Nordic contact man, a relatively high level civil servant in each government department in each of the five countries who is responsible for co-operation with the other Nordic countries within the particular field covered by his department. Through these contact men, as well as through other channels, policies are co-ordinated over a wide range of domestic issues but without resulting in any formal inter-state negotiations or treaties.[14]

More important in our context, however, are the attempts at co-ordinating foreign policies in order to gain more influence than the countries could exert individually. Illustrations of this can be found in OECD, EFTA, the UN, and its specialised agencies. The Nordic countries in the International Monetary Fund, for example, have been formally recognised as a group and have thereby secured a directorship in the organisation. Another example, often cited in the domestic debate, was the common Nordic negotiator in the Kennedy Round, where the effort to negotiate as one group did succeed with positive results. This, however, was facilitated by a combination of circumstances unlikely to recur.

Such attempts at co-ordinating foreign policy stands (outside the area of security and defence policy) have been most extensive within the United Nations. The voting record shows a very high degree of similarity in the voting behaviour of all five Nordic countries. In general, agreement is highest among the three Scandinavian countries and lowest between Iceland and Finland. However, on some issues the allied/neutral dimension places Denmark, Iceland, and Norway in one group and Finland and Sweden in another.[15]

In the preceding sections we have pointed out a number of external forces at the global and European levels which have had a major influence on the foreign policies of the Scandinavian countries and which have tended to pull the three countries in different directions. One could ask, however, whether Nordic co-operation could be seen as a counterweight diminishing extra-regional influences on the Nordic countries?

Faced with the choice between Nordic or broader Western co-operation, one or two of the Scandinavian countries chose the latter in all the most important situations. However, following several such situations, attempts have been made to renew Nordic co-operation. For example, Norwegian and Danish NATO membership was followed by the creation of the Nordic Council and the proposal for a Scandinavian Customs Union. The applications for membership of the EC in 1961 were followed by a Nordic Co-operation Agreement in 1962. And finally, after Danish membership of the EC, the Nordic institutional framework was strengthened and an 'action programme' adopted. Contrary to the neo-functional theory of integration, one could almost say that Nordic integration is spurred on by failures! How effective Nordic co-operation will be in counterbalancing external forces in the future remains, however, to be seen. The areas of potential conflict between European and isolated Nordic co-operation are many.

Societal level

Following a few words about the social homogeneity of the Scandinavian countries, this section deals with the differences in foreign policy outlook as derived from different recent historical experience of the three countries, the main differences in economic structure relevant for foreign policy, and finally, the role of interest organisations in the political process.

Homogeneity and social cleavages

Generally speaking the three Scandinavian countries are ethnically very homogeneous and they are probably also among the socially most homogeneous countries in the world. This should mean that factors relating to varying ethnic and social composition of the population are not relevant when trying to explain their foreign policies or the differences in the foreign policies between the countries. In later years Sweden in particular, but also Denmark, has had a large influx of Southern European migrant workers and consequently some social problems not experienced before, but no foreign policy problems seem to have followed, with the possible exception of the problem created by Croatian migrant workers for Swedish-Yugoslav relations.

The most important social cleavages with implications for foreign policy in Scandinavia seem to be the split between rural and urban – or central and peripheral – Norway. There are fundamentally different political cultures to be found in Oslo and on the south and west coasts. The traditional issues separating the two have been temperance, fundamentalist religion, and language. The split asserted itself most clearly in the debate and referendum on membership of the European Community, where the 'traditionalists' (lined up with the political left) fought a fierce battle against membership.[16]

Historical experience [17]

Although situated in the same geographical region and sharing a common heritage in many respects, the most important recent experience with relevance to foreign policy differs considerably. Sweden's more than 150 years of successful armed neutrality has given the doctrine of neutrality a status in Swedish political thought which has no equivalent in the other two countries. The doctrine of 'non-alignment in peace aiming at neutrality in war' as it is officially formulated, is the ideological basis for all Swedish foreign policy and is supported by almost all sectors of the population. Thus any foreign policy move by government or opposition parties must demonstrably accord with this doctrine to gain acceptance and credibility. On the other hand, the doctrine is sufficiently broad and vague to allow for a wide range of policies. This can be seen in the change to the much more enterprising policy of so-called 'active neutralism' which Swedish governments have followed since the middle of the 1960s.

The success of armed neutrality has no doubt resulted in a general support for a relatively high level of armament and the consequent large defence expenditure which stands in clear contrast to the situation in Denmark. In Sweden, defence planning and budgeting has been strongly influenced by the military experts whose recommendations have seldom been called into question for party political purposes. Of course, exceptions can be found, as for example when during the 1950s the military argued for the development of tactical nuclear weapons. The traditional acceptance of military appropriations has also suffered somewhat in recent years. The steeply rising costs of maintaining an independent defence effort have been the subject of increasing political debate. In 1968, the decision on future defence policy was the first example in the post-war period of a failure to achieve an all-party agreement (not counting the Communists) on a major question of defence policy.

The Danish historical experience is very different from the Swedish and has contributed to the creation of a spectrum of political attitudes quite different from those to be found in Sweden. In particular three historical situations have profoundly, though in different ways, influenced Danish political thought. A hazardous foreign policy based on unrealistic evaluations of its own military strength led to the war of 1864 and the subsequent loss of two-fifths of the Danish kingdom. This traumatic experience laid the foundation for a general conception of Denmark as a small and powerless state very much dependent on Germany. In some quarters it created the belief that any Danish defence effort was inherently futile. In the 1880s and until the turn of the century defence policy furthermore became the major issue in domestic politics by being the chosen instrument in the constitutional battle over the issue of parliamentary government and parliament's sole right to appropriate money. Thus, as opposed to the situation in most other countries, including Norway and Sweden, Denmark developed a tradition of defence as a major issue of party political infighting.

The policy of the inter-war years was one of almost unarmed neutrality. The defeat and German occupation during the Second World War made the Social Democrats finally give up the policy of unilateral disarmament. It also set in motion the development which made the Social Democrats, the Liberals, and the Conservatives give up neutrality. But the Radical Party, with its tradition of anti-militarism, could not accept the entry into NATO. Though never very large, the Radical Party has been important because it occupied the political centre in a parliament where no party had an absolute majority. And when the Radical Party gradually began to accept NATO membership, the Socialist People's Party, founded in 1958, picked up and carried the mantle of anti-militarism.

Norway also experienced defeat and occupation during the Second World War, although its topography helped make resistance by military means a bit more credible and effective than in the Danish case. The German occupation definitively discredited neutralism and, contrary to Denmark, Norway established a Government-in-exile in London which came to see close co-operation with Britain and the United States as essential for post-war Norwegian foreign policy.

The other historical factor must be mentioned in the case of Norway, namely its relatively recent independence. Until 1815 Norway was under Danish rule, but Denmark's alignment on the losing and Sweden's on the winning side in the Napoleonic Wars caused the transfer of Norway from the Danish to the Swedish monarchy. Norway did not emerge as an independent country from its union with Sweden until 1905. This recent development combined with Sweden's dominant economic position within the Nordic region no doubt has contributed to Norwegian fear of very close and formal relations with Sweden, fears which asserted themselves in recurring debates over closer economic integration in the Nordic area. Some writers also claim that the consciousness about newly gained independence was a factor behind the negative attitude towards membership of the European Community. Obviously, the existence of such influences are hard to prove, and at least the fear of Swedish economic domination may dwindle under the impression of the new riches derived from off-shore oil and gas. It is, however, true that the word 'union' in Norway carries with it connotations of the unhappy union with Sweden and implies a closer and more formalised relationship than envisaged by many who use the term in discussing the future of the European Community.

Economic structure

We have already noted that the three Scandinavian countries are industrially highly developed, and very dependent on international trade. With foreign trade accounting for about one-third of the net factor income, external economic relations become the most important aspect of domestic as well as foreign policy in periods of military stability and non-crisis. There are, however, a number of important differences in their economic structure which influence their foreign policies.

Denmark is the only one of the three countries which is a net exporter of agricultural products. About 60 per cent of the land is cultivated, compared to 9 per cent in Sweden and only 3 per cent in Norway. But at the same time, the proportion of the population employed in agriculture is about the same in Denmark and Norway and only a little less in Sweden. Until the late 1950s agriculture accounted for more than 50 per cent of Denmark's total exports, but this percentage steadily declined due to the agricultural protectionism of the EC, the industrialisation of the Danish economy, and the growth in industrial exports during the EFTA period. Sweden, partly for strategic reasons, has tried to curb the decline of agricultural production in order to retain about 80 per cent self-sufficiency. In Norway unfavourable climatic and topographical conditions necessitate a high degree of protectionism and subsidy of agriculture.

The three countries also differ significantly in their industrial basis. Denmark has hardly any natural resources, and must import almost all raw materials for its industry. Norway and Sweden are rich in forest; both (but especially Norway) have large actual and potential hydroelectric resources, and both (but especially Sweden) have large deposits of iron ore. Finally, the recent discoveries of large oil and gas reserves on the Norwegian part of the continental shelf have dramatically changed the prospects for Norway's future economy.

Size and concentration of industry in the three countries vary considerably. In Denmark there is a large number of relatively small firms, often working as sub-contractors to foreign firms; in Sweden, the firms are larger but relatively fewer in number; Norway falls between the two. However, not even Sweden has many firms which would be considered large by international standards. Although no detailed description of industrial structure will be attempted here, the strong position of fisheries and shipping in Norway should be mentioned. Norway's position as the owner of one of the largest merchant fleets is important to several aspects of its foreign policy, and it provides foreign currency earnings which make Norway less dependent than, for example, Denmark upon the existence of trade blocs.

The 'oil crisis' in 1973–74 emphasised strongly a new difference in the economic and international position of the three countries. Norway's strengthened economic position as a consequence of its hydrocarbon reserves and the new price level was unmistakable, but with it followed a number of new problems of foreign policy such as its position *vis-à-vis* OPEC and IEA and its relations with the Soviet Union and the major NATO countries on the issue of rights to the continental shelf in the Arctic Sea around Svalbard. To Sweden the 'oil crisis' demonstrated the vulnerability of its neutrality. In Denmark, the weakness of a country totally dependent upon import for all its energy needs was dramatically demonstrated. In contrast to the two other countries, Denmark accepted IEA membership without any reservation or hesitation. Sweden joined after some hesitation and in spite of its neutrality. Norway only became an associated member of IEA.

Interest organisations

The three Scandinavian countries are among the most thoroughly organised countries in the world. Almost any conceivable aspect of social, economic, and political life has its formal organisation and the membership ratio (the ratio between actual and potential members) of the socio-economic interest organisations is high compared to other countries. The relationship between interest organisations and government is formalised through rules and practices of communication before the making of decisions and through representation on public and semi-public consultative and decision-making bodies.

Lobbying, in the American sense, does not take place. Interest organisations do send spokesmen to parliamentary committees considering bills, but for the major organisations this is only of marginal importance. Relations with the administration play a much larger role. The administration's consultation of the relevant interest organisations for facts as well as evaluations is considered not only legitimate and useful but most often politically and administratively necessary. The formal integration of the socio-economic interest organisations into the decision-making process, although its extent occasionally has been the subject of political debate, is a characteristic feature of the political system in the Scandinavian countries. In Sweden, this process gave rise to the term 'Harpsund Democracy', named after the Prime Minister's holiday resort, where many meetings between leaders of government and organisations were held.

The particular role of Danish interest organisations in decision-making has changed to some extent following EC membership. The major organisations have established offices in Brussels and all socio-economic interest organisations work directly or indirectly through community level interest organisations. On the domestic side of the decision-making process the role of the organisations has also changed. Although difficult to predict what the pattern will be in the long run, it seems so far as if the interest organisations have lost some of their former direct influence. This is due to both much more complicated governmental and administrative decision-making in EC-related matters and the Government's desire to have greater direct control over policy-making, especially with regard to agriculture.[18]

Besides the formal and informal relations with government and administration, interest organisations can influence policy through the political parties. In all three countries there are, though brought about through different organisational linkages, close relations between the trade union movement and the Social Democratic Party. These linkages are both established through formal organisational linkages, economic support and overlapping leaderships. In Denmark and Sweden trade union leaders have been prominent members of Parliament, as illustrated by Arne Geijer who was Secretary General of the LO (the Swedish Trades Union Congress) and chairman of the Foreign Policy Committee of the Swedish Parliament, or as illustrated by Mr Anker Jorgensen, who before becoming Prime Minister was chairman of the Danish General Worker's Union.[19]

Employers' unions and industrial organisations are traditionally allied with the conservative parties or one of the other 'bourgeois' parties, but this relationship is seldom formalised and direct personal overlap is rare. The relationship depends more upon common outlook and financial contributions.

Finally, in all three countries there are political parties (Agrarian, Centre, or Liberal) closely linked to agricultural organisations, though the smallholders in Denmark have traditionally been connected with the Radical Party, and in Norway with the Labour Party.

In this way the views of the major interest organisations become represented in Parliament without the process of formal lobbying. In all three countries the Labour Movement is strong and asserts an influence on all aspects of domestic and some aspects of foreign policy. The structure of organised interests and the relative strength of interest organisations varies among the three countries according to the economic structure of each country. It is thus not surprising that in Denmark we find a politically strong and effective agricultural organisation, and that the Shipowners' Association's influence in Norway extends to several questions of foreign policy. However, the influence of interest organisations is not uniform but varies from issue–area to issue–area, as we shall see in a later section.

Besides these permanent socio-economic interest organisations there are, of course, also 'promotional' interest organisations, often created in order to influence specific decisions and with membership open to all who support the organisation's goal. Since these organisations normally do not receive any formal recognition and are not given direct access to the consultative and decision-making bodies of government they have to rely on mobilisation of public opinion and the press and on influencing individual members of parliament. Such organisations have also from time to time tried to influence foreign policy. One example, is the campaign against nuclear weapons, which for a period was quite active in all three countries. The most recent major examples are the campaigns for and against EC membership in Denmark and Norway, which played an important role in the mobilisation of voters prior to the referenda in 1972. These EC campaign organisations are, however, among the only ones where one can say with confidence that promotional organisations did have a major direct impact on the making of foreign policy. But the situation was unique in the sense that the decisions were made through referenda and by the fact that the promotional groups in these campaigns were closely linked with political parties and socio-economic interest organisations, a situation which gave them organisational and financial resources seldom available to promotional groups.[20]

Governmental level

By discussing the role of interest organisations and their direct participation in decision-making processes we have gradually moved from the societal level to what in Rosenau's terminology is called the governmental level.

The characteristic features of the political systems in the three countries are very similar. They are all constitutional monarchies with a parliamentary system of government. The institutional structures have roughly the same roots in nineteenth century constitutional ideas, and in many twentieth century reforms the three countries have freely borrowed from each other.

Although differences in the political institutions do exist, they are minor when seen in a global or even Western European perspective. It is not plausible that these differences can contribute to an explanation of the main differences in foreign policy. Instead of looking at the formal institutional structure of government, this section mainly deals with the party system and the role of the political parties.

Parties and party systems [21]

Until 1973 one could say that the party systems of the three countries were roughly similar. In the post World War II period, which we are dealing with in this essay, the Social Democratic Party (in Norway called the Labour Party) has been the largest party in each of the three countries. To the right of the Social Democrats there have been three to four so-called 'bourgeois' parties. Each country has its Conservative Party and a Centre or Liberal party originally founded as an agrarian

120

party. Furthermore, each country has a non-socialist radical or social-liberal party. The most important difference on the right of the political spectrum was the existence in Norway of a Christian People's Party which, until recently, had no parallel in either of the two other countries.

To the left of the Social Democrats one originally only found the Communists, who with the exception of the first post-war elections, never became very powerful in Denmark and Norway. Since 1958 and 1961 respectively Denmark and Norway have had a Socialist People's Party somewhere on the political spectrum between the Social Democrats and the Communists. The creation of these parties took place partly in reaction to the political development in Eastern Europe. In Sweden no new socialist party was established but the Communist Party, already less dogmatic than its Danish counterpart, developed an independent line, and became a serious political force to the left of the ruling Social Democrats. Finally, Denmark, in contrast to the other two countries, has experienced a number of small break away party groups all over the political spectrum. Though small and often short-lived, they have had a disproportionately large influence in periods of minority government or on the creation of majority coalitions.

The pointing out of similarities in party system and parallelism between parties should not, however, obscure the differences in the foreign policy attitudes of corresponding parties. The traditional anti-militarism of the Danish Radical Party has no parallel in the other two countries, and, of course, the attitudes towards the EC in the Danish and Norwegian agrarian parties could not have been more incompatible.

Several of the similarities of the three party-systems which existed up till 1973 do not exist any more. In 1973 a number of dramatic changes took place in Norway and Denmark. In the case of Norway, there can be no doubt that the prime cause was the long and bitter debate over the Common Market issue. It split the 'Venstre' (the social-liberal party) into two political parties defined according to attitudes towards membership of the EC and the campaign was instrumental in creating the alliance between the Socialist People's Party, the Communists, and a number of smaller left wing groups. It also resulted in a considerable internal weakening of the Labour Party.

In Denmark the 1973 election even more dramatically changed the party system but here, although possibly serving as a catalyst, the Common Market question was not the prime cause. First of all the election not only brought the anti-tax so-called Progress Party into Parliament, but in one sweep made it the second largest political party. The election also brought in another new party called the Centre Democrats as well as the Christian People's Party, established a few years before. The Communists and the Georgists were brought back into Parliament after several years in the wilderness. Thus a party system which had been known for its stability over more than half a century was suddenly changed and ten parties now sat in Parliament.

No similar or equally dramatic change has taken place in Sweden. No new parties have found their way into the Swedish Parliament, and the change in votes in the 1976 election which led to the creation of the first non-Social Democratic

121

government in forty-four years was only marginal. Although the result of the election was remarkable by Swedish standards, by any other standard it was a confirmation of the stability of the Swedish party system.

We have emphasised the similarity and stability of the party systems up till 1973. A more detailed study would, naturally, have uncovered a number of differences. The most important of these has to do with the parliamentary base of Scandinavian governments. When turned out of office in 1976 the Swedish Social Democrats had been continuously in office for forty-four years, and only during a period in the 1950s were they forced into coalition with another party in order to secure stable government. In Norway, the Labour Party has been less dominant. It held an overall majority up to 1961, continued as a minority government (with a short interruption) until 1965, when a majority coalition of the four 'bourgeois' parties was formed. Since 1971 Norway has again been governed by a minority Labour government, though interrupted for a year by a minority coalition of anti-EC parties following the referendum on EC membership. The Danish parliamentary scene has been much more complicated. While the Social Democrats have been the largest party, they have never held a majority of seats. The government, although often led by the Social Democrats, has been based on changing combinations of parties in majority coalitions, minority coalitions, or minority government by one party with or without semi-permanent support from other parties not in government. Since 1945 Denmark has had seventeen governments, Norway ten, and Sweden six.

The differences between the three countries up till 1973 remain, however, minor when compared to the differences between the Scandinavian countries on the one hand and other European countries on the other. It is inconceivable that the minor differences that did exist between the Scandinavian countries in this respect are important in accounting for major differences in foreign policy, but possibly the difference in governmental base and stability can explain, at least in part, differences in consistency and relative influence.

It is even difficult to point to changes in foreign policy as a consequence of the dramatic political changes recently. Although the setback, suffered by the pro-EC forces in Norway, could discourage a new attempt at membership, there are much more important reasons why such a policy is not realistic in the foreseeable future. The change in government in Sweden does not seem to indicate any change in substance, but maybe in style, of Swedish foreign policy. It has, for example, been said that a change in government would lead to an improvement in Sweden's relations with the United States. But relations were already improving following the termination of the war in Vietnam which had been the main topic of disagreement. Even in Denmark, no direct consequences for foreign policy seem to have followed from the dramatic rise of the Progress Party although its programme calls for the complete abolition of the diplomatic service and a total stop to development aid, and its colourful and dominant leader also wants to see the armed forces dissolved. The most important domestic as well as foreign policy consequence of the recent developments in Denmark seems to be the further weakening of the parliamentary possibilities of the government and thus of its ability to conduct coherent and long term economic policy.

Finally, a few words about the internal decision-making in political parties, which is relevant in at least two respects. First, the organs of the ruling party (congress or executive committee) often are the locus of important decisions. For example, the Norwegian decision to join NATO was made by the Labour Party Conference and once it had decided overwhelmingly in favour, the question was, for all practical purposes, settled. The subsequent decision by Parliament was never in doubt.

Secondly, but closely related, is the fear in the leadership of splitting its own party on a major issue. The mere anticipation of a split will influence policy. Since the Social Democratic Parties have been dominant in Scandinavian politics and since the dividing line on many controversial issues seems to go through these parties they provide a host of examples of how a governing party modifies its position, at least in part, out of fear of an open disagreement. One example is the Swedish government's attitude towards the development of Swedish nuclear arms. Development of tactical nuclear weapons was advocated by the military and the Conservative Party but was strongly opposed by groups within the Social Democratic Party. The question would no doubt have split the party had the Government decided to go ahead with a nuclear programme. An extensive public debate took place, but no explicit decision was made. The question was postponed until international developments such as the Test Ban and Non-Proliferation Treaties had made it irrelevant for all practical purposes.[22]

The Common Market issue, however, provides an important exception to this way of arriving at major policy decisions. In Sweden in 1970–71 the Government's initial relatively positive attitude of at least considering full membership was modified in the course of the debate because of, among other things, the influence of opposition within its own ranks. This was not the case in Norway and Denmark. Here the Social Democratic governments went ahead determined to join the EC in spite of strong internal party opposition. The Danish party leadership had originally tried to overcome internal disagreement by making its positive attitude dependent upon Norwegian membership, but as the final decision approached and the uncertainty of the Norwegian referendum became apparent, it tried quietly to drop the 'Norway proviso'. However, from a purely party political point of view, the experience of the Danish and the Norwegian party hardly encourages repetition.

A note on 'bureaucratic politics'

The term 'bureaucratic politics' denotes an approach to explaining foreign policy which has gained substantial interest in recent years. It explains foreign policy decisions and actions (or 'resultants', to use its own terminology) in terms of competing bureaucratic perspectives and interests. Several American foreign policy decisions have been reinterpreted in the light of the new approach.[23]

How important is this perspective when it comes to explaining the foreign policies of the Scandinavian countries? Naturally, bureaucratic battles are also fought with much energy and enthusiasm in these countries. The battle over control over co-ordination of Common Market policies in Denmark was almost paradigmatic for 'bureaucratic politics', and the Swedish decision to build the 'Viggen' multi-purpose military aircraft has been explained in terms of bureaucratic politics although without the use of the specific terminology of the fashion.[24]

The basic assumptions of the 'bureaucratic politics' approach have been heavily criticised.[25] However, even if one accepts the relevance of the approach, the sheer difference in size between the American foreign and defence policy bureaucracy on the one hand and the bureaucracies in the Scandinavian countries on the other, must make the approach less important as a general approach to explaining the foreign policies of the Scandinavian countries. Furthermore, if one accepts the basic line of argument of this chapter, bureaucratic battles, however energetically fought, are not the main determinants of policy. International and societal forces, as well as other factors at the governmental level, narrowly limit the area within which purely bureaucratic factors can shape foreign policy.

One point about bureaucracies must, nevertheless, be mentioned and that is the phenomenon which has been called 'bureaucratic interpenetration'. In Sweden, due to its non-alignment, the making of security and defence policy is a strictly national affair, whereas in the two NATO countries it is a much more complex process involving NATO institutions and other NATO governments. Not enough information is available for a systematic description of interactions between the alliance and the national decision-makers. But a Norwegian study of the administrative decision-making processes in foreign policy [26] has shown that of the international communication (which accounts for 37 per cent of the total volume of communications) between the Norwegian Ministry of Defence and the outside world, 36 per cent was with the NATO organisation, 28 per cent with the permanent delegations to NATO, and 18 per cent with other defence ministries – mainly in the other NATO countries. Although not surprising, these figures illustrate the importance of interaction at the bureaucratic level.

Another example, which includes all three countries, could be the so-called 'confrontation procedure' used in the OECD when preparing the yearly economic reports on each of the member countries. Informal 'bureaucratic interpenetration' is an important phenomenon in inter-Nordic co-operation, as has already been mentioned. The most far-reaching phenomenon of 'bureaucratic interpenetration', however, has been in the Danish decision-making processes since becoming a member of the European Community. Its principal character is not different from what is well known from the original member countries. In Denmark an elaborate structure for administrative co-ordination of EC policies has been established. The reasons behind the attempts to centralise and co-ordinate EC policy have been political as well as bureaucratic, but the tendency since 1973 seems in practice to be a development in the direction of less strict centralised co-ordination.[27]

Individual level

In terms of the framework used here, explanatory factors at the individual level are not very important in explaining the foreign policies of small, developed, and democratic states, they seem mainly to be of a residual nature. This hypothesis seems to hold true as far as the three Scandinavian countries are concerned. No major foreign policy posture or decision can reasonably be explained with primary emphasis on the private preferences of individual political leaders.

We have already noted the difference between governmental stability in the Scandinavian countries. The Danish Government has generally been in a weaker position *vis-à-vis* parliament and civil servants than the governments of the other two countries and particularly the Swedish. This seems to have some implications for the role of individual political leaders. During the forty year period from 1936 to 1976 Sweden has only had three prime ministers, and one of them, Mr Tage Erlander, served in this capacity for twenty-three consecutive years. The longest serving Norwegian prime minister, Mr Einar Gerhardsen, served for sixteen years, whereas Mr J. O. Krag only served seven years as Danish prime minister, but he had previously had responsibility for foreign affairs. In Sweden, Mr Östen Undén was foreign minister from 1945 to 1962,[28] and in Norway, Mr Halvard Lange from 1946 to 1965. They both, like their prime minister, gained an immense amount of authority in relation to their civil servants, their own parties, and their parliaments as a whole. No comparable situation has existed in Denmark since Dr Peter Munch was foreign minister in the 1930s.

Yet, it is difficult to point towards examples where one can convincingly argue that a major decision was made or policies outlined due to the personal views even of these long serving and comparatively 'strong' political leaders.

Issue–areas

So far we have only listed a number of rather general factors at different levels of analysis and with them a number of illustrations indicating the possible relevance of each. But not all factors and not the same factors are at work in each situation. One aspect of Rosenau's pre-theory which has not yet been mentioned is the concept of 'issue–area'.[29] Issue–areas are defined as clusters of issues having some similarity. Whereas issues can be short lived, issue–areas are of a more permanent character. The idea of dividing foreign policies into different issue–areas rests on the notion that there is no single general process of foreign policy making, but different processes depending upon the issue–area. Varying groups are mobilised in relation to different issues and procedures change. We, therefore, cannot go on discussing in general terms what variables explain the foreign policies of the Scandinavian countries. In order to be more specific a distinction between issue–areas must be made. Unfortunately, however, Rosenau's own proposal for a distinction between issue–areas is very abstract and difficult to apply in conjunction with the other elements of the pre-theory. In the following section a much cruder distinction is made between: 1 security and defence policy, 2 foreign economic relations, and 3 value promotion. Within each of these three areas we shall select the crucial variables and attempt an evaluation of how they interact in explaining the foreign policies of the three Scandinavian countries.

Security and defence [30]

The different roads chosen by the Scandinavian countries after the Second World War on matters of security and defence policy, Denmark's and Norway's membership of the Atlantic alliance and the confirmation of Swedish neutrality, is primarily to be explained in terms of the bipolar confrontation between the United States and the Soviet Union, the strategic location of each of the three countries and the extra-Scandinavian territories of Denmark and Norway, and the political attitudes in each of the three countries as shaped by historical experience, primarily the success or failure of neutrality in the recent past. In other words, when explaining the basic posture on questions of security and defence the main factors are to be found at the systemic and societal levels and it is not necessary to go further in the search for explanatory variables.

When looking at the numerous other decisions taken over the years within the issue–area it is important to emphasise that they are made within the framework established by the basic decisions on alignment/neutrality and thus indirectly influenced by the same factors as the basic decisions. But when it comes to explaining the specific content of these less far-reaching decisions other factors do enter into the explanation. Let us take a brief look at the main differences between the three countries in this respect.

In Sweden, the making of security and defence policy is a strictly national affair, whereas in the two NATO countries, it is part of a complex process involving NATO institutions and the governments of other member countries. We have already illustrated this in the discussion of 'bureaucratic interpenetration' above.

Another example of NATO involvement in national policy-making, which became publicly known, occurred when the Danish Social Democratic Government in 1971 proposed a Defence Bill significantly restructuring the armed forces. The bill was viewed with some scepticism in NATO quarters and several criticisms were expressed, including some by the Secretary-General. His comments were made known to the public and subsequently used by the political parties opposed to the bill. This may have been a particularly pronounced example of NATO involvement, but in Denmark and Norway, 'NATO requirements' – as interpreted by the political parties – always play a role in decisions on defence policy.

Looked upon from another point of view, a distinction could be made between the policy-making processes in Denmark on the one hand and Norway and Sweden on the other. Within all three countries a large measure of consensus exists among the major political parties on basic questions of security and defence. In Norway and Sweden this consensus has until recently been almost total; and security and defence policy has normally been kept outside party politics. As a consequence, such policy is normally made at the governmental and administrative levels. The Danish situation has been somewhat different. We have already touched upon the reasons for the politicisation of these questions in Denmark. The result is, that many issues, which in Norway and Sweden are settled at the governmental or administrative level, in Denmark often require substantial negotiations between the political parties. The historical and ideological reasons for this situation, mentioned above, are reinforced by two other factors. The first has to do with the normally weaker parliamentary basis of Danish governments, especially when compared to Sweden.

The second factor, again separating Denmark from the other two, has to do with the role of the military. In Norway and Sweden the defence establishments have normally been able to put forward unified appraisals of the strategic situation and consequent proposals for organisational structure and appropriations, thereby presenting a united front of military expertise to the politicians. In Denmark, whether for historical, strategic, or political reasons, such agreement among the military experts has not always been the case. Inter-service disagreements have, in situations of major reform, diminished the weight of military recommendations, enabling politicians to select the military advice most similar to their own views. For example, during the 1960 negotiations for a new defence structure the Danish army, mainly in co-operation with the Conservative Party, secured a decision which the navy and air force felt gave undue strength to the army at their expense. Maybe it was this experience which in the following years helped bring about a somewhat greater consensus between the services.

Interest organisations play hardly any role in the making of Danish and Norwegian security and defence policy. And although Sweden has a rather large and sophisticated defence industry, it would probably be misleading to talk of a 'military-industrial complex', although a study of the decision to produce the 'Viggen' aircraft actually sees the decision primarily as the result of the interests of such a 'complex'.[31] Another analyst talks about the 'military-labour market complex'.[32] But at least in Sweden we find very active and large private organisations distributing information about defence problems and propagandising for strong armed forces. Nothing similar exists in the two other countries.

Foreign economic relations

The issue-area of foreign economic relations is a very broad one, and a very important one for these three small and highly industrialised countries with only limited resources. The linkage between foreign and domestic policies - or should one say the futility of making such a distinction? - is seen most clearly within this issue-area.

When explaining the overall policies on foreign economic relations and economic integration, in particular the relationship to the European Community, the most important factors have to do with the evolution of economic co-operation in Western Europe and particularly with British policy towards the EC, and the domestic economic structure of the three countries, in particular the high but varying dependence upon exports and the consequent interests of the socio-economic groupings in each of the three countries. This alone, however, cannot explain the Swedish reservations about membership of the EC. Here we also have to add the 'spill over' effect from the general foreign policy posture of non-alignment – i.e. the consequences of security policy for other policy areas.

Again we see that the general policy stand is primarily to be explained in terms of systemic and societal variables and it is not necessary to include variables from Rosenau's other categories. However, although the basic variables in explaining foreign economic policy are to be found at the same level as the variables used in explaining security and defence policy, the particular variables are not the same, except to some extent in the case of Sweden.

The decision-making processes within the area of foreign economic policy seldom becomes highly politicised. The major exceptions to this rule are the decisions on the great schemes for economic integration such as the two abortive Nordic attempts, the creation of EFTA, and especially the situation around the EC membership negotiations and decisions. The final EC debates leading up to the referenda in Denmark and Norway were truly 'great debates' with an unprecedented mobilisation of all political groups and a larger portion of the public than had been stimulated by any other issue since the Second World War.

In Norway, where the debate was most bitter, attitudes cut across several party lines. Farmers and fishermen, supporters of NATO, worked together with the political left against the establishment and the political centre. The debate reinforced traditional cleavages and at the same time broke up traditional political alignments. In Denmark, although differences were more clearly expressed according to the normal left–right division, the dividing line also cut through both the Social Democratic and the Radical Party. The most important difference from the Norwegian situation was the wholehearted support for membership found in the farming community. The strongest opposition came from working class constituencies in Copenhagen.

The smaller and much more numerous decisions on foreign economic policy seldom become politicised. They are normally made without the active participation of parliaments, parties, and the public. They are taken by ministers and civil servants in close consultation with the major interest organisations. It is particularly within the issue–area of foreign economic relations that the role of interest organisations, mentioned earlier, is most clearly demonstrated. Several examples could be given of policy areas where decision-making and execution has been permanently delegated to the interest organisation concerned, or where interest organisations have – acting on behalf of the government – been negotiating trade agreements with foreign governments. These latter examples, however, mainly belong to a period before economic questions became as central a concern in the conduct of foreign policy as they have in recent years. But, for example, before the diplomatic recognition of the German Democratic Republic the necessary relations concerning trade were established through interest organisations.

Value promotion

'Value promotion' is the least generally used term for the description of an issue-area, and may need some explanation. All foreign policy can be seen as an attempt to promote certain values or to influence value distribution in the international system. However, in Scandinavian political science, the term seems to have been accepted as the 'terminus technicus' for that aspect, or issue-area, of foreign policy which is not directly related to security, defence, trade, and monetary matters, but which could also – with an equally imprecise term – be called the ideological aspect of foreign policy. It refers to the attempts to influence international relations, and sometimes also the internal policies of foreign governments, in a direction more compatible with the norms said to be honoured in the domestic politics of the promoting states themselves, such as 'rule of law' and 'social justice'.

This aspect of Scandinavian foreign policy is often looked upon with some irritation by other states, including some of those with whom the Scandinavian countries have close relations. It is seen as a nuisance and unbecomingly self-righteous. Such criticisms are also heard in the internal debate over foreign policy in the Scandinavian countries themselves, particularly when the policy by some groups is considered to interfere with the two other issue-areas, by for example harming exports, or, in the Danish and Norwegian case, weakening NATO, or, in the Swedish case, being in conflict with a strict neutral posture.

Whatever the political or ideological attitudes, the rationale for such a policy is that small states have a clear interest in an international system which is highly organised and regulated by mutually accepted norms. To the extent that the international system develops in that direction, the importance of military and economic power in inter-state relations is minimised. Voting rules in international organisations normally favour small states and international norms might limit at least some unwanted actions by other states.

One characteristic of this issue-area is that it does not have the same direct relationship to survival and development as the two issue-areas mentioned above. Here, decision-makers are less constrained by external forces, and policies derived from ideology and domestic experience can be given more weight.

While the three Scandinavian countries have followed divergent roads concerning security and economic integration, they have found it much easier to co-operate within this less demanding sphere. However, the forces and concerns which led them in different directions over security and economics do penetrate into this issue-area from time to time as do ideological variations within the common culture.

The Swedish policy of so-called 'active neutralism' to a large extent falls within the issue-area of value promotion. Part of its background has been the growing *détente* between the superpowers which indicates that external factors are at work even within this issue-area. The most prominent feature of active neutralism has been the outspoken criticism of American policy in South-East Asia, and thus seems to have been designed not to interfere directly with Sweden's own vital security and economic interests. The more active line in Swedish policy has also put some strain on Nordic co-operation on foreign policy, especially when non-Social Democratic parties have held power in the other two countries.

The organisational framework of the value promotive foreign policy is primarily the UN, the Council of Europe and the Nordic institutions. But other fora may from time to time be used also, as when military aid to the Greek junta was criticised in the NATO Council of Ministers. More effective than criticism in NATO, however, was the initiative taken by the three countries in co-operation with the Netherlands to bring the Greek junta before the European Commission on Human Rights. This resulted in the withdrawal of Greece from the Council of Europe, although it achieved little for human rights in Greece.

Most important in this area is the United Nations, and as already mentioned, here Nordic co-operation has been extensive. Denmark, Finland, Norway and Sweden undoubtedly consider their contribution to UN peace-keeping operations as a major element in their UN policy. In the early 1960s they created an inter-Nordic standby force of approximately 5,000 men to be used for peace-keeping operations at the request of the Secretary-General subject to national approval. Second only to Canada, Sweden and Denmark have contributed the largest number of troops for such operations.

Attitudes towards the UN among the citizens of the three countries are generally positive, and one would expect a high degree of public debate in the formulation of UN policy. Furthermore, in all three countries political parties and some interest organisations are represented on the delegation to the UN General Assembly. Part of the rationale for this representation has been to increase information and discussion of UN activities.

Nevertheless, there is generally very little public and parliamentary debate on the majority of issues dealt with by the UN, and it is clear that the decision-making processes are normally confined to foreign ministries and diplomatic missions. From time to time, UN related issues do catch the interest of politicians and the public, but it is difficult to establish clear criteria for which issues do and which do not. Keeping a common Nordic line in the UN seems, if one has to judge from the public debate when this has not been maintained, to be a subject of more public debate than the actual stand taken on the issue.

An illustration of this can be found in policy towards South Africa, not an atypical question within this issue–area. At a meeting of Nordic foreign ministers in 1963 a common policy on apartheid was decided. However, in the UN no resolution was proposed because of disagreement on the problem of sanctions between the African countries and the Western Great Powers. But in 1965, when a resolution was proposed by the Afro-Asian countries, Denmark was the only Nordic country to vote for the resolution. This splitting of the Nordic vote gave rise to quite a debate in the Nordic countries and the matter was also taken up by the Nordic Council. Denmark was criticised for not consulting the other countries before voting, and interestingly enough the whole problem was seen more as one of failure of communication than one of differing interests.[33]

Should the foreign policy co-operation between the members of the European

Community in the future result in effective co-ordination of voting in the UN, Denmark could from time to time be forced to make a choice between following the EC or the Nordic countries. Whatever the Government chooses it could lead to considerable domestic criticism.

Conclusion

We have in this chapter tried to outline the major variables determining the general foreign policy posture of the three Scandinavian countries. Our findings have roughly been in accordance with the hypothesis of the pre-theory in the sense that as far as small, developed, and democratic countries are concerned systemic and societal variables were found to be more important than governmental and individual variables. However, since the pre-theory does not delineate specific variables within each category, we had to select a number of rather crudely defined variables at each level. The foreign policy behaviour of the three countries was divided into three broad issue-areas. It was found that different variables explain policy within different issue-areas; that although both systemic and societal variables were used in order to explain security policy as well as foreign economic policy, the explanatory variables in each category were different depending upon the issue-area. Furthermore, the systemic variables seemed to be less potent in explaining the value promotive foreign policies, and societal variables, particularly those pertaining to political attitudes and ideology, were more important within that particular issue-area.

These findings are either in accordance with the pre-theory or do not contradict it. The way the foreign policies of the Scandinavian countries have been explained is, however, in one respect slightly at odds with the assumptions of the pre-theory. In all formulations of the pre-theory, be it the original version, later revisions or empirical applications, the central concern has been the relative potency of variable categories. Variables and variable categories seem to be considered one by one and then added together. The underlying assumption could be called an additive model, indicating that the relative potency of each variable can be studied in isolation and the different variables then added together. However, this assumption of additivity is problematical and does not accord well with several other theoretical assumptions in the study of foreign policy nor with the way in which most explanations of foreign policy are made.[34]

We cannot say that the bipolar structure of the international system accounts for a certain amount of the variance in the behaviour of the three countries, or that geographical location or historical experience accounts for some other fraction of the variance. The explanation of the alignments of the three countries lies in the interaction of these three sets of variables: none of them alone explains anything. Thus, even if we accept that governmental and individual variables were less important we cannot say whether systemic or societal variables were the more important. Neither of them can stand alone, and the explanation lies in the interaction between them.

Likewise, in the area of foreign economic relations, it was not British membership of the EC alone which led to the parting of the ways of the three countries, nor their different economic structures, nor concerns for the effects of membership on security policy. It is in the interaction of these three sets of variables that one has to find the explanation. And even though we have explained the value promotive foreign policy mainly in terms of societal variables, there are other variables at work, such as the domestic parliamentary situation or changes in the international system.

Notes

[1]   Richard C. Snyder, H. W. Bruck, and Burton Sapin (eds), *Foreign Policy Decision-Making*, Glencoe, Ill. 1962.

[2]   Stephen J. Andriole, Jonathan Wilkenfeld, and Gerald Hopple, 'A Framework for the Comparative Analysis of Foreign Policy Behaviour', *International Studies Quarterly*, vol. 19, June 1975, pp. 160-98.

[3]   Ib Faurby, 'The Lack of Cumulation in Foreign Policy Studies: The Case of Britain and the European Community', *European Journal of Political Research*, vol. 4, no. 2, 1975, pp. 205-25.

[4]   Arend Lijphart, 'Comparative Politics and the Comparative Method', *American Political Science Review*, vol. 65, Sept. 1971, pp. 682-93.

[5]   Arend Lijphart, 'The Comparable-Cases Strategy in Comparative Research', *Comparative Political Studies*, vol. 8, no. 2, July 1975, pp. 158-77.

[6]   James N. Rosenau, 'Pre-theories and Theories of Foreign Policy', in R. Barry Farrell (ed.), *Approaches to Comparative and International Politics*, Evanston, Ill. 1966, pp. 27-92.

[7]   James N. Rosenau and Gary D. Hoggard, 'Foreign Policy Behavior in Dyadic Relationships: Testing a Pre-theoretical Extension', in Rosenau (ed.), *Comparing Foreign Policies*, New York 1974, pp. 117-50.

[8]   Ralph Pettman, *Human Behaviour and World Politics*, London 1975, pp. 32-51.

[9]   For an interesting study which disagrees with many of the explanations given in the following, see Barbara G. Haskel, *The Scandinavian Option. Opportunities and Opportunity Costs in Postwar Scandinavian Foreign Policies*, Oslo 1976.

[10]   Arne Olav Brundtland, 'The Nordic Balance', *Cooperation and Conflict*, vol. 2, no. 2, 1967, pp. 30-63, and Erik Moberg, 'The Nordic Balance Concept', *Cooperation and Conflict*, vol. 3, no. 3, 1968, pp. 210-14.

[11]   Claes Wiklund, 'The Zig-Zag Course of the Nordek Negotiations', *Scandinavian Political Studies*, vol. V, 1970, pp. 307-36.

[12]   Arild Underdal, 'Diverging Roads to Europe', *Cooperation and Conflict*, vol. 10, no. 1-2, pp. 65-76 explains the different policies of the Nordic countries towards the EC. See also Carl-Einar Stålvant, 'Neutrality and European Integration', *Scandinavian Studies*, vol. 46, no. 4, pp. 405-28.

[13] *Nordiska Samarbetsorgan*, Stockholm, Oslo, Copenhagen 1974.

[14] 'Kontaktmandsseminar', *Nordisk udredningsserie*, 1966, no. 6.

[15] Kurt Jacobsen, 'Voting Behavior of the Nordic Countries in the General Assembly', pp. 139-57, and Jaakko Kalela, 'The Nordic Group in the General Assembly', pp. 158-70, *Cooperation and Conflict*, vol. 2, no. 3-4.

[16] Henry Valen, ' "No" to EEC', *Scandinavian Political Studies*, vol. VIII, 1973, pp. 214-26.

[17] For another interpretation of historical experience, see Haskel, op. cit., pp. 52-8.

[18] Svend Auken, Jacob Buksti, and Carsten Lehmann Sørensen, 'Denmark Joins Europe', *Journal of Common Market Studies*, vol. XIV, no. 1, 1975, pp. 1-36.

[19] Ingemar Lindblad et al., *Politik i Norden*, Stockholm 1974, p. 73.

[20] Nikolaj Petersen and Jørgen Elklit, 'Denmark Enters the European Communities', *Scandinavian Political Studies*, vol. VIII, 1973, pp. 198-213, and Ottar Hellevik and Nils Petter Gleditsch, 'The Common Market Decision in Norway, *Scandinavian Political Studies*, vol. VIII, 1973, pp. 227-35.

[21] Lindblad, op. cit., pp. 113-26.

[22] P. Ahlmark, *Den svenska atomvåpendebatten*, Stockholm 1965.

[23] Graham T. Allison, *Essence of Decision*, Boston 1971.

[24] Ingemar Dörfer, *System 37 Viggen*, Oslo 1973.

[25] Stephen D. Krasner, 'Are Bureaucracies Important?', *Foreign Policy*, 1972, pp. 159-79.

[26] Nils Ørvik et al., *Departmental Decision-Making*, Oslo 1972, p. 99.

[27] Auken et al., op. cit.

[28] Furthermore, Mr Undén had been Foreign Minister 1924-26.

[29] Rosenau, 'Pre-theories . . .', op. cit., pp. 71-88.

[30] Johan Jørgen Holst (ed.), *Five Roads to Nordic Security*, Oslo 1973.

[31] Dörfer, op. cit.

[32] Nils Andrén, 'Sweden's Security Policy', in Holst, op. cit., p. 145.

[33] Nils Amstrup, *Dansk udenrigspolitik*, Copenhagen 1975, pp. 90-1.

[34] Kjell Goldmann, 'The Foreign Sources of Foreign Policy' (mimeo), The Swedish Institute of International Affairs, Stockholm 1975.

Selected literature in English on Danish, Norwegian and Swedish foreign policy.

Monographs

S. Abrahamsen, *Sweden's Foreign Policy*, Washington DC 1957.

Stanley V. Anderson, *The Nordic Council: A Study of Scandinavian Regionalism*, Stockholm 1967.

Nils Andrén, *Power-Balance and Non-alignment*, Uppsala 1967.

Philip M. Burgess, *Elite Images and Foreign Policy Outcomes. A Study of Norway*, Columbus, Ohio 1968.

Ingemar Dörfer, *System 37 Viggen: Arms, Technology, and the Domestication of Glory*, Oslo 1973.

Erik S. Einhorn, *National Security and Domestic Politics in Post-War Denmark. Some Principal Issues, 1945-1961*, Odense 1975.

Barbara G. Haskel, *The Scandinavian Option. Opportunities and Opportunity Costs in Post-War Foreign Policies*, Oslo 1976.

Johan Jørgen Holst (ed.), *Five Roads to Nordic Security*, Oslo 1973.

Helge Hveem, *International Relations and World Images: A Study of Norwegian Foreign Policy Elites*, Oslo 1972.

Einar Løcken, *Norway in European and Atlantic Cooperation*, Oslo 1964.

Kenneth E. Miller, *Government and Politics in Denmark*, Boston 1968.

Nordic Economic and Cultural Cooperation, Nordisk Udredningsserie, Stockholm 1970.

The Role of the Nordic Countries in European Cooperation, Nordic Council, Stockholm 1973.

Max Sørensen and Niels J. Haagerup, *Denmark and the United Nations*, New York 1956.

Niels Morten Udgaard, *Great Power Politics and Norwegian Foreign Policy*, Oslo 1973.

Nils Ørvik et al., *Departmental Decision-Making*, Oslo 1972.

Nils Ørvik (ed.), *Fears and Expectations: Norwegian Attitudes Toward European Integration*, Oslo 1972.

Nils Ørvik and Niels J. Haagerup, *The Scandinavian Members of NATO*, Adelphi Papers, no. 23, London 1965.

Egil Ulstein, *Nordic Security*, Adelphi Papers, no. 81, London 1971.

Yearbook of Nordic Statistics, 1975, Stockholm 1976.

Articles

A large number of articles is to be found in *Cooperation and Conflict*, Nordic Journal of International Politics, Oslo.

Some articles on foreign policy can be found in *Scandinavian Political Studies*, a yearbook published by the Political Science Associations in Denmark, Finland, Norway, and Sweden (Oslo, Beverly Hills and London) which also contains a yearly bibliography.

6 Foreign policy at the European level: beyond the nation-state?

DAVID ALLEN

Whilst, as is suggested by the title of this chapter, foreign policy making at the European level may well go 'beyond the nation-state', foreign policy analysis as developed primarily by American theorists[1] most certainly does not. Although many aspects of contemporary thinking about foreign policy are of relevance to the recent European experience none actually faces up to the problems of foreign policy analysis at this new level. A survey of recent literature, both empirical and theoretical, leaves one with the vague impression that here one has a 'new international actor' which in some ways both illustrates and embodies a variety of the concepts that have become common parlance in the study of contemporary international relations; what we discover however is a process that defies immediate categorisation, involving as it does elements of integration, intergovernmentalism, transnationalism and bureaucratic politics all operating within a framework that encompasses both international organisations and nation-states struggling to attain or maintain an independent identity in an interdependent world. Whilst comparison can be made with the policy process as it is known to operate in various nation-states (so that we can, at the European level, usefully comment on the place of public opinion, the difficulties of distinguishing between foreign and domestic policy and the role of the individual leaders and their perceptions) it is essential to bear in mind that in so doing we are not necessarily comparing like with like. Whilst Europe does indeed represent a new level for foreign policy analysis, it does not yet embody the familiar features of statehood that we rely on for organising our thinking about, say, British or French foreign policy. Thus whilst Europe is to a degree institutionally distinct, policies that might be described as 'European' are still, to a large extent, the product of national policies formulated within familiar national frameworks. Many of the characteristics of foreign policy making at the European level are the consequences of developments that observers of national policies have noted elsewhere in this volume, so that in concentrating on Europe rather than its constituent states, we tend to end up looking at what are essentially the same set of problems only from a different perspective. Thus the close links that are evolving between the Foreign Offices of a number of European states can be viewed either as an extension or development of national policy frameworks[2] or as the beginning of something that one might wish to term the 'European' policy framework. Similarly the difficulty that students increasingly face in attempting to define the substantive nature of foreign policy is carried over to the European level where it should be noted all attempts at policy co-ordination or integration, be it foreign or domestic, are to a large extent the product of the 'foreign' policies of individual nation-states. Those analysts who have attempted recently to come to grips with the question of Europe's foreign policy remain cautious as to the exact nature of the beast under examination. Thus whilst Goodwin[3] in a recent article attempts to separate achievements of substance from those of 'a more shadowy or procedural nature', Wallace [4] remains uncertain as to whether in looking at European foreign policy we are faced with 'mirage or reality'.

The proliferation of books and articles [5] concentrating on the international aspects of European integration that has taken place in recent years contrasts significantly with the obsession prevalent in the 1960s with the internal development of the EC and the nature of the integration process that appeared to be under way. Since the early 1970s, which were marked by high hopes for the raising of the level of integration and the expansive dreams of the 1972 Paris summit that preceded the enlargement of the EEC from the Six to the Nine, progress towards common internal economic policies has been minimal. The trend within the European Communities has been if anything negative, with member states increasingly seeking national solutions to problems that they once sought to solve together. The exception to this has of course been external policy, for the pressures that have tended to divide Europe internally have also served to expose the need for, and thus provide the stimulus to, common external action. Thus recently we have seen a twofold development. First the EC itself, most noticeably the Commission, has come to play an increased role in international affairs; and secondly the member states, as part of a development that has its origins in the proposals for a European Political Community of the 1950s,[6] have constructed a machinery for discussing and where possible co-ordinating policy on matters of international political significance that lie outside the limited economic competences of the Treaty of Rome. All this activity has led academics and advocates of European integration alike to raise once again the question of the long term future of the European Communities and the place within that future of a European foreign policy. For many, be they academics or politicians or both, this renewed interest in external affairs is motivated less by a clear conception of substantive policy issues and the stance that Europe should take than by a perception of the role that common foreign policy activity might play in the construction of a United Europe. Thus when the Heads of Government of the EC, following the summit meeting in The Hague in December 1969, instructed their Foreign Ministers to 'study the best way of achieving progress in the matter of political unification'[7] it was within this context that they responded with proposals for co-operation in the foreign policy sphere. Thus, as with the debate on EPC/EDC and the Fouchet proposals [8] of the early 60s, discussion of foreign policy and the correct framework for its development is inextricably bound up with the arguments, often of a theological nature, about the present and future content of the whole European construction. This tendency goes further than the dispute between those who would advocate a Europe built on federal lines and those in favour of a move

136

towards the construction of a confederal 'Europe d'Etats', for both sides in this argument make clear assumptions about the role of foreign policy in the construction of a new international edifice which distinguishes their interest in foreign policy analysis from that of students of national policy. One thing seems clear, and this becomes the more apparent when one attempts to fit what is happening at the European level into a comparative framework, and that is the difficulty that is experienced when one tries either to advocate or analyse foreign policy outside the reassuring framework provided by the nation state.

Foreign policy analysis derives its two central organising devices from the existence of the nation state, namely those of a sovereign government and a national interest or interests that the government attempts to pursue externally. Thus Hugo [9] in providing students of international politics with an admirable working definition of foreign policy as 'that general conception of national aspirations, interests and capacities which influences the government in the identification of disputes with other governments and in the choice of methods for the prevention, determination or limitation of such disputes', serves only to underline the difficulty faced by those who seek to order their thinking about such policy at the European level. For within the framework of Europe there is no state and thus no government to identify its interests; therefore foreign policy takes on a different meaning in relationship to the community that it is meant to serve. Despite the great interest that has been expressed in recent years in the subject of non-state actors in international politics, analysis of their behaviour, be they multinational companies or international organisations, has not advanced beyond the descriptive stage simply because the tools available for such analysis are restricted by their dependence on the very organisational form that some believe is becoming redundant – namely the nation–state. Thus to date those who have sought to examine the external activities of the Community or the Nine have continually looked for indications not of a process that goes 'beyond the nation–state' but for one that approximates to those that exist within the nation–state. It is argued here that to comprehend fully the nature of what passes today as 'European' foreign policy it is necessary to accept the reality that the Europe of the Six or Nine has never been a nascent nation–state and that states have joined the Community not to give up their sovereignty but to protect it. Several writers have sought to break away from such opposed but nevertheless state-centric concepts as intergovernmentalism and supranationalism (the creation of a larger quasi-state) in their efforts to find a useful conceptual framework for analysing policy making at the European level. Carole Webb,[10] after examining the theoretical basis of the two extremes mentioned above, uses the literature developed by Keohane and Nye [11] on transnationalism and transgovernmentalism to construct a third conceptual framework that is less dependent on familiar state structures and thus enables consideration of the partial, often informal, coalitions – both bureaucratic and governmental – that are beginning to emerge at the European level, particularly in the foreign policy sphere. David Calleo,[12] too, adopts the concept of coalition ('a temporary combination between parties that retain distinctive principles')[13] to describe the essence of the 'actor' Europe that is beginning to emerge on the world scene.

The concept of coalition enables us to examine the foreign policy practices of the Community within the context of an accepted global reality of interdependence; a state of affairs which makes a nonsense of traditionally absolute concepts such as sovereignty upon which our familiar identification of foreign policy is based. Thus it is argued here that the way to study foreign policy at the European level is with an intellectual framework that does not rely upon traditional conceptions of the state and its interactions with other states. The EC and its constituent member states represent not just another actor but a new form of actor on the international scene. That the institutions for foreign policy making that have been developed do not entirely correspond with our state orientated conceptions should indeed be a cause of puzzlement and reason for analytical innovation; it should not be a cause for regret. Our emphasis in attempting comparison should be on process not structure. Instead of searching in this context for the European equivalent of a Foreign Office, we should attempt to examine the extent to which tasks in the international sphere correspond or not at European and national levels, whether the interest of the 'coalition' can be defined in similar ways to those of states, and whether the traditional national means of satisfying these interests are of relevance at this new level of policy determination. To reject the traditional conception of foreign policy in the state context as a useful criterion for analysing European foreign policy should not of course lead to an abandonment of attempts at comparative study. The very fact that policy-makers at the European level are in many cases the same men who also operate at the national level, and the fact that the problems that they are dealing with are essentially the same, despite being viewed from different perspectives, indicates that comparison is both worthwhile and possible. My plea is a rather simple one: a request that foreign policy behaviour at the European level be studied for what it is rather than for what it might be. Whilst there is obviously a case for an examination of what might eventually emerge from the complex of contemporary European activity, be it a 'superpower Europe'[14] or a 'civilian power Europe',[15] there is still a need for an analysis of present reality free of the restraints that attempts to theorise about the nature of international society impose. Until recently the analysis of foreign policy at the European level has been regarded as being outside the province of those who seek to examine foreign policy *per se* and thus best left to those whose specialism lies in either integration theory or European Community studies. It is perhaps understandable that analysts such as Allison [16] and Brecher [17] who have played such a major role in advancing hypotheses about foreign policy making in the national context should steer clear of the European phenomenon, relying as they do on the notions of state and government. What is surprising is that many of those writers whose work tends to move their focus of attention away from the state-centric view of the world have not turned to the European example to illustrate the effects of the forces that they identify on a new policy-making structure.

At the state level a major revolution in foreign policy analysis occurred when students abandoned in large part the purely historical approach of describing what a state did in the international system and concentrated their efforts on examining the sources of such conduct. This led to attempts to explain behaviour in terms of the ways that states organised themselves for decision-making. As yet such a perspective has not been brought to bear on policy making at the European level, although in recent times several authors have felt the necessity to comment on the fact that at this level there seems to be a greater emphasis on procedure than on substantive policy.[18] In the main however the examination of European foreign policy has followed two distinct lines of thought. The first, which we have already rejected for the purpose of this analysis, seeks to examine, usually to advocate, the contribution that the foreign policy sphere can make to the achievement of European unity. Some see such co-operation as an essential prerequisite for further advance, others are critical that developments to date are taking Europe away from, rather than closer to, the unity conceived of by the founding fathers of the Treaty of Rome. The second approach conforms exactly to the traditional historical approach, concentrating as it does primarily on a description, again often tinged with prescription, of the developing relationships between the EC, the Nine and various parts of the world. Examples of this literature[19] do however illustrate the fact that, whatever the definitional problems that academics are faced with, for many other international actors, be they states or international organisations, Europe represents a growing force in world politics that they must come to terms with. There is not however a body of literature that deals with the foreign policy making mechanism as a whole; policy as such tends to be explained in terms of the balance of interests between member states rather than in terms of the machinery that produced it.

Analytically two sets of general comments dominate the conclusions of this body of writing. First there is an emphasis on the fact that the policy of the EC and the Nine towards the outside world tends to be reactive in nature. There is usually a suggestion in such comment that this state of affairs compares unfavourably with the positive (active?) nature of national foreign policies, although the two broad generalisations are rarely substantiated. Whilst it is undoubtedly the case that at the European level policy does tend to be initiated by the need to respond to external events, this is also true to a very large extent of foreign policy at the national level, particularly as far as the individual European nation–states are concerned. Secondly great emphasis is placed on the nature of the distinctions that are made in the European context between economics and politics, 'low' and 'high' politics and external relations and foreign policy-distinctions which are less frequently made at the national level. Much has been written about the validity of this set of distinctions used by Hoffman[20] to argue that whilst the EC may successfully create common procedures for resolving low key issues between states it was not likely to make any impression on the issues and arenas of diplomacy and strategy (high politics) where governments jealously guard their sovereignty. As we shall see the two policy-making systems that operate within the European Community framework owe their nominally separate existence to an initial recognition of the validity of these distinctions; thus to quote Morgan:[21]

It is sometimes tempting and to a degree useful, to distinguish between the concepts of 'foreign policy' and 'external relations' by arguing that 'foreign policy' as traditionally practised by nation states through their foreign offices and their diplomatic agents, concern such matters of 'high policy' as prestige, political influence, national security and the pursuit of diplomatic objectives, whereas 'external relations' covers more mundane activities such as the regulation of international trade, migration across frontiers and other issues which might not unfairly be characterised as 'low politics'.

Nevertheless as Morgan goes on to say,[22] 'the artificiality of the distinction has already become clear in practice, in the functioning of the institutions which the Nine have set up to conduct their relations with the rest of the world'. Not only have matters such as trade, tariffs and exchange rates become recently politicised whilst security issues seem less important in the European contemporary situation; it has also become apparent that policy issues are best categorised not in terms of their inherent qualities but in terms of the way that they are perceived. Thus at the European as well as the national level the areas of policy activity that are liable to provoke political reactions from the rest of the world have become greatly expanded, and so also has our conception of the substance of foreign policy.

To the extent that much of the literature on European foreign policy is prescriptive, the overwhelming tendency is to rue the non-existence of a common foreign policy of the type that is held to exist at national level, and thus to advocate the creation of such policy or policies as the best means of ensuring that 'European' interests are promoted in the international system. As was noted above, many writers, having failed to identify at the European level something which they recognise as foreign policy at the national level, have thus drawn the conclusion (logically if one accepts the timeless nature of the state model) that Europe will not be a significant actor in the international system until it too has a coherent and co-ordinated foreign and defence policy. There is something of the 'chicken and egg' argument that used to surround debate on the question of additional powers and direct elections for the European Parliament about this line of reasoning; rather than argue that for Europe to become politically united, a common foreign policy is an essential prerequisite, one can equally put the case that until Europe is politically united under an identifiable central government, a foreign policy as conceived in national terms cannot be realistically anticipated. All of which serves to distract one from an attempt at analysing and comparing with the national level the policy process that actually exists in Europe today.

At this point, mention should be made of a further definitional problem related to the arguments made above for moving away from the rigidly imposed conceptual framework of the state. We have already suggested that the concept of coalition best describes the nature of the actor whose policy processes we are attempting to analyse. The point needs to be made that this coalition is a shifting one; thus although when discussing Europe we naturally focus attention on the activities of the European Community, this does not however represent the sum total of foreign policy activity that can be labelled as European. Members of the EC also play significant roles within the framework of NATO, OECD, and IMF, the North/South dialogue and the economic summits of the major industrialised countries. In studying the development of European foreign policy we are not therefore merely witnessing the transfer of decision-making power from one fixed locus to another. The EC is but one manifestation, albeit the most important and significant, of an evolving framework for the conduct of European affairs in an interdependent world. Within this framework European states pursue their individual and mutual interests at a variety of levels and in a variety of fora. Although the nation–states remain as relatively cohesive identifiable units, and although as they always have done they continue to pursue state-centred foreign policy, some of their activities together can be said to go beyond the nation–state. Thus although the analysis will now concentrate on the Europe of the Nine acting within the framework of the Treaties of Rome and within political co-operation, the effect of activities in other fora such as those mentioned above must be recognised to the extent that they in turn affect policy within the EC.

The place that the European construction now has in world politics cannot be described as one that it has actively sought. Throughout the 1960s, mainly due to the indulgence of Europe's major ally, the United States, the original six member states pursued their integrative path in a manner that made little concession to the rest of the international system. Europe, such as it was, was essentially inward-looking, concentrating its efforts on the two pillars of economic integration, the customs union and a common agricultural policy. The Common Market was not viewed either by its members or indeed other significant actors in the outside world as an international force to be reckoned with. After the failure of the EDC/EPC proposals and the Fouchet plans, the member states relied either on bilateral relations or other multilateral fora such as NATO in defining their international role. Of course some contact with the outside world was inevitable, given the sheer size of the economic unit that had been created (particularly when one considers its prominent role in world trade). The Treaty of Rome had itself made provision for trade and association agreements and for a common commercial policy [23] whilst one of the conditions of French acceptance of the EEC had been the multilateralisation of aid relations with former colonies and dependencies. Furthermore the existence of the common external tariff, ruled over by the supranational Commission meant that this body had an obvious role to play in the conduct of global trade negotiations within the context of GATT (in the sixties known as the Kennedy Round).[24] Similarly the Treaty made the Commission responsible for maintaining appropriate relations with all other international organisations such as the United Nations, OECD and the Council of Europe. Nevertheless contacts of this nature were still universally regarded at that time as coming within the sphere of 'low politics' and thus not touching upon the traditional role of national foreign offices, who continued to concern themselves with the pursuit of 'political' objectives on a relatively independent basis. However, as we have seen, the distinction that this division of labour implied has always been a dubious one, even before the politicisation of economic matters became so apparent. The EC itself, despite the political assumptions of its founding fathers, owes its existence and its development to agreement between its major constituent states on those very issues of 'high politics' that the Common Market initially avoided. Thus throughout the sixties, despite the proliferation of contacts between the EC and the outside world, external relations were essentially pursued within a limited technical and economic framework.[25] Although at the European level a form of external relations machinery was devised, with the Commission negotiating agreements on the basis of briefs prepared by the Council of Ministers and their deputies, this machinery operated within the strict confines of the Treaty of Rome. Such consultation as existed between the European states on matters of international political significance tended to take place within the NATO context (from which France by choice excluded herself in 1966). Indeed differences over the Communities' role in the world had been among the reasons for De Gaulle's distaste and distrust of the European Commission. At the time of the 1965 Community crisis the French President had sharply criticised the tendency for non-member states to establish delegations to the EEC in Brussels: he did not wish to see the Commission indulging in what he described as 'striped pants diplomacy', for he regarded such matters as being the rightful task of member states and member states alone.

Thus by the end of the 1960s, with its initial internal integrative tasks completed, the EC could be and was described as an 'economic giant and a political dwarf'. That such a state of affairs could not continue was the subject of much discussion in Community circles, most obviously at the summit conference held in The Hague in 1969. At this conference significant decisions were taken both about the future internal development of the Community (the commitment to economic and monetary union and a host of future common policies), the enlargement of the Community (most significantly to allow British entry) and the re-awakening of proposals for co-operation in the foreign policy sphere. The proposal to allow British negotiations for entry was frequently justified in terms of the Community's future external role; it was felt that the addition of Britain with its tradition of involvement in the major issues of world politics would enable the Community to break out of its rather constrained, and inward-looking situation and begin to play a political part that was commensurate with its significant world economic position. That such a shift in the Community's role was no longer a matter of choice for the member states was best illustrated by the growing signs of a shift in American attitudes towards European integration. The Nixon presidency had by the end of the sixties given every indication that an American reappraisal of its position in the world, following the changes that were taking place in south east Asia, would have repercussions on the European position. It did not seem likely that the process of economic integration, which had been viewed by the United States in the past with great indulgence, despite the fact that many Community policies could be regarded as opposed to American interests (in particular the tariff barrier against US agricultural exports and the discriminatory nature of the preferential agreements that the EC had signed with a number of third countries) would be allowed to continue unchallenged. Pressure from the United States was twofold and was to be of particular relevance to the question of the establishment of a European mechanism for the co-ordination of foreign policy. First the concept of an evolving 'pentapolar' world, which both Nixon and Kissinger had spoken of, implied the need for Europe as a unit to play a role similar to its proposed partners, namely China, the USSR, Japan and the United States. This was a role that the limited decision structure of the Communities as it existed in 1970 could not sustain. Secondly the United States, mindful of the contribution that it was making towards the defence of Western Europe and mindful also of the lack of support that it had received from European states in its pursuit of a global policy, sought to link discussion of economic, political and security matters together. Such a linkage was of course likely to prove detrimental to European interests, for the United States could rightly argue that EC trade discrimination against the US was hardly the best way of ensuring continuing US military support for Europe. It also presented the Community countries with an institutional problem in that they did not have at the time a policy-making framework capable of handling negotiations across political, economic and military boundaries. Precisely because the institutions of European co-operation did not resemble those of a state there was no central locus capable of co-ordinating multi-issue negotiations.

Furthermore other parts of the world were beginning to put pressure on the Europeans to act in a more united fashion on the world scene. Even before the drama of the Middle East war and the subsequent oil crisis the Arab states of the Middle East were beginning to see in Europe an attractive alternative to the two superpowers. Similarly as the developing countries began to appreciate their new power position it was to the integrated (as it appeared to them at least) Europe of their ex-colonial masters that they began to shape their demands. The Chinese, too, having split with the Soviet Union, seemed anxious to pursue the age-old policy of regarding their neighbour's neighbour as their friend, and thus also sought ways of encouraging the Europeans to act as a united bloc. Finally the tendency for bloc negotiations to replace bilateral dealings as the dominant practice in the international system, which was just beginning to manifest itself at the end of the decade, again put pressure on the European states to organise themselves in order to act effectively within this new environment. It was these pressures which positively favoured moves towards European co-ordination of foreign policy, and which were as strong as the arguments put by those who advocated further integration in Europe on the assumption that because individual European States were now relatively weak they could only achieve their objectives by united action.

Yet apart from a defensive desire to maintain the *status quo* as best possible, the European states did not have particularly clear demands to make of the international system or indeed much of a conception of the role that they would ideally like to play within it. Thus the charge that we have noted above as being frequently levelled against European foreign policy initiatives – that of mere reaction to events – must be put in the context of a set of national policies which were themselves not particularly positive. It is important to bear this in mind when turning, as we now must, to an examination of the policy-making mechanisms that have been created at the European level. The major ingredient that existed at the beginning of the seventies was a growing pressure from the outside for the European Community to act as a single unit in the international system; a pressure that the European states were singularly unprepared to cope with, given their inability to articulate national as well as European postures. The framework that we are about to examine would undoubtedly have looked different if at least some of the member states of the Community had had clearly articulated ideas about their own national positions, which might have led them to give at the maximum leadership and at the minimum a positive and substantive injection of ideas to the Community's response to international pressure. As it was, the framework that evolved represented an attempt, if a relatively successful one, to avoid problems by institutional ingenuity rather than to solve them or play an active part in their resolution.

In strictly institutional terms the European Community has two distinct sets of machinery for framing its policies and responses to the outside world. The first operates under the principles that have evolved from the Treaty of Rome within a framework of formal legal procedures, involving a dialogue between the Commission and the member states acting in the Council of Ministers (supplemented by the Committee of Permanent Representatives beneath it and the institutionalised summit conferences now known as European Councils above). In addition, since 1970 a mechanism for foreign policy co-operation on matters outside the formal provisions of the Treaty of Rome has been developed,[26] known as the Davignon or political co-operation procedure, which consists essentially of regular exchanges between officials and ministers from the foreign offices of the Nine, meeting with the following objectives (to quote the Luxembourg Report):[27] 'to ensure, through regular exchanges of information and consultations, a better mutual understanding on the great international problems; to strengthen their solidarity by promoting the harmonisation of their views, the co-ordination of their positions and where it appears possible and desirable, common actions.' Whilst on the face of it these two policy-making mechanisms remain separate, indeed during the early part of the decade their separation was insisted upon by those states anxious to maintain the distinction between supranational and intergovernmental practices,[28] in reality they must increasingly be considered as part of the same network. As the theological barriers have been broken down, partly by a softening of French attitudes, partly by the nature of the issues involved, the European Commission has come to play a significant role in the political co-operation procedure, and equally the national governments have exercised greater control over areas that are nominally within the jurisdiction of the Communities. (A good example of the latter is the attitude of the member states towards the Commission's negotiating role on matters such as industrial co-operation agreements.)[29] Whereas once the existence of the two separate mechanisms served only to illustrate the nonsense of attempting to differentiate competences using economic and political criteria, they can now be used much more flexibly to develop appropriate European responses to issues that defy such categorisation. Nevertheless despite a more flexible interpretation of the uses to which these structures can be put, the Europeans are still faced with a number of difficulties that arise from those differently constituted structures and because of this it is still necessary to describe them separately before discussing the ways that they can be used in harness.

External policy which arises out of or involves the legal competence of the Commission is handled according to clearly laid down procedures for decision-making that were described in the Treaty of Rome and which have been modified by subsequent practice. The Treaty of Rome deals with external relations in a number of places. Articles 110-16 [30] deal with commercial policy and thus with agreements with third countries, Part 4 (articles 131-6) deals with the relationship with overseas colonial territories, whilst various articles in the general and final provisions of the Treaty cover the question of new members (article 237), association agreements (article 238) and relations with other international organisations (articles 228-31). Article 228 provides for general negotiating procedures, giving the Commission in effect powers of negotiation and the Council rights to conclude any agreements made, after consulting the Assembly.

Within the Commission responsibility for dealings with the outside world rests ultimately with the President, who also plays the chief representative role. Two other Commissioners also have key parts to play: the Commissioner responsible for the external relations portfolio and the Commissioner in charge of development policy. Until 1977 Sir Christopher Soames held the former post; during his period in office he was sometimes described as Europe's foreign minister, usually in countries such as China and particularly the under-developed world for whom the Community represents their major contact with Europe. In addition as more and more issue-areas that traditionally could be categorised as 'domestic' become internationalised or have foreign policy implications, so other areas of responsibility such as economic and monetary affairs, energy and finance policy within the Commission become involved in external relations, thus reproducing the problems of overlap and co-ordination that already exist within nation-states. Since the inception of the political co-operation machinery the General Secretariat of the Commission has come to play a particularly important liaison role between the two policy structures, in addition to its strong co-ordination position within the Commission itself. The Secretary-General or one of his deputies also plays a representative role at external meetings which take place below the level of minister on the national side. Within the regular hierarchy of the Commission Directorate-General 1 (External Relations) and DG 8 (Development) handle most of the external relations work; their field of competence is best indicated by listing the directorates that operate within them.

DG 1 is divided into six directorates dealing with:

1 Relations with international organisations.
2 Relations with North America, Australia, New Zealand and South Africa; commercial questions with respect to agriculture; protocol; and external offices.[31]

3 General questions and instruments of external economic policy; commercial and industrial matters; Middle and Far East.

4 Bilateral and multilateral relations with Latin America and Asia; United Nations, except UNCTAD, general tariff preferences and co-ordination with DG 8 on relations with developing countries.

5 Multilateral relations with planned economies; credit insurance and export credit.

6 Relations with countries of northern, central and southern Europe.

DG 8 has four directorates:

1 General development policy and liaison with DG 1.

2 Africa, the Caribbean and the Pacific (the ACP countries of the Lomé convention.

3 Projects.

4 Operations.

Attempting to compare institutions at the Community and national level is, as we noted above, not a particularly fruitful task; especially when at the Community level we find a Parliament that has no legislative powers, a bureaucracy with policy-making competence and an executive body that acts as a legislature. However if one wished to draw an analogy, then DG 1 is the equivalent of the old British Board of Trade, DG 8 of the Colonial Office and the political co-operation machinery of the Foreign Office. What is lacking of course is the equivalent of a Cabinet and of clear political leadership.

Beneath the Council of Ministers the Committee of Permanent Representatives (COREPER) has a number of working groups and committees (on which the Commission usually participates). One of the most important of these is the Article 113 Committee which is consulted by the Commission on all commercial matters under negotiation. Thus in the Kennedy Round of GATT the Council of Ministers laid down a general mandate for the Commission whilst day to day negotiations were conducted in co-operation with the Article 113 Committee. This institutional structure has generally worked well and the achievements of the Community in developing external relations make a marked contrast with the relative lack of progress towards internal common policies. In addition to the Lomé Convention [32] which has broken new ground in the provision made for the stabilisation of the export receipts of the forty-six associated countries, the Community has entered into free trade agreements covering most industrial goods with the remaining members of EFTA; it has association agreements with Greece, Turkey, Cyprus and Malta; a co-operation agreement with Canada; preferential trade agreements with Morocco, Tunisia, Algeria, Israel, Spain and Egypt; non-preferential trade agreements with Yugoslavia, Argentina, Uruguay, Brazil and Mexico; and commercial co-operation agreements with Bangladesh, India, Pakistan and Sri Lanka. Negotiations are also at present under way with Jordan, Syria and Iran. Furthermore the Community has participated as a cohesive bloc in the Conference on International Economic Co-operation, in the Conference on Security and Co-operation in Europe and is now the prime European negotiator for dealings with all countries who wish to fish in what are now Community waters. That the EC is an international actor is beyond doubt; as the largest trading bloc in the world it could hardly be otherwise. Whether or not the issue-areas that we have discussed above can continue to be regarded as 'low politics' and thus whether the distinction between external relations and foreign policy remains useful is however open to doubt. The Community's attempts to develop an external posture have produced substantive policies, in marked contrast as we shall see to the output of the political co-operation machinery whose work at present tends to be limited to the discussion of policy rather than the active pursuit of objectives. For many parts of the developing world the interesting thing about Europe is the European Community, because for them economic and commercial matters are 'high politics'. Furthermore it is the European Community as established by the Treaty of Rome which possesses some of the traditional 'tools' of foreign policy. Thus the common commercial policy has 'given the Community leverage which it used against Greece in 1967 to express disapproval of the Colonels' coup and used again in the complex bargaining within the Conference on Co-operation and Security in Europe'.[33] Similarly the lure of possible membership of the Community is currently contributing to the moves towards democracy in Spain, Portugal and Greece; in Portugal after the coup the European Investment Bank was used as a lever to strengthen democratic forces within the military leadership by offering loans with informal political conditions. Finally the network of association agreements, particularly with Mediterranean countries, provide economic instruments for political ends. Nevertheless, doubts are still expressed as to whether all this activity adds up to something recognisable as foreign policy; the Commission is frequently and often rightly criticised for its lack of sensitivity to the political significance of the external acts that it undertakes. It is argued that only a bureaucracy lacking the sensitive touch of a foreign office could envisage selling cut-price butter to the Russians, or signing a trade agreement with Israel the day before the opening of delicate negotiations with the Arab states. The arguments about the competence of the Community institutions to participate in the sensitive area of diplomacy are similar to those that are currently being debated within the administrations of the member states. They centre on the changing perceptions of the nature of foreign policy; as more and more aspects of domestic life become part of the international arena so the traditional role of foreign offices and diplomats comes under challenge. Arguments about whether the Commission and other Community institutions are competent to participate in global affairs, indeed whether the nature of their work is significant enough to be described as 'foreign policy', are similar to those that are put in Britain about the ability of home civil servants as opposed to foreign office officials to handle the delicate job of dealing with foreigners, regardless of the fact that they have the expertise in the issues involved.

Before turning to examine the work of those who would claim that they, not the Commission, are in the business of European foreign policy, some qualifications should be made about the external relations work of the Community. First the success of the Community in developing a set of external economic relations needs to be put in perspective by reference to its lack of success in the internal field. The main bargaining tool of the Community, the asset that leads so many countries to wish to form a relationship with it, is of course its continued existence both as a major trading bloc and as a significant market for all types of imports, most particularly raw materials; to the extent that the Community as a relatively cohesive and united economic bloc is threatened by its inability to solve internal problems it will be perceived by the outside world as having less and less to offer. Such a decline of the Community's role in the world is likely if the member states continue to challenge the co-operative basis of the enterprise by seeking national solutions to what are essentially a common set of problems. Many parts of the world have been forced to deal with the Communities because they perceived that on trade issues at any rate there was very little to be gained by attempting to deal bilaterally with individual members. Thus eventually even the Soviet Union, which has steadfastly refused to recognise the EC over a number of years, was forced to negotiate not with the member states but with the Commission over the question of fishing in Community waters. Recognition by other international actors is essential for any body that wishes to pursue its objectives in the international system. To the extent that the Community has achieved that recognition, be it formal or merely tacit, then it can claim to be in the business of foreign policy regardless of the existence of the political co-operation network. However, if the internal unity were to break down or if member states were to revert to an active seeking of unilateral solutions to their economic problems, then the very basis of the Community's external posture would be undermined. If on the other hand, the Community prospers as an economic unit, then it will continue to retain the attention of third countries. It would certainly seem to be the case that the standard mode of international economic negotiation within the global international system will continue to be on a bloc to bloc basis. As it stands the Community derives certain advantages from its display of unity; though increasingly that unity is maintained less by the will of the member states, more by the binding legal nature of the Treaty of Rome. This legally enforced unity goes some way towards making up for the disadvantages that the Community faces in developing relationships with other international actors, namely its lack of internal sovereignty which is the basis of a nation–state's bargaining position *vis-à-vis* the outside world.

Discussion of the role that the Treaty of Rome has played and continues to play in the development of a European foreign policy provides us with an important introduction to that other manifestation of European external policy – the political co-operation network. Political co-operation lies entirely outside the reassuring competence of the treaties; it has no legal framework other than the text of the communiqué of The Hague summit [34] at which it was conceived and two reports [35] by the foreign ministers to the heads of state and government of the Community. However, since its inception in 1970 the political co-operation procedure has grown into a considerable network for the discussion, and where possible, the co-ordination of foreign policy amongst the member states of the EC. In the process of development it has by and large managed to divorce itself from the arguments that surrounded earlier attempts at integration in the 'political' sphere. The distinction between the activities of the Nine and the work of the Community under the Treaty of Rome is no longer rigidly maintained at the European level, although the organisational structures of a number of the member states lead to a number of co-ordination problems at the national level which in turn adversely affect cohesion at European level. The problem is however increasingly organisational rather than theological.

The essence of political co-operation is a growing web of intergovernmental contacts between the foreign offices of the Nine. The institutions that have been established, although they do not have the legal identity of Community institutions, are similar to those of the European Community. Thus at the top of the policy-making pyramid we have the European Council (consisting of the heads of government), whilst below them are the meetings of foreign ministers which now take place regularly and frequently, either in the capital of the country holding the presidency of the Community (which rotates alphabetically on a six-monthly basis) or within the context of Council of Ministers meetings in Brussels or Luxembourg. The body that is charged with the preparation of these ministerial meetings (the equivalent of the COREPER in the Community context) is known as the political committee; its members are the political directors of the nine foreign offices. Beneath the political committee, which is the core of political co-operation, a number of working groups, some permanent, some *ad hoc*, meet to discuss particular issue-areas of common concern. The participants in these working groups, of which there are now at least seventeen, are predominantly drawn from the desk officers within the national foreign offices. Thus the Middle East working group consists of the responsible officials from the Middle East sections of the national offices. The whole exercise is managed by the country holding the presidency, and the extra volume of work generated by political co-operation (there are at least two working groups meeting every week) has added a considerable strain to that task, particularly for the smaller countries.[36]

The Community institutions themselves have come to play a significant role in the political co-operation procedure. Although the Parliament has now established the right to ask questions about foreign policy matters that lie outside the areas covered by the treaties, by far the most important role falls to the European Commission. Originally excluded from meetings within this intergovernmental framework, the European Commission now has an important co-ordinating role. The Commission is represented at all meetings of the foreign ministers and the political committee, usually by the relevant commissioner and either the Director-General of DG 1, or a member of the Secretariat-General respectively. It also participates in most of the working groups and within the context of the Euro-Arab Dialogue, now one of the most active areas of political co-operation, actually chairs those groups whose work impinges on Community matters. The importance of the Commission's role is emphasised by the fact that at national level considerable co-ordination problems arise between the two frameworks below the ministerial level (where of course the foreign ministers are responsible both for formal Council business and political co-operation). The main problem arises from the fact that the two senior official committees, COREPER and the political committee, draw their membership from individuals who are not only based in different centres but who are also heavily burdened by their other tasks. Thus the members of COREPER are based in Brussels whilst the political directors travel from their national capitals. As the demarcation line between Community business and political co-operation matters becomes blurred, as in the handling of say relations with the Arab states or the Soviet Union, there is a growing danger that the two European bodies will end up either discussing the same issue oblivious of the other's deliberations, or worse reaching contradictory conclusions as to the policy to be pursued. This has already happened within the context of dealings with the Soviet Union and the countries of Eastern Europe. At one point whilst COREPER was involved in consultations with the East over the relationship between the EC and state-trading countries, the political committee was also dealing with the Soviet Union in Helsinki within the context of preparations for the European Security conference. It was only when post mortems were held much later that member states realised that bargaining points that had been conceded in one forum were still being held back in the other. It is here that the role of the Commission has become significant, for it is Commission officials who by and large are the only people to attend both sets of meetings and who are thus able to keep the political directors informed of the work of the COREPER in Brussels. Despite this co-ordination problem the two frameworks have displayed an ability to be operated successfully together. The best example of this was at the CSCE conference, where the Europeans were able to maintain a unified position even though the many issues under negotiation overlapped the areas covered by the Treaty of Rome and yet extended far beyond them.

The challenge to the traditional role of foreign offices which is such a striking feature of contemporary foreign policy making within the member states has not surprisingly led diplomats to be extremely enthusiastic about the political co-operation formula, precisely because its relatively secretive nature (political co-operation attracts little publicity in marked contrast to that which surrounds the working of the Community institutions in Brussels) and the lack of any legal commitment to agree ensures that success can safely be claimed in the knowledge that failure is virtually impossible. Furthermore the practice of political co-operation accords more closely to the traditional conception of the work of diplomats; as such it is perceived by many as an attractive line of retreat in the face of pressures from competing bureaucracies at the national level.

Political co-operation has had however some notable successes. It enabled the Community, as we have noted, to maintain a united front in the CSCE talks. It has provided the basis for an ongoing dialogue with Arab states, a dialogue which potentially goes far beyond the questions of trade and development currently under discussion. More importantly it has provided a framework for the establishment of a satisfactory relationship with the United States, following the debacle of the

Year of Europe and the frictions that were generated by the European response to the Middle East war and the energy crisis. It has provided a forum for discussion of issues like that of Rhodesia, Angola, Cyprus where pressure has been put on the Europeans to produce common postures; and finally it has enabled a number of the smaller countries in the European Community, not previously noted for their involvement in global affairs, to participate in new areas of foreign policy.

Nevertheless, despite the successes mentioned above, along with the achievements of the Community in the external relations field, doubts still exist as to whether all this activity adds up to a European foreign policy. One of the traditional tools of foreign policy, namely a defence policy, is missing from the European level; although within the separate context of the Eurogroup and their efforts at joint collaboration in weapons procurement the Europeans are making some headway. A number of observers have laid stress on the fact that such policy as exists is still essentially reactive; since there is no clear decision making locus, there is a subsequent inability to take the necessary decisions that we associate with crisis management. Others have argued that the informal nature of political co-operation contrasts unfavourably with the legal basis of the EC's external relations; L. Tindemans, in his report on European Union,[37] concluded from this argument that the basis of political co-operation should be merged with the treaties, thus obliging the member states formally to consult one another and produce common policies, possibly by majority voting. This obsession with legal formulas and common policies is in the classic *communitaire* mould, but one may doubt its relevance to certain areas of foreign policy. Whilst the member states undoubtedly have an interest in acting together wherever possible, not all their interests coincide; furthermore there may well be occasions (such as at the United Nations) where nine relatively strong individual positions are still better than one weak common position. However, if the Europeans are to play a greater role on the world's stage, then some changes are obviously desirable; some better means of co-ordinating and organising European foreign policy is called for. The question of the creation of a 'political secretariat' to replace the rotating presidency as a managing device is still likely to cause concern amongst those states who continue to treat with suspicion any moves that they detect towards expanding the supranational capabilities of the Community. However some form of permanent body is clearly desirable; recently suggestions have been made to the effect that this role could be well handled by an unofficial group working within the present Council Secretariat. The need is for a body that is permanent enough both to relieve the strains on the presidency and to provide some form of ongoing contingency planning that would put the Europeans in a better position to react positively to whatever surprises the international system has in store.

Another motive for a more central co-ordination of all the various European mechanisms relates to the instruments of foreign policy. At present the political co-operation machinery, to the extent that it is capable of reaching common positions, does not have the wherewithal to carry them out. Most of the instruments of foreign policy lie within the EC itself. So frequently the best that can come from the political co-operation network are either agreed statements, some of which like the 1973 statement on European identity are of little consequence or meaning, or decisions to use the economic instruments available to the Community institutions. There is thus an obvious case for further binding the two policy mechanisms together. It may well be however that within the twin frameworks of the Community and political co-operation something which resembles a 'European' diplomatic service may be emerging as a future instrument of European foreign policy. At present partly in response to the domestic pressures that they face at home, co-operation between the nine diplomatic services is tending towards a possible future division of labour. Already political co-operation has extended to the embassies of the Nine in third countries. As Guinea Bissau approached independence a proposal was floated to establish a joint embassy; although in this instance agreement proved impossible the proposal may well be an example for the future. Similarly the foreign offices of the Nine are now linked by a common telex system known as COREU. Many of the officials from these offices now know each other probably better than they know home civil servants in their own countries; although they are still capable of occasionally surprising each other, it is undoubtedly the case that in terms of foreign policy the member states of the EC have taken great strides in recent years towards establishing the environment at least from which a 'European' foreign policy may well emerge.

The major reservation remains however the internal state of the Community, particularly as it might be affected by an enlargement that brought Greece, Spain, Portugal and possibly Turkey into the Community. If this development were to lead to a break-up of the internal unity of the Community, as it might well do, then the foreign policy that emerges under the European heading may well prove to be more an interesting extension of national policy than something that truly goes 'beyond the nation-state'.

Notes

[1] See, for instance: Richard C. Snyder, H. W. Bruck and Burton Sapin, *Foreign Policy Decision-Making: An Approach to the Study of International Politics*, ed. 1962; George Modelski, *A Theory of Foreign Policy*, 1962; Joseph Frankel, *The Making of Foreign Policy*, 1963; James Rosenau, *The Scientific Study of Foreign Policy*, 1971; Graham Allison, *Essence of Decision: Explaining the Cuban Crisis*, 1971; and Michael Brecher, *The Foreign Policy System of Israel: Setting, Images and Processes*, 1972.

[2] See, in particular Chapter 2 by William Wallace.

[3] Geoffrey Goodwin, 'The External Relations of the European Community – Shadow and Substance', *British Journal of International Studies*, vol. 3, no. 1. April 1977.

[4] William Wallace, 'A Common European Foreign Policy: Mirage or Reality?',

New Europe, Spring 1977.

[5] See, for instance: Kenneth J. Twitchett (ed.), *Europe and the World: The External Relations of the Common Market*, 1976; M. Kohnstamm and W. Hager, *A Nation Writ Large*, 1973; Werner J. Field, *The European Common Market and the World*, 1967; Gordon L. Weil, *A Foreign Policy for Europe: The External Relations of the European Community*, 1970; Roger A. Reiber, 'The Future of the European Community in International Politics', *Canadian Journal of Political Science*, vol. 9, no. 2, June 1976; Ralf Dahrendorf, 'Possibilities and Limits of a European Communities Foreign Policy', *World Today*, April 1971; and Gianni Bonvicini, 'The Foreign Relations of the European Community and Political Co-operation', *La Spettatore Internazionale*, April 1976.

[6] See F. Roy Willis, *France, Germany and the New Europe, 1945-1967*, 1968, p. 130-85.

[7] Communiqué of the Conference of the Heads of State and Government of the European Community's Member States of 2 December 1969 in The Hague, para. 15.

[8] For a discussion of the 'Fouchet proposals' see Geoffrey Goodwin, 'A Foreign Community Foreign Policy?', *Journal of Common Market Studies*, XII, no. 1, Sept. 1973, pp. 17-18.

[9] Grant Hugo, *Britain in Tomorrow's World*, 1969, p. 27.

[10] Carole Webb, 'Introduction: Variations on a Theoretical Theme', in Helen Wallace, William Wallace and Carole Webb (eds), *Policy-Making in the European Communities*, 1977.

[11] R. Keohane and J. Nye (eds), *Transnational Relations and World Politics*, 1972, and 'Transgovernmental Relations and International Organisations', *World Politics*, 27 January 1974.

[12] David Calleo, 'The European Coalition in a Fragmenting World', *Foreign Affairs*, vol. 52, no. 1, 1975.

[13] *Concise Oxford Dictionary*.

[14] J. Galtung, *The European Community: A Superpower in the Making*, 1973.

[15] Horst Menderhausen, *Civilian Power Europe*, 1975.

[16] Graham Allison, *Essence of Decision: Explaining the Cuban Missile Crisis*, 1971.

[17] M. Brecher, B. Steinberg and J. Stein, 'A Framework for Research on Foreign Policy Behaviour', *Journal of Conflict Resolution*, xiii, 1969.

[18] William Wallace and David Allen, 'Political Co-operation: Procedure as Substitute for Policy' in Wallace, Wallace and Webb *Policy Making in the European Communities*, pp. 227-48.

[19] See Note 5.

[20] S. Hoffman, 'Obstinate or Obsolete; the fate of the nation-state and the case of Western Europe', *Daedalus*, Summer 1966.

[21] Roger Morgan, *High Politics, Low Politics: Toward a Foreign Policy for Western Europe*, 1973, pp. 8-9.

[22] Ibid., p. 10.

[23] See Stanley Henig, *External Relations of the European Community*, 1971, especially pp. 9–39.

[24] See David Coombes, *Politics and Bureaucracy in the European Communities*, 1970, chapter 8, pp. 166–216.

[25] See S. Henig op. cit. for an account of the development of external relations in the sixties.

[26] See Wallace and Allen, op. cit., for a full account of the development of the political co-operation procedure.

[27] First Report of the Foreign Ministers to the Heads of States and Government of the Member States of the European Community of 27 October 1970 (Luxembourg Report) Part 11 (1).

[28] Wallace and Allen, op. cit., pp. 230–1.

[29] Goodwin, op. cit., p. 40.

[30] *Sweet & Maxwell's European Community Treaties*, 1972, provides full texts of all the relevant treaties. A useful guide to interpretating the treaties is P. S. R. F. Mathijsen, *A Guide to European Community Law*, 1972.

[31] At present the Commission has six external delegations; to the OECD in Paris; to the international organisations in Geneva; to the United States in both Washington and New York (UN); to Canada in Ottawa; to Latin America in Santiago and Montevideo and to Japan in Tokyo. The Commission also has a number of representatives in the ACP countries of the Lomé Convention.

[32] Isebill V. Gruhn, 'The Lomé Convention: inching towards interdependence', *International Organisation*, vol. 30, no. 2, Spring 1976.

[33] Wallace, op. cit., note 4, p. 23.

[34] Op. cit., note 7.

[35] Op. cit., note 27 (First Report and Second Report of the Foreign Ministers to the Heads of State and Government of the European Community's Member States of 23 July 1973 (Copenhagen Report).

[36] See Helen Wallace and Geoffrey Edwards, 'European Community; The Evolving Role of the Presidency of the Council', *International Affairs*, vol. 52, no. 4, October 1976.

[37] L. Tindemans, *Report on European Union*, 1976, chapter 11.

Index

Committee of Permanent
Representatives (COREPER, EC)
146, 149, 150
Comparative method 106-7:
framework of 108-31; global and
Atlantic variables 109-10;
governmental variables 120-4;
individual variables 124-5; issue
areas 125-31; operative variables
107, 108-31; regional variables
111-15; societal variables 115-20
Competency, dispute of 67
Conceptual models 8
Concorde project 45
Conference on International Economic
Co-operation (CIEC) 13, 33, 41,
51, 146-7
Conference on Security and Co-
operation in Europe 147, 150
Conservatism 17-18, 84
Constraints 22, 23, 41, 49:
international 52, 69, 91-2
Content analysis 9
Co-ordination 19, 45, 67
Council of Europe 34, 130, 141
Crisis and crisis decisions 11-14
Crisis of sovereignty 34-5
Cross-national linkages 23-5; see also
interdependence
Cuban missile crisis 12, 15, 87
Cultural imperialism 11
Currency 'snake' 37
Czechoslovakia: Soviet invasion of 12,
109

Davignon, Etienne 56, 68, 78
Davignon co-operation procedure 144
Deboutte, Jan 2
Decision-making 7, 11, 24-5: collective
and individual attitudes in 14,
16; comparative investigation into
10; domestic and international
pressures 58; group-think 15;
and public opinion 21-2
Defence 33, 151: British policy 39;
French policy 37
De Gasperi, Alcide 85-6
De Gaulle, President Charles 32, 37-8,
43, 45, 89, 111, 142
Denmark 113: bureaucracy 124;
defence and security policy 126-7;

and EC 111-12, 114, 119-21
passim, 123, 128; economic
structure 117; historical experience
116; interest organisations 119,
127; and NATO 72, 107, 110, 116,
124, 126; party system 121-2;
value promotion 130-1
Den Uyl, Joop 62, 63, 75
Departmental and ministerial
competition 19, 22, 44-8
Determinism, geo-political 23
Diplomatic service, see Foreign service
Domestic policies 42, 48, 72-8;
internationalisation of 66-7
Domestic sources, see Foreign policy,
domestic sources of
Dosetti 86

East, Maurice 57
Economic development: levels of 19
Economic growth 23
Economics 7
Economic Summit, Puerto Rico
(1976) 70
Economy: integrated international 35
Eden, Anthony 12
Energy 42
Environment: external 23-5;
particular images of 16
Erlander, Tage 125
Eurocommunism 92
Eurogroup 34
European Commission on Human
Rights 34, 130
European Community: Agricultural
Guidance and Guarantee Fund
93-4; aid relations 141; British
entry, see Britain; common
agricultural policy 14, 91, 141;
common commercial policy 141,
147; and common European
foreign policy 13, 136-41; concept
of 137-8; Council of Ministers 13,
70, 142, 144-6 passim, 149;
customs union 141; Declaration on
Middle East 71; and domestic
issues 22, 136; Fouchet proposals
136, 141; within framework of
international organisations 34-5,
143-4; Hague Summit (1969) 40,
136, 142, 148; influence on foreign

156

109-10, 126, 131; and Western
European States 85, 86-7, 148

United Nations 109, 114, 130, 141
UNCTAD 41
United States: Congress and Senate
4; exports and imports 32-3;
foreign policy 4, 18, 51; foreign
policy studies 1, 83; and oil crisis
96-7; political coercion by 70, 95,
97; President's role 4; State
Department 4; theory-building 8,
11; and West European
interdependence 31-2, 85, 142-3

Values 16-17, 18, 129-31
Van der Beugel, E. H. 67
Van der Stoel, Max 64, 69, 71-2, 75
Van Elslande, Renaat 67-8
Vannicelli, Primo 90, 94, 99
Van Staden, Alfred 2

Vatican, the 86, 88
Vietnam 15, 74-5, 78, 90, 98, 122
Vredeling, Henk 71

Wallace, William 1, 2, 136
Watergate 20
Webb, Carole 137
Weber, Max 17
Western European States: attitudes
towards US 3, 37, 85-6, 150;
bureaucracies 18; interdependence
24, 31-3; integration, see European
integration; political co-operation
144-5, 146-52
Wilkenfeld, Jonathan 106
Wilson, Sir Harold 39

Yom Kippur War: see Arab–Israeli War
(1973)

Zinoviev Letter 20